SICK AS MY SECRETS

Ann
God bless
Patricia
9-53-83

Happy New Year! 2021

Happy

Sick as My Secrets

Patricia L. Brooks

Sick as My Secrets

For more information
Brooks Goldmann Publishing, LLC
www.brooksgoldmannpublishing.com

Edit and interior format by Ann N. Videan

1. Memoir. 2. Alcoholism. 3. Spirituality 4. Recovery
Sick as My Secrets/Patricia L. Brooks

ISBN 13: 0-978-0981788166
ISBN: 10: 0-981788165 (paperback)
And available in e-book

First Brooks Goldmann Publishing Company, LLC
trade paperback edition June 2018

Also by Patricia L. Brooks
A Memoir: *Gifts of Sisterhood – journey from grief to gratitude*
A Memoir: *Three Husbands and a Thousand Boyfriends*

Dedication

This book is dedicated to my dear friend,
Charmeon Louise Opie Richey.

She was killed in a car accident July 5, 1970
at the hands of a drunk driver.

She died instantly at the scene.

TABLE OF CONTENTS

PROLOGUE

A lcohol became my liquid courage, my confidence, as well as my consoling partner. I fell in love with alcohol, with the feeling it gave me. It felt good, it worked for me for a long time, even with all the chaos around me.

If you learn to drink excessively and the hard way, just as I did, you eventually learn alcohol is a cozy soothing friend... who turns on you. Eventually, you will no longer count on this friend, who becomes downright ugly.

That is my story of how alcohol made all things possible. This is where the beginning was for me, with fun and romance. Then, I *needed* to drink. It was not just wanting to drink with friends, I counted on a drink to help my stress, ease my pain, and to help me sleep.

Every disappointment, every celebration, called for a drink. If I was lonely and overwhelmed, a drink was in order. If I was successful in my career, drinks were on me. Suddenly, as if my ship hit an unexpected iceberg, the damage was done. I was drinking at lunch, after work, every evening, and before and during any occasion.

Alcohol controlled my life, causing me trouble with husbands, family, friends, clients, the police, and my employer. Alcohol took over, and I was alone with my wine, and scared. I wanted to quit, but I couldn't, even when enough was enough.

I bargained with wine to drink only a little, but I always lost that game. It was tough to admit defeat, so I didn't. I kept drinking. My life took its course, and my dependence on alcohol went to a new level until God's intervention. This memoir is how it happened for me.

It is my sincere hope you will be open minded to my lessons learned during my alcoholism journey. This is my recovery path and my spiritual transformation that crossed many lives, some who deserve one more apology.

Many of you will look for the truth in these stories, be assured it is here in detail. This story does not include lies of any kind, just a little deceit from my past washed down with alcohol. This is what it was like for me in the days of wine and a few roses. The whole tale, one I wanted to tell for some time, is now written and I feel free.

Now that I am coming up on thirty-five years of sobriety in the fall of 2018, it is time to share my story openly, despite my fear. I had days and weeks and months with therapists prior to sobriety, but many more in meeting rooms of recovery. I did my best to allow you into my most private therapy sessions, my conversations with my sponsor, and my inner thoughts.

I apologize again to my husband Alan for my part in our relationship. He was fooled as much as I was as to what we were getting into with my teenage marriage and, for that, I am truly sorry. With no blame to him or our seminary friends, or his family, all of whom disowned me at the time, I humbly apologize. They owed me nothing. I disowned myself first. In many ways, those years seem like they happened to somebody else.

The story I tell about my second marriage is how I drank regularly, got drunk too often, and made a mess of things, while still wanting my marriage to succeed. Being drunk got increasingly hard for me as time went on in my late twenties. Not being drunk was even harder, until I had to stop or go to prison. I was thirty-three years old.

With the arrival of my thirty-five years of sobriety, and now that I am older and sober half of my life, I am most objective. I hope these pages will show you the thinking of an alcoholic younger woman, and how she found peace.

Finally, thank you to my current husband Earl who has only known me as a sober woman active in recovery circles, while leading a happy and productive life. With him, I am free in my sobriety and open with my recovery. I have come back from beyond the depth of a bottle of wine to share a healthy relationship with my husband and my other sober friends. For that, I am most grateful.

FIRST DRUNK

I suppose we always remember the first time we got drunk, like the first kiss. I do. But, then again, there is a lot about high school I remember.

I liked high school in a lot of ways, even if I felt like I was on the run, running away from, and running to something and somebody. I was anxious on the inside.

I acted confident and self-assured on the outside: freshman class president, cheerleading captain for junior and senior years, and first-chair flute. In junior high I was also on the cheerleading squad and played flute in the band. On the inside, though, I felt different. I feared somebody would find out I wasn't perfect, and neither was my family.

TOMMY

My first boyfriend drank beer and smoked cigarettes like a lot the high school guys did in 1964. I was fourteen. Tommy was sixteen, good looking, a strong athlete, and smart, too. The girls liked him, and he liked the girls. Tommy drove a black '57 Chevy. That sealed the deal.

1

He was my first boyfriend kiss. It took place on the merry-go-round in the state park. He took me to Junior Prom when I was a freshman. I wore an auburn-colored false ponytail, and a mint-green knee-length chiffon dress. I looked like I should have been atop an angel food birthday bunt cake. Just like the ones I had as a little girl.

"You look pretty," he said and handed me a wrist corsage.

I feel beautiful tonight, for the first time in my life, all grown up. Tommy is so proud of me. I can tell by the way he holds my hand. I am smitten. He drinks beer when we park in his car near my house. He talks, I mostly smile and listen. He is not pressuring me tonight. I am sure my dad is watching the clock and pacing the floor. I will be home on time.

Tommy broke my heart that summer after I had been away for two weeks on vacation. He decided an older girl visiting from Detroit was more interesting than me. I made a fool of myself hiding in the back seat of his car, while I waited for him at the movie theatre. He had her with him, and they had no idea I was hiding under the blanket in the backseat. They headed out to the drive-in. I knew no other way to get his attention, so I popped up at the drive-in to surprise them.

I didn't like myself for doing that and embarrassing myself. I made him angry and her laugh at me. I was humiliated when they brought me home. I did not let anyone see me cry, though.

DAVID

My boyfriend in my sophomore year was also on the football team. David and I were friends with Ronny and Sandy. The four of us were inseparable. We often congregated at school, laughing and enjoying each other. Ronny played football, too. I was a cheerleader and Sandy just, naturally, looked pretty all the time. They were all juniors.

The guys drank beer and talked football, and Sandy and I giggled a lot. We were always planning to be together. Ronny had a truck, and we double dated often, especially to the dances. Sometimes Sandy and Ronny wanted to be alone and go out parking in the woods. It shocked me the day I learned Sandy delivered a very small baby girl, weighing just over two pounds. She recovered at the hospital, while the baby struggled to live.

My dad said I was not allowed to see her or David or Ronny, and grounded me for two months. I finally knew what they did out in the woods. She never told me anything. I felt abandoned, left out. My happiness depended on those three relationships, and their loss made me sad.

I snuck off of the school bus near the hospital the day after I heard the story, *needing* to visit Sandy. I saw her baby girl before she died. She resembled a tiny puppy, helpless and struggling. I never told anyone I went there, only that I had missed the bus and walked home from school. I did not go to the burial, but heard it was difficult for her, and her mother and four sisters.

"She had to be held up by her sisters," her neighbor told me later.

I never dated David after that, and saw Sandy only a little that summer. She seemed changed by it all, and I heard she wasn't with Ronny anymore either.

DARRYL

I worked at the Indian Village curio shop in downtown St. Ignace, Michigan, during the summer of 1966 with Nancy, another one of the cheerleaders. I was sixteen, and she was fifteen. We shared a lot of fun with the tourists, and also playing pranks on each other. On occasion, her brothers would come in the store. They were older than us, and good looking. I liked it when they came by the store for no reason and stayed long. They were charming. My dad called them reckless. They had a reputation for girls and beer, marijuana, and speeding cars. I found them exciting. They liked to flirt, especially Darryl, and that was okay with me.

"You smell nice. Can I take you to Chief's drive-in?" Darryl asked with his winning smile.

My parents argue, and my mother leaves again without me or my younger sisters. My dad can't take care of us. He must go to work on the Great Lakes until the lakes freeze over, which is usually with the gales of

3

November. He must find us a place to live. Our cousins have too many kids, but my friend Nancy's house has a basement apartment.

I quickly moved into that apartment. Nancy's brother Darryl immediately began peeking in the windows and knocking on the door. He also liked playing footsie with me under the table at dinnertime. He was eighteen, his brother Jacque was nineteen. I was curious and a little afraid to think I wanted to have Darryl visit me downstairs.

Nancy's mother told me to lock myself in the apartment. Her dad watched me constantly. He knew his sons well, especially Darryl. I liked their parents and was grateful for their kindness. I didn't want to disappoint them.

Darryl was my boyfriend as soon as I returned home a month later. My mother came home again, and life went on for our family. But, my life grew crazy. I skipped school one day to be with Darryl. I chanced being kicked off the cheerleading squad and out of band, two things I loved, just for the thrill of being with him.

The foolishness of youth convinced me I would not be missed from the attendance list and, even if I was, the school's secretary would not call my parents. But, they figured it out when Darryl wasn't there either. I never missed school, so somebody worried.

That day, Darryl was into the liquor when I arrived, but I said no. I heard myself saying, "I don't want to be like *him*," meaning my dad. But, my lifestyle choices pointed to my changing destiny.

The next day, my mother confronted me after receiving a call from the school. She took me to the principal's office to get me back in school.

"My daughter made a huge mistake, this won't happen again. Her dad will see to that. She's a good student," my mother pleaded.

Mr. Dahms' reprimanded me harshly. "She's on thin ice with this. I will be watching her closely."

The wrath of my dad came down on me when he found out… his yelling, the accusations of things that didn't happen, and things that could happen. His rage hurt me and my sisters. We were all punished with fewer privileges. My dad and I barely spoke for almost a week. He told me he was extremely disappointed. He always wanted me to do better than he had done with his schooling. He had left school in the eighth grade and regretted it.

Darryl remained my boyfriend after that day. We snuck around to see each other when we could. The rumor mill at school buzzed about my bad decision and what really happened that day at his house: what we did, and what my parents knew, but I ignored it. My virginity was intact.

Darryl hung around more and more with his friends after that day; guys who seemed to like trouble and who always had beer and marijuana. They attended school less and less as the year progressed.

Darryl showed up the next semester in my American History class, as he needed to repeat it to graduate. He sat behind me and looked over my shoulder to cheat on quizzes. I was a good student and usually on the honor roll.

Mr. Mac taught history and was a tough old bird… mean by most teaching standards. I thought the flask in his desk drawer helped him deal with the stresses of teaching. He thought we did not know, but we did. His bad mood in class gave it away.

He saw Darryl's wandering eyes and punished me with a C grade. I was not given the opportunity to do extra work in the class, a class I enjoyed and knew well. He was hardnosed. Negotiating my C was not an option. Allowing Darryl to cheat when I didn't cheat myself, pounded another nail in my coffin of shame.

My relationship with Darryl faltered that Christmas when he gave me a bottle of Playboy Club perfume shaped like the trademark bunny in a beautiful black and white box. He had ordered it from the infamous magazine. My parents were livid, and my older sister voiced her disapproval.

"You are too young for that. I am old enough, and I don't want *anything* from that kind of magazine!" my sister yelled. In her vehemence, she accidently spilled some of the perfume on the floor.

"You did that on purpose!" I screamed. "You are jealous, you are always jealous!"

My mother stood firm. "It is the wrong gift for you. You have to give it back to him."

I did not give it back. I hid it in my locker for the rest of the year. I wore it only at school and washed it off when I left at the end of the day.

Since Darryl was more than a year older than me, and nineteen, he was drafted into the Army shortly after his miraculous graduation. He left for Vietnam that summer of 1968, about the time I was planning my senior class pictures and thinking about college. Our lives came to a fork in the road. I put his large silver class ring with the blue stone, angora yarn wrap and all, in my jewelry box for safekeeping. I wrote to him often, but heard very little from him over those first few months.

"He's busy with training and playing Army," I told my friends. "He'll write."

I hear from others at school that Darryl has lied to me often, has other girlfriends, and is not a good guy. I am told by several in his class not to wait for him. I am hurt and angry, and out to prove them wrong. I write diligently to him for most of the semester.

My sadness grew during his great silence, but I told no one. I did not want to admit I had made a mistake with him. I felt alone and misunderstood. My life had been chaotic my junior year; I wanted my senior year to be better. Drinking or marijuana was not for me, even though there was plenty of that to go around. I turned to finding somebody else to fill that hole in me, while waiting for something to happen, somebody to help me. Who would that be?

JIMMY

That last summer before graduation, I worked as a waitress at the truck stop. It sat on the highway parallel to Lake Michigan, heading west out of town. The late-night shifts paid the best tips, and were always busy with tourists and truck drivers. I had no real experience waitressing, but the owners knew my dad from the American Legion, so they hired me.

6

A guy from my class named Jimmy pumped gas next door. He came in once in a while and sat at the counter to drank black coffee. He was friends with guys I knew from the band, Skip and another Jim, who dated a couple girls, Julie and Melody. I knew them from my mom's church. The band guys had been trying to fix Jimmy up with me for quite a while.

Friendly Jimmy had a great smile. He flipped his long blond hair around when he came and went. I noticed he always wore cowboy boots, even though we were in northern Michigan and not the west. A little bit of rebelliousness in his long, lean frame enticed me.

One night, he asked me to a party at the Sand Dunes Beach off Lake Michigan. Because of our jobs we would be a little late, but the party would last well into the night. He made a quick stop on the way to pick up a case of beer, though we were more than three years shy of the legal age. I said nothing and sat next to him in his turquoise and white '54 Chevy. I belonged there.

I drank nothing at the party, saw a lot of kids from high school drinking, and talked to a couple girls I knew from the band. We could smell marijuana, but said nothing about it. It was part of our world now. I watched Jimmy drink a lot of beer and joke around with his friends. I liked the atmosphere with the flames flying high across the beach and the roar of Lake Michigan rushing the shore. It was exciting, almost erotic, a warm summer night, and a happy time.

Several couples were coming and going behind the sand dunes as the evening progressed. We laughed and enjoyed the party for hours until Jimmy handed me his keys.

"Can you take me home? I want you to drive."

That was the first time I met his mother, and I spent the night in his sister Lou Ann's room. After going upstairs, I heard his mother talking to my dad on the phone.

"Patty and Jim are spending the night at our house." My dad knew his dad from the American Legion, so it was okay.

My mother liked Jimmy… she liked all my friends. My dad raised an eyebrow when he saw the length of Jimmy's hair. He often asked when he was getting a haircut.

Jimmy usually picks me up on time, why not all the time? He is reluctant to wear a tuxedo on Prom Night. He shows up at basketball and football games late and waits for me. He takes me home the long way after my cheerleading duties were done. Am I happy?

He was not a sports guy; he was one of the other guys. I often said we didn't match. I never saw myself marrying him. He was a fun guy, he knew how to get beer and marijuana, and he always had cigarettes. I wanted nothing to do with beer and certainly not cigarettes. It would be a long time before I would own a pair of cowboy boots.

I made plans to go away to school in the fall and said I never would come back, at least not permanently. He was not going to college, but I was going. Even if part-time, with work and studying all night. I was not staying in our little town for anybody.

BLANEY PARK

Senior Class Skip Day was always a big deal at LaSalle High School. Our class of 1968, the largest class ever to graduate from LaSalle with more than one hundred students, would not be outdone. Even though the class before us had made trouble for themselves, they had not ruined it for us. We headed to Blaney Park in the Seney National Wildlife Refuge about an hour northwest of our hometown, St. Ignace. This beautiful place situated in the eastern upper peninsula of Michigan, tempted us with a top-notch lodge offering the outdoors, the north woods' smells, and a day at Lake Anne Louise.

I will pack an extra blouse, a blanket, a book, and snacks. Jimmy, Melody and Jim, and Julie and Skip will be there, and a lot of my friends from band and cheerleading. It is going to be a great day in a peaceful place. I love that park and the outside activities.

I was in total denial about my issues, and what was happening between me and my friends. I had no idea that Skip Day would be a turning point in my life, and no clue I would someday use this day as a starting point to say, "My name is Pat, and I am an alcoholic."

Halfway through this beautiful seventy-degree sunny day of fun on the walking trails scouting for deer, my friend Jimmy handed me a bottle of orange-flavored sloe gin.

"This is for you. Happy graduation," he said. "Bottoms up!

I looked at him and my other friends in our inner circle and said nothing. They were smiling. We all kept walking. I was the only one who had never tasted alcohol before. I did not push away from this initiation to drinking. Though I felt pressure, I also felt excited. As one of the oldest kids in my class, I was already an adult, though not yet of legal age to drink in Michigan. No one this day was, except the teachers, and they appeared to not be drinking.

"Come on, we have to go, the bus is leaving!" Jimmy yelled as he tugged at my arm.

I did not remember anything between the first drink and waking up near the shoreline of Lake Anne Louise. I had a tremendous sense of exhaustion, a headache, and nausea. The lodge was a blur, my eyes refused to focus. The sounds of the Finnish women chattering near the lodge kitchen's open window sounded muffled in my brain fog. I had a severe sunburn and my legs shook. I missed the entire afternoon in a blackout.

I was ashamed and angry, frustrated with myself for allowing this to happen. What had happened to me for those hours? What did I say? What did I do? I was fearful and felt lonely, even though Jimmy held my hand and my other friends walked behind me. Did they drink, too? Had they made fun of me? Had they used me for entertainment?

"Please God, do not let this happen to me again." I prayed under my breath.

This was my end-of-school-year memory. I would have this for the rest of my life, and the moment weighed heavy on my heart. Senior Skip Day had gone all wrong, and I had no idea how to make it right again.

9

THE POLICE

Jimmy dropped me off at my friend Sandy's house in the older part of town. I was living there at the time due to another argument with my parents. Her family had no money, their father no longer supported them, and their mother worked nights in a bar. She could hardly afford her five daughters who mostly depended on her.

It was not a welcoming place that night, cold and dark, but I entered the kitchen slowly and went straight upstairs to bed, sad and hungry.

About two hours later, a banging sounded on the door. I peeked out the upstairs window above the stoop. Two policemen stood rigidly outside the door. I had to open it. Sandy and her younger sister Betty were awakened and afraid. They knew the police were looking for me.

The officers took me to the police station. I was not questioned about alcohol use, as I suspected, but for use of a needle and a syringe found at the park. Somebody in my class had told the police I had used it and I was out of it all afternoon on the beach. I was being accused of drug use.

I am in shock and trembling with fear. There is no one to help me, not even God. All of this for my first mistake with alcohol? God, how can this be? What will I tell my parents? I must go home to them; the writing is on the wall where I was living.

I could not include my boyfriend in my explanations to the police. He already had a history with them. What will happen to me at school? Can they keep my diploma? Graduation is next week. How about my reference for college? This thought engulfed me with fear.

"God," I prayed silently. "I will never drink another drop of alcohol again. This is the worst thing that has ever happened to me. I promise."

"There was a syringe found at the park where your class picnic took place. One of the students turned it into us," he began. "She said it was possible you used it, that you were in bad shape most of the afternoon. What do you have to say about that?"

I was speechless. Who would do this to me? What girl hated me so much? Who wanted to hurt me like this? My head was spinning. I was so afraid for my life, my chest hurt. I could hear the men in the jail behind the officer's desk talking amongst themselves. I was so ashamed, but it was familiar; I never quite felt on the right side of the tracks.

Drugs were so foreign to me, and so scary and bad. Did the men in the jail they know me? Or, know why I was here? Were they talking about me? I froze. I could not answer the police officer. He waited a few more minutes and asked again. I finally blurted out my answer.

"I don't know anything about any of this. I am so surprised by this I can't answer you. Please believe me. I would never do that. There are people who will vouch for me."

"Were you drinking on the trip?" he asked.

"I drank sloe gin. It was the first time drinking for me. A friend gave it to me. It was a joke really, for graduation. I didn't bring it to the picnic. I do not remember a thing, not the entire afternoon." I added, in a hurry, "That is the truth, I swear it is. I'm so sorry."

The policeman somehow believed me and did not ask me who supplied the gin. He was not somebody who recognized me, but I knew his name. God took care of the rest.

The officer did question me about who would do this and why. I had no answers. He did not tell me who called him or what information she provided him. All of this was a mystery to me. I was afraid just thinking about somebody hating me enough to cause me so much trouble. This incident added to my shame of having made a fool of myself that day. I needed to validate myself, to be loved and accepted.

This one mistake, one decision, changes Senior Skip Day for me forever. My last summer as a high school student is going to be different. I have my plans to go to college, to leave home, and to not drink like my friends. I am no longer running away. I was eighteen and running toward my new plans, just a little faster than before.

Patricia L. Brooks

LEARNING TO DRINK

I t didn't come naturally. I had to work at it. I was a teenage bride on my way to seminary with my husband, which seemed an unlikely place to learn to drink. Drinking held mixed messages for me, but I learned to rely on it and love it. I had a good teacher and was a willing student.

I didn't want to be a heavy drinker or an alcoholic; I suppose nobody does. Most start out like me, drinking socially, experimenting with different drinks and habits until it weaves its way into the fabric of life.

APPLE RIVER

I took the receptionist position at Apple River Chemical Company to help support our meager household. My new job was across a bridge over the Mississippi River from Iowa. We lived in married housing on the campus of the University of Dubuque. They were small houses in the form of one room with a kitchenette, a bathroom, a desk area, and a hide-a-bed.

They had been built for Army families during World War II and were still being used by the university in 1969 when we arrived. They needed updating, but I did the best I could to make ours feel like home. Although not much bigger than the dorm suite I shared with my girlfriends the year before at Northern Michigan University, it was ours.

Alan began studies in the university's Presbyterian seminary graduate program. We lived a simple life. His parents expected we would both work while he went to school full-time. They didn't expect I would have interests away from seminary life… a life that included training for the wives, too. We were all being prepared to take on church life.

I finished my business program the year before at NMU and had a certification in stenography. I'm not sure if it helped me get hired or not, although those qualifications, and my other clerical skills, were in high demand in 1969. My position changed soon after being hired. My new boss, a charismatic sales manager named Jack, decided I should be in the sales department as his secretary and not waste my talents answering the phone in the reception area.

We quickly began our relationship both business-like and playful. He had a great sense of humor and a good head for sales. I quickly learned a lot about the fertilizer business, and about the sales department, as I wrote letters and proposals for him. Apple River Chemical Company produced anhydrous ammonia for fertilizer for most of the larger farmers in the Midwest. They were environmentally friendly and ahead of their time, a highly successful company.

It is a treat to see Jack's enthusiasm during sales meetings. I lose all my fear of being able to do my job just being around him. There are no regrets about the extra time I spend with him. I don't think twice when he asks me to go to lunch to discuss a big proposal. We have these marketing projects for several weeks, and we work well together.

EAST DUBUQUE

It didn't take long before my high-energy boss invited me to happy hour at one of the popular taverns along the river; near where the nightly card games and girlie shows took place. I knew about all of this, because the men on the sales staff talked about those places around the office—including what went on in the back rooms.

On the east side of the river in Illinois anything went, a much more liberal state. It seemed miles away from my life in seminary when I walked through the door of that job and began to learn the culture. It was okay to drink in a tavern in Illinois, but it was alcohol from a State Liquor store in Iowa. I was nineteen and not of legal age to order a drink anywhere. My boss ordered for me. Nobody asked questions, nor requested my ID.

"What would the young lady like?" the waitress boomed with a smile.

She knew him. He had a tab there and frequented the place on his expense account.

"Bring us a couple of martinis."

She raised her eyebrows, acknowledging a new experience for all of us. I had no idea what to expect. I had drunk wine with my husband at dinner, but I rarely drank anything. I was five years younger than my husband and fifteen years younger than Jack.

I was curious to know what was in a martini, how hard it would hit me, or if I would like the feeling it gave me. I did not expect to wear a smile the rest of the day, but I did. Like the Cheshire Cat, I was sneaky and getting away with something.

"You took a long lunch today?" one of the girls in the office asked at the three o'clock afternoon break.

"No. Not really. Business, too. We have a big proposal due next week, a new campaign for the second quarter. It's going to take a lot of extra time," I said, feeling a bit dizzy.

Jack was in meetings the rest of the day. I fielded calls for him and shuffled papers, wondering if every time I drank my day would be unproductive. Jack saw me as a woman. I wanted to be worthy of his respect, to grow up quickly, and handle the job and the responsibilities he gave me. The martini did relax me. It took the edge off, but getting used to the bitter taste was another thing.

IOWA JAYCEES

"I'm running for president of the Iowa Jaycees and need your help," he said one day out of the blue. "I want to run a unique campaign. I have some big ideas. I need a right-hand gal, and I think you could help me. We work well together."

Wow. Is this a working relationship heading to personal interests? Does he want to be closer to me? Am I reading more into this than is there? Am I looking for more with him? He is exciting and funny. I like being around him a lot. What would this mean for my marriage?

"I'll be able to pay a small stipend for your help, but it means working late several nights a week." He continued, "Would you be able to do that with your home-life situation?"

"It sounds like fun. I would enjoy it. I've always wanted to do something like that," I chirped. "My husband studies at night. It should work out."

I worked full-time at the chemical company and ran a jewelry home-sales business on the side for extra money. This campaign would eat up all my free time, yet I didn't hesitate to commit. It was the beginning of me losing interest in my marriage, seminary life, and wanting more excitement to keep me happy. I liked the taste of wine and the feeling I experienced from alcohol.

THE CAMPAIGN

Running for president of the Iowa Jaycees in 1970 meant high energy, new ideas, and being on top of what was best for the State of Iowa. The Dubuque Jaycees organization afforded young men an opportunity to grow and develop as leaders. They were very effective, and the leading networking group in town… therefore, Jack's choice. The relationships he formed there were keys to his advancement personally and in business. It was the best young people's organizations in the Dubuque area, and all members were expected to represent it well.

My husband didn't fully support what I was doing, and he quickly learned that the duties of a seminarian's wife did not fill my passion. He also knew I asserted myself more and more each day; demanding what I wanted. He did not have the time or the energy to fight it. His graduate classes and incidental preaching demands consumed him.

"We need to be in Ames on Sunday. I preach at the Collegiate Presbyterian Church at nine in the morning. I hope you are going to make this one," he fished as he dressed for school that morning.

"I need to be here that day. We have a big rally at Loras College. I need to be there. We have worked on this event for a long time," I commented, knowing it would cause a rift.

"Your responsibility is to the church and our life, first. Have you forgotten that? Is this campaign that important to you?"

"I enjoy what I am doing, and you enjoy what you are doing. I cannot always be excited about what you are excited about."

"Why did he ask you to do this?" He raised his voice. "You have only six months on your job, and you have commitments with the seminary, too."

"I work well with him, and he knows what I am capable of doing. He feels we can work well together on the campaign, too. He needs somebody he can count on."

I did not tell my husband that Jack and I went out a couple times a week for lunch and drinks to discuss the campaign. Nor did I mention that I worked on the campaign at the office and happy hour, or that our relationship was already being discussed at the office. Jack was exciting, handsome, funny, and interesting. And, I was in.

THE KEY

The campaign led to connections I did not expect, people I would have never met. Seminary life was confining and often boring for me. The people with the campaign and Jack's friends and supporters were fun, enthusiastic, and exciting. Then there were the guys from the bank, who provided the key to our relationship going forward. They liked Jack. They were strong supporters of his desire to win, and they found me entertaining. I liked them enough and appreciated their sense of humor.

"If you two ever want to use my apartments, I almost always have one vacancy," one Key Bank guy kiddingly told Jack one night at the campaign office.

Jack laughed. "Whoa. You're way ahead of me."

I pretended I didn't hear this, as we had only flirted with the idea of being alone. Some members of the campaign knew what was on the horizon. Most chose to ignore the obvious, but some knew.

"The boys offered us a place to be alone," Jack said as we headed to our cars.

"I know. I overheard them," I admitted sheepishly. "I can't tonight. I must be home soon. My husband's class does not meet tonight. He is waiting for me."

I embraced him with more than a friendly hug. He held me close. An opportunity to cross-the-line had presented itself. Infidelity was in the air.

When I walked through the front door, Alan tossed his textbook onto the table. "You're late. When does this end? Do you need to be so involved?"

I shrugged, though my heart beat hard against my ribs. "The election is in a month. We're just starting to gear-up. It's going to be even more work over the next few weeks."

THE APARTMENT

The Key apartment building was in a newer section of Dubuque, up on a hill, and at least a half hour from the campus, closer to the river. I arrived first and waited in my car. Watching the street from my rear window, I was like an undercover detective on the job. I thought he might not show. He was new at this, too. We were the brutally honest types, almost to a fault. We surely had that in common. How could he lie to his wife and six kids? I could not comprehend it nor think about it.

I had a half bottle of wine with me in a bag below the seat, one from home. I removed the cap, put my head down below the dash and took a swig of confidence. It was left over from a spaghetti dinner I cooked recently for us and the neighbors. The spaghetti was sticky and the dinner mediocre, but the wine was a plus. It made life palpable, while my husband kept apologizing for my cooking. The rest of the bottle would work tonight.

Jack's car appeared in my rear-view mirror as if he was looking for a safe place to hide. He left his car in a hurry, running to me. His smile was happy, but taut. He reached for my arm.

"The stairs are at the end of the building." He pointed. "The second-floor end apartment is ours. We have it anytime we like."

I noticed he was carrying a brown paper bag, too. Jack was certainly old enough to buy at the state liquor store. He liked a good drink, but found wine the romance drink, the precursor to a good night. Would this be a good night?

The apartment was small, but well appointed, sparsely decorated and somewhat cold. But then, it was for clients not lovers, business conversations not a tryst. Or, was it?

Jack led me in by my hand. He pulled the bottle from the bag ceremoniously, as if it was a ritual to the scene, and placed it on the table. Two wine glasses emerged from his trench coat pockets. I smiled, and he did, too. He poured wine for us without asking. He came close to me for a toast. We were playing cat-and-mouse, and having fun.

"Here's to our good health and long-lasting love," he said as he raised his glass.

"Yes, to us."

My inhibitions are only slightly noticeable here. My guilt is falling away. My heart races like a sailor's in the final surge of a race on a gusty day. I drank wine in the car, but I'm not woozy, I'm energized. How many glasses of wine will it take before I melt into his arms where I have been

19

dreaming of being for hours, maybe days? How much small talk will it take before he approaches me with no pause? Or, will it be me?

The apartment loomed dark and still as I lifted my pulsating head and moved from him to find the bathroom. I looked for my clothes. My head ached. I needed aspirin. My head spun. What happened? Will I remember? I want to remember. I want to remember every little detail forever. Even the part where I puked.

I took my time feeling my way around the unfamiliar furniture. His bottle of wine was empty, too. The two glasses sat on the nightstand on his side of the bed, near his personal things. I moved about slowly so as not to disturb him. But, why? He had to get up and leave, too. He had a big family waiting for him, for God's sake. We had to sober up quickly, but how would we do that? I was new at this, I needed advice. I had drunk too much.

"What time is it?" he asked, beginning to stir. "I'm afraid it's pretty late."

"It's ten-thirty on your watch," I said as I leaned over him. "It's late, I need to leave."

"Don't hurry away without a goodbye. Remember, we're supposed to be together. I want to be with you. I don't want this to be our only night."

"It won't be," I said as I gathered my things, trying not to forget anything. "I need to go. This is going to be hard to explain to my husband."

"Wait for me," he begged as he scrambled to get dressed. "Let's leave together. It would mean a lot to me."

"Okay, but please hurry, I'm feeling very nervous."

The front porch light of our small campus house shone brightly. All the inside lights were off, and Alan was pretending to sleep. I crept to the closet, changed, and crawled into bed. I laid there a long time coming to grips with how my seminary life was no more, and how wine and romance were now a part of my work and social life away from this campus. I thought about how infidelity was becoming my normal way

20

of life, and getting easier and more justifiable. I made no plans that night to change any of it or to apologize to anyone.

The Key Bank boys' apartment was ours every week, usually Thursday night, but sometimes Wednesday to mix it up. Jack or his friends made sure the night included a bottle of wine. Usually, we had a nice dinner before the adventure began.

My husband often asked a lot of questions and was regularly irritated with me. He demanded the seminary intervene and require counseling for me. I had stopped going to my "seminary wives training classes." The other women worried about me.

My neighbor Charm often showed concern in her voice when she called. I had not talked to her much since we took a trip to Florida months earlier to attend a writer's conference. We took turns driving her VW bug on the thirty-six-hour trip. We got to know each other some while handing off the driving. We also had beach time and workshop time, and time to laugh and time to cry. We shared an incredible adventure from Dubuque to Ft. Lauderdale, including snow in Atlanta, and a flat tire in Nashville.

Recently, she worried because I was not confiding in her or seeking her out for conversation. What was I doing? Why was I abandoning her friendship?

GOING HOME

Some things are meant to be, and some are not, and then some are fought hard for before we let them go. This affair was one of those hard-fought obsessions. Jack lost the campaign. A lot of time and energy was spent, but it was not God's plan.

Soon after the defeat, a confrontation at work with Jack, an ultimatum, meant I had to go. The affair had to end, or he would lose his job. He was distraught when he called me to his office to end it.

"We can't continue, and we have to say goodbye," he said with a shaky voice. "They are threatening me with my job, and I cannot afford that."

"I know. I have been thinking a lot about leaving here and going back to school in Michigan. I am ready to leave my husband and Dubuque."

"I am so sorry. I wanted you to leave him and be with me. I want to help you. What can I do?" he asked with a pain in his voice I had not heard before.

"Nothing. Just remember we cared about each other. It was not possible with six kids… you need to be with them. I need to be back in school. I am in the wrong place here."

My parents came to Iowa the next week with a small U-Haul to pick me up with most of my wedding presents. The fine Lenox china from J. L. Hudson's in Detroit, and the matching crystal and silver were still in their original packaging, but I would take none of it to college.

I made plans to move into a dormitory at the Central Michigan University campus, and said hurried goodbyes to my neighbors and Alan the night before I left. Not feeling guilty, but free and excited about going back to school, I was not even sad about leaving Jack. Why was that? Had I not loved him a little? Would I forget about him as soon as I hit the CMU campus in Mt. Pleasant?

As we loaded the U-Haul, Jack showed up to say goodbye, and insisted on taking all of my family out for pizza. My younger sisters were there, too. It was awkward, and not the final goodbye I had anticipated. I thought our goodbye occurred that day at the office, clean and simple, the way affairs ended in the movies. We laughed a little at lunch, but my parents were quiet. The scene was surreal, odd really, and I regretted the affair had happened.

MARRY ME

I enrolled at Central Michigan University in January of 1971, less than three years after embarking on the seminary path at the University of Dubuque with Alan. It had been a whirlwind, but not a waste of time. I learned a lot about myself and grew up a little, and was

22

newly determined to put my nose to the grindstone, study, not date, get good grades, finish my degree and not look back.

Late one afternoon, after about a month on campus, a call came in to the dorm for me. A visitor waited for me at the front desk.

Who can it be? My parents would not surprise me. I'm not dating anyone and have only a few friends who live in the dorm with me. My sisters are north of me in community college and high school. Who can it be?

"You look beautiful," Jack said without hesitation. "I had to see you. I could not take you saying no on the phone," he blurted out. "I had to talk to you again about us being together. I am miserable and need to be with you."

The image of Jack standing there in his trench coat will forever remain my memory. With his sheepish grin and long swag of dark hair over one eye, he proceeded to beg me to leave the dorm and spend the night with him. He had driven all day from Iowa to get to the campus.

My jaw dropped. I had thought about him, but not in that way. I had wondered how he was doing. Had he made amends to his wife, had he spent more time with his kids? Were things better for him at work, and who took my place at the office? But, this scenario never entered my mind. I had moved on.

Oh, dear God, what had I done to this poor man? This father and husband was so much older than me, but not so much wiser. How does the heart do this to us? Why do I not feel the same?

He saw the disappointment about us in my face. His shoulders slumped, and his face winced. His hands and legs shook visibly. We found a quiet place in the lobby of the dorm to talk.

"Jack, please sit down," I begged. "I can't leave here. I have a lot of studying to do. I have an exam tomorrow. Your being here is not fair to either of us," I said. "That life we had in Iowa is gone. I haven't had any wine since the last time we drank at the apartment. I don't go out to parties or the bars near the campus. I stay focused on my studies and finishing school. I thought your intent was to go home to your family."

I had told him all this a couple of times on the phone since saying goodbye in Iowa, but obviously he did not hear me. He wanted to know I missed him, that I loved him and was miserable. I couldn't tell him that. I could not pretend. Had I pretended in Iowa?

Jack left a sad man. I was sad, too. For the second time in a short period of my adult life, I had hurt two men who had loved me. It was not fair. Love hurts. I knew that. Would love ever to feel good and wonderful? The thought of going out with my roommates for a few glasses of wine that night crossed my mind. I went back to my suite to look for them.

LET THE PARTY BEGIN

GOLF ANYONE?

"**W**e need to head to the course early, about six o'clock," he announced over dinner. "I'm managing the beer delivery for the tournament. Even if it looks like I play golf and drink beer for a living, I do work hard."

I had taken the Greyhound bus to John's apartment in Grand Blanc the day before, a couple hours from the campus. I had no car at Central Michigan University. He had offered to pick me up, but I wanted my independence. We had met only a couple weeks earlier.

I had a new sundress to wear, but my sandals would not do to walk eighteen holes on the golf course. He bought me a pair of canvas PF Flyer sneakers at a shoe store near his apartment. We agreed immediately on the navy color. The other women would have golf attire, but I was his guest and had never walked a golf course before. Tomorrow would be interesting.

I don't quite feel like I can be myself with him, but I am trying. He is so different from anyone I have known. He has a lot of energy. I listen to him and say very little. This weekend is his party, so I will stay behind the scenes. A glass of wine later will help.

THE GAMES BEGIN

The music was loud, the large crowd mostly men. The party began in the morning with an eight o'clock shotgun start. A canon

25

boomed behind the first tee, keeping people on their toes. It was a beautiful Michigan morning in May at the Fenton Farms Golf Club.

John shouted over his shoulder for me to browse the pro shop or watch golfers on the driving range and as he disappeared into the crowd. Since I did not know any of the professionals, and even fewer celebrities, I was oblivious to who was there, but fun was in the air. I enjoyed the sunshine on my hair while taking in the sights.

As I approached the driving range, a man dressed in stylish golf attire, walked toward me. "Would you like to have a drink?" he asked.

I was a bit surprised and thinking more of a glass of wine at lunch as my treat for the day.

"I'm a golf pro playing in the tournament, he said. "I didn't mean to startle you."

"I'm Pat. I'm a guest today."

He was friendly enough, so I tried to have a conversation with him, but my knowledge of golf was limited. I was not ready for the bar, but he quickly had an alternative plan.

"The "booze buggy" will be along soon and we can have a Bloody Mary or a Screwdriver here at the putting green," he suggested with a grin.

"It's a little early isn't it?"

"No. Not at a Saturday golf tournament with celebrities and professionals. There are no clocks here—like Vegas," he responded. "Who invited you, but isn't paying attention to you?"

I explained John was selling beer before playing. I liked his attentiveness a bit, but not all the questions. Shy, and not used to this banter, the situation took me aback slightly. I considered his drink offer.

Dave bought me a Bloody Mary without any answer from me. Soon, I grew chatty. I tasted the juice and became a giddy little girl. That warm red spicy liquid relaxed me. Even my new shoes felt better. I began to fit in and feel pretty in my red and yellow striped sundress. With each sip, more confidence built in me. I was ready for anything.

Can I envision myself with this life? Will this be a fun day? Is this for me?

THE FRONT NINE

John found me soon after, near the putting green with that zesty red drink in my hand and Dave long gone. He seemed amused I was drinking at that early hour. He held a beer in his hand: the golfer's norm as I looked around the crowd.

"Get in. My start is on the third tee. We will meet up with my foursome there. You can ride with me or walk." He smiled wickedly. "I am playing with a couple of guys from the Detroit Tigers. This will be fun."

The Alex Karras Golf Classic was a fundraiser for Cystic Fibrosis. I realized it was a special event in a unique place when, on our way to the course entrance, we drove down past the beautiful old farm houses on Torrey Road.

We heard the shrieks of wild animals echoing on the golf course as we made the last curve toward the clubhouse. Alex Karras was a character of TV sports, eccentric really, but a football great. He had an off-the-wall sense of humor and was one of the golf course's investors.

I did not follow professional football even though I had been a high school cheerleader a few years earlier. My ex-husband was not a fan, and neither was my dad. But, that day, I found an interest in football. I wanted to be a part of the activities.

Bizarre antics occurred everywhere. I heard intense car crash sounds from loudspeakers behind the trees at every green, and recorded sounds of people screaming to distract the golfers. The recordings startled me at first, but successfully amused the golfers. The elephant sauntering around made no more sense to me than the musicians serenading golfers as they walked toward various holes. It was crazy, but a good time for a charity fundraiser stamped with Karras's quirky expression of life.

Tiny Tim parachuted onto the golf course at the start of the tournament with his band playing *Tiptoe Through the Tulips*. After his parachute landed, the golfers heard the gunshot and stepped up to tee off. By now I was ready for anything.

27

Finding a new man in my life with high energy was just what I wanted at the end of a long school year. I was born too late. I was an old soul, the Sixties and Seventies often didn't fit me. Alcohol seemed to lessen my longing for love. I had pushed my yearning for love deep inside while I studied at CMU and finalized my divorce. Drinking was not an option. Here, though, drinking was legal and acceptable, and it promised fun. I was not into marijuana and hoped no one would offer me any.

The golf course was buzzing with young men in colorful clothes, some in funny little hats that reminded me of fishing hats. A few even wore knickers. I owned what women called "pedal pushers," but never expected to see men wearing anything similar. The golfers appeared ready for fun, as if they were anticipating wild times to come. The day would surely not disappoint.

I stepped off the cart at the third tee when John parked it below an embankment under a large tree. He hurried up to the others, although I constantly stepped back as golf carts whizzed by me.

Many of the men said hello and chuckled when they saw me. "Hello beautiful, have fun today. Keep your head up."

I smiled and waved. New at this confidence thing, I was breaking in a new pair of shoes and a new lifestyle, embarking on country club life. My dad did not golf, my ex-husband did not golf. I had never visited the golf course in my hometown. I grew anxious, thought about the "booze buggy," and wondered where it was stationed.

"Do you want some refreshment?" a cheery voice asked from behind me.

A pretty girl in sky-blue hot pants and a matching tube top magically appeared as if she had read my thoughts. She had a full bar set-up on the back of her golf cart. Temptation urged me to ask for another Bloody Mary, but it was before lunch.

"A Screwdriver or a Bloody Mary? They are premixed, but fresh. Done this morning." She beamed and licked her bright pink glistening lips.

I was uncomfortable, trying to find an answer. I had to say no.

"Make that three Bloody Marys please, one for me, one for George here, and one for the young lady," boomed a voice on my right, followed by a barrel of laughter.

"Yes, Mr. Karras," said the cart girl, moving about in a hurry.

"Thank you," I responded like a puppet. "I am not sure I need another one. It's pretty early for me, and I don't drink."

"You will today, honey." He laughed loudly again. "This is a golf party and we are celebrating. I'm Alex, and this is George. Welcome to my tournament."

"I'm Pat, and I'm happy to be here." I offered. "I'm a guest. Do you know John, the beer guy? He is with Schlitz."

"Yes, the beer guy. I am glad to know him," he bellowed. "He asked to have his special lady here today. That must be you."

"We are a men's-only tournament, but we are making some exceptions today," George said in a much softer manner. "Let us know if you need anything or are harassed by any of these guys... except for us, of course." A smile accompanied his tease.

"By the way, George is a famous writer," Karras quipped. "This is George Plimpton."

In one morning, to meet Alex Karras of the Detroit Lions, a notorious football rebel, and George Plimpton, author of *Paper Lion* and serial prankster, was surreal.

I read once: "When you see crazy coming, cross the street." They lived large, everything around them was larger, and it was getting even larger now that they had bought me my second drink of the morning. It was not yet ten o'clock. I took a sip of my drink and the Karass/Plimpton cart sped off as quickly as it had appeared.

My adrenaline rushed. I was a little buzzed. I only wanted to walk the golf course, drink water, stay in the shade as much as I could, talk to a few people, and watch good-looking men play golf. I was caught up in the excitement of it all.

Drinking made me comfortable in a new situation. Especially when it was over-the-top, I was in tune. This was happiness.

29

John had long since headed down the golf course in his cart. I realized he assumed I wanted to walk the course and catch up with him later. That hurt. I wanted him to invite me to come with him in the cart. I wanted him to stop teasing me about the drinks. I could not keep up with him in so many ways. Would I ever use him the way he used me?

He exhausted me with his constant need to tell fabricated stories. I heard him tell a few more that morning. I tried to catch up at every turn, to feel a part of his fast-paced life. I wanted to catch up now, but my drink was fresh, so I would walk and enjoy it.

I am excited some of the time. I don't miss him when he walks off. There is a full bar driving around on the golf course and men flirting. Dangerous temptations for me lie everywhere.

THE BACK NINE

John surfaced again nine holes later as he made the turn near the clubhouse. I had walked the first couple of hours, following the others. He noticed me drinking a Screwdriver and grinned, but didn't offer a hug or any sign of affection. I didn't say anything more than hello, nor did I move toward him. It was impossible to read his signals. Did he want somebody around for him?

"How many drinks have you had?" he asked with a chuckle. "I would keep track of those if I were you. You're not used to all this excitement."

I smiled as I approached him, only to realize he was in a hurry to get back on the course. I backed off. The people in the gallery observed us, but seemed unaware I had any relationship with him or felt rejected. He gave them no real indication otherwise, and neither did I.

The hubbub of the golf tournament, the scantily clothed women walking around, and the constant flirting by the men in the tournament is the norm for the day. I can go with it. I don't want a hangover, but having fun sounds good. I must pace myself to be my best and impress people.

GOOD NIGHT

"I am staying in Grand Blanc on Saginaw Road." I told the cab driver after learning the evening dinner was for men only. "Can you take me there?"

"Get in. It is a bit of a drive, but I can do it," he said as a man got in next to me.

"Hi. I'm going your way, mind if we share the cab to save a few dollars?" he asked with a big smile. "Remember? I'm Dave, I bought you a drink early this morning."

He looked more handsome than I remembered, in a rugged sort of way. I guess golfers get better looking the more you drink. He had been drinking all day, too, but didn't act drunk. Yet, he had a drink with him in the cab.

Dave sat too close to me, but I said nothing and answered his small-talk questions, while not being too receptive. I was not as friendly as eight in the morning had allowed me to be. I was tired, and something did not feel right. It made me happy to see the cab driver glancing often to the back seat. My shyness had come back in a wave of nervousness. I cleared my foggy head by opening the window.

I was feeling my drinks as the cab lunged forward out of the drive—not myself, tired with too much sun, and needing rest. It had been an eventful day, and certainly not a typical one for me. Meeting a lot of people and talking, drinking, and eating all day, I had begun to understand the game of golf. In some ways, it mirrored the game of life.

"Where are your friends?" he asked. "Did you come to the tournament alone?"

"No. I was invited by a friend. I thought I told you earlier. His company supplied all the beer for today. He is now at the tournament dinner, men only."

"Those things aren't for me. Besides, I would never leave a pretty girl like you alone for a rare steak," he said with a laugh.

I can't do this anymore. Small talk bores me. I feel sick. I want to get back safely and get to bed. Why am I shaking? What does it take for me to say, "No, leave me alone?"

The cab driver continued to look in his rearview mirror, but I felt abandoned and out of sorts, wanting another drink. I needed to have my wits about me, though, and could not have both. I felt more anxiety coming on, and concern about this person knowing where I lived. I prayed the car driver took him home first.

"Sir, what address do I take you to?" the cabbie asked, almost intuitively. "I will take you home first." `

"No, let's take the lady home first. Seems like the right thing to do."

I quietly handed my address to the cabbie and look pleadingly into his eyes. I huddled closer to the window and tried to think clearly.

Dave leaned even more toward me to talk privately. "What do you do? Work? Go to school? Live the life of leisure?

"I go to CMU in Mt. Pleasant. I am getting ready for summer school."

I refused to discuss anything more. Dave was scaring me. I felt deceived by John, though I had no commitment to him. The guilt of past relationships crept over me. I yearned for the apartment and a glass of wine.

I looked out the window as the dark whizzed by us. Is this my fault? Did I deserve to be harassed because I drank too much and put myself in a precarious position? Would this be typical of my time with John? Would I be unhappy with other nights out? Would he buy me things, take me to exciting events, and nice places to eat and drink, then disappoint or put me in a difficult situation? Would a new lifestyle with him be worth it?

Close to an hour later, the cabbie pulled into the large wrought iron gates at Knoll Wood Apartments in Grand Blanc. The large brick building for me was at the last turn of the small manicured golf course that encircled the complex. A quiet night, the grounds lay still and beautiful with gas lamps reflected on the water areas along the course.

The circular drive twinkled and welcomed us. I liked the place. I had only been there a couple days, trying to get used to the idea of moving in, but it felt like home at the moment.

"May I walk you to the door?" Dave quickly asked as he grabbed my arm.

I did not respond or look at him. I shook off his hand and stepped out of the cab on the driver's side as soon as the cabbie opened the door for me. I handed him the money he asked for, along with a generous tip.

My anxiety was a volcano ready to erupt, a rising tide of red lava. I couldn't function socially without a drink. I was struggling to care for myself.

"Please wait until I am safely inside," I whispered to him.

He nodded, and I knew he would do that for me. I hurried toward the door, picking up the pace across the parking lot with my heart pounding in my chest and my knees shaking. The night was beginning to cool, but I felt only the fire in my head.

What is going on at the dinner? Are they drinking and celebrating? Will John worry if I get home okay? Are there women there to entertain them? The end of my fun day was anything but fun.

I could have easily lost my self-respect with more alcohol and advances from a charming man, but that did not happen. This time, I did the right thing for myself.

I remembered the code for the main door and quickly entered the well-lit private lobby. I bounded up the stairs to the second floor. It was eerily quiet. My key jingled in the apartment lock. No one stirred as I quickly shut the door to the comfortable rooms that waited for me.

The place was dark except for the pool glistening below, off the deck through the dining room door. I hesitated, afraid to turn on the lights. I was alone in his apartment for the first time. A man's apartment, a place I might live in soon. It did not quite feel like my home, but a half-bottle of red nectar in the refrigerator smiled back at me, and all that changed. I was once again okay for the night. I did not loath myself now, and settled down on the deck in a soft chair.

I put my feet up on the small wrought-iron fence and looked down at two lovers chatting in the pool, treading water in each other's arms. I watched them with curiosity and enjoyed my wine, knowing they did not see me. I envied them without jealousy.

I weighed the pros and cons of the situation I was in as I sipped the red sweetness. I saw only opportunity ahead, attending University of Michigan-Flint and living in the lovely town of Grand Blanc. This was a life more exciting than the one I had in seminary in Iowa, or my life as a college student with no car and little money.

I finished another glass of wine in the stillness of the night and waited for him to come home to me. I had no thoughts of a hangover, the highs and lows experienced that day dissipated.

John has asked me to move in with him, to change schools. He offered to pay for me to attend the U of M-Flint. We've known each other a month. I will move in after summer school ends at CMU. Will I feel loved by him someday, or just a satisfaction for him at certain times?

Going to the Chapel

Love

"Look for the experience," the campus therapist said softly. "Not the excitement. Don't try to control love."

"I'm trying to pace myself with him," I told her.

"You're in lust or desperation if you have to control anything around him," she continued.

I had been in therapy for a while now, since back at school. It was helping me deal with being an older student and divorced at twenty-one years old, and to understand John better. I needed to talk to her twice a week.

I knew right away after meeting him there was something unique about it all. It was the end of finals week when I was more open to a social life. He influenced my daily life, especially his determination to get me to move in with him after summer school. Things happened quickly and now getting married was on the agenda.

He focused intensely on me from the start, valuing my looks, my ideas, and my desires. I was fabulous in his eyes. He had his college degree and a busy career in the business world of sales and marketing. He was confident. I coveted a business man in my life again.

He was handsome, well dressed, from the west coast, and different from the guys I had known before him. He was interesting and intriguing in a new way. It was icing on the cake when he told me he had a busy social life and I could be a big part of it.

An athlete all his life, in college he played baseball and football. He had also played a lot of golf all his life, since his teen years. He was positive and outgoing, just what I needed. I was hooked into his charm immediately.

Is this love, love at first sight? He is a real boyfriend who takes me places, shows me off, and introduces me to people. I change my plans for him and feel happy about doing it, even before he asks me to do it. I like our life.

PEACE

I didn't fit in on campus in the late Sixties or early Seventies. I was not the bohemian type. I liked classic preppy-style clothes. I followed fashion magazines and icons like English model and actress Jean Shrimpton. I wanted a marriage to a businessman who would support and help me have a career, too. I had no desire to have children, at least not any time soon.

I was rebellious in my political views, but not with drugs. The legal issue of drugs stopped me. I did not want to deal with the police or jail, or the shame of anything that came with an arrest. It would not be worth the risk. I liked doing the right thing. I didn't like the smell of marijuana anyway, and other drugs scared me. The fear of flashbacks and hallucinations from taking LSD, and the fear of blindness from marijuana frightened me. My parents' scare tactics worked.

Besides, I did not want to lose control. That was not my style. I avoided people doing drugs and the places where they hung out. That meant not hanging around with the hippies who smoked marijuana and followed the teachings of Harvard professor Timothy Leary and his urgings to "turn on, tune in, and drop out." The tie-dye shirts and the sit-ins were not me either. My generation was fast becoming a part of the heyday of drugs. A culture that would shape the society I would live in and around for many years.

36

I saw a lot of drinking at home growing up and, though I had my guard up, I knew alcohol was legal for me at age twenty-one. It became my drug of choice. It was acceptable.

Drinking alcohol was different for me. I suspected pot could be, too. Alcohol was easy to get, wine as part of dinner and champagne, part of celebrating. I was not much into hard liquor.

Loud music or lyrics not easily understood did not interest me, yet I wanted to escape into The Beatles. Long-haired guys were not attractive to me, especially with hair longer than mine. I had no intention of protesting the Vietnam War, even though the killing appalled me. Being more reserved than most my age, and naïve—due to going from living at home to dorm life, to marriage and seminary, then another dorm and another college—this was all new. A second marriage wouldn't change any of it.

I want to expand my mind, but not with drugs. I want to be noticed, to be somebody, but I don't have the wherewithal on my own to do that, or the confidence to make it happen. I need to be around the right people.

LOST

"You're an old soul," my therapist offered at one of our next sessions. "Be careful who you pick for your life companion or you'll likely be disappointed."

"I feel like I was born in a past generation. The immediate post-World War Two era has gone by along with hope," I told her. "I am out of place here."

She smiled and nodded for me to continue.

"I befriended a guy in my political science class during summer school. He had recently returned from Vietnam. I held him at a distance. His life was not for me. He was fun, but not going anywhere. This new guy is much more to my liking. He is five years older than me."

My classes and my grades were important to me. I took my studying seriously and spent a lot of time at the library. I had student loans, Pell grants, and a small scholarship to be able to be there. I did not waste time. I abstained from drinking and was too serious most days for the people I met on campus. I had a closet full of clothes that looked out of place.

Who out there is trying to do something with their life? Who out there is more like me? Who out there doesn't want to get stoned every night? Where should I be?

AGREE

I met Mr. Right in a student bar during finals week when at last I agreed to go out with one of my roommates and her sister. I had not had a drink that entire school year. A glass of wine seemed well deserved to celebrate what I knew would be good grades going into summer school classes. I would be living alone for the first time in my life.

John was there at the student bar—The Cabin, near the Central Michigan University campus—on business as a marketing representative for Schlitz Brewing Company. He was having fun being the big guy giving away beer. I was there to unwind, and maybe to find somebody to amuse me. He liked that idea, and so did I the minute we met and began to talk.

"You two make a cute couple," my roommate said after only a little wine and a lot of loud music. "You look good together."

We laughed and ordered another drink, wine for me and beer for him. I thought we were happy that night, telling stories and leaning in close so we could hear each other. I felt we were right for each other. All his charm made me feel good, and my smile seemed to satisfy him. We had known each other for three hours when he asked for my phone number. I gave it to him without hesitation, and our dance began.

Immediately, I started traveling on weekends to his apartment. He came to the campus at least once during the week to take me out to dinner while he was in the area promoting Schlitz beer. We had drinks and intimate romance to complete the occasions. We talked, early on, about closing the miles gap and living together. We often entertained his clients when I visited him, but it was just the two of us when he was near the campus.

38

It wasn't romantic conversation when we talked about living together. It was as practical as if it was only about the miles, the money, and a decision of convenience that mattered. Neither one of us talked about commitment nor how much we loved each other. We hardly discussed our previous marriages. We were still in our twenties. I was barely able to visualize our life together, we had only spent weekends together over that summer. I did not even fully understand what he did for a living, and maybe did not even care at that point. I was just ready to not live in a dorm with other women. I was beyond living on or near a campus. In some small way, I had grown up a bit.

I am still uncertain. Am I willing to change schools? Take up housekeeping again so soon? Change my school plans for him? Do I want his life? Could it be my life, too? Our time together is so much centered on alcohol.

MOVE

We drank every time we met. We even drank Bloody Marys for breakfast. It involved cocktails before dinner, wine with dinner, and a sweet liqueur after dinner. Schlitz beer was around all the time, but I did not like beer. There was always talk about drinking. Drinking was what he did for a living. He lived and breathed it.

"You're going to move in with him?" my former roommate asked on the phone. "What do you know about him?"

"I know him pretty well. I know a lot about him now. I am going to do this. He is a good guy," I responded.

"He's a traveling salesman, and he moved to Michigan from California for God's sake. You don't know any of his old friends. How can you trust him?" she asked.

"I can, and I do," I blurted out. "I have met his new friends from work, and I like them, and I like him a lot. He likes me, too, and includes me in his life."

At one of the first company functions I attended with him, I learned from one of his business colleagues there was another woman in a city an hour away. He had been seeing her for about a year. He apparently had made no effort to stop seeing her, despite seeing and committing to me.

I was stunned. I was hurt. And, I was angry.

"You're a pretty girl, a nice girl," his friend said. "You would be enough for me."

This man was drinking when he told me, but I believed him. Some things a woman knows. I felt it in my gut. I kept it to myself. When we marry, I told myself, there will be no others. I will make sure of it. I was unhappy about it for a while, but then school demands kicked in, and life went on.

I stuff my hurt feelings with a little wine. There is no broken heart, no devastation on my part. I am a tough girl. I will get what I want with this move. I will be in control while sharing this household. I will make a commitment and ask him to do so as well.

THOUGHTS

I wished I had not known. On occasion, when I was alone and he was traveling, I'd drink over the idea. I finally told him she was no secret to me. We talked about it only briefly, and he told me I was wrong, and had no right to accuse him. He was angry, and we drank that night and bickered about a few other little things. We talked very little about how it bothered me, or how I was hurt. The subject never came up again.

Drinking with these thoughts solves nothing. Will we be okay? Will he adore me again? Will we go on? Will we ever get married? Will I forget and play house? Will I move out? Did we move too fast? A glass of wine will take the edge off.

COMMITMENT

Each week I started preparing for his return from a business trip with a meal plan, and a cold bottle of wine. This required a lot of effort from me, since cooking was not my thing, nor did I care to learn. He was the better cook.

I was not leaving. Infidelity was something we had to work on in our relationship. We had a big life ahead of us. My moving into his apartment meant no looking back. Life was not so bad; in fact, it was good. There was always something exciting to look forward to with his schedule and his friends who were now my friends, too.

I drink several days a week, but don't make note of it. It's as if the year of abstinence never happened. It's a busy life with classes now at the Flint branch of the University of Michigan. Being a smiling face when he needs me to greet his clients is what I do best.

"I'm a commuter, so I don't know a lot of the students. I wait until I'm home to have a glass of wine, sometimes with him, sometimes on my own when he's on a business trip," I told the school therapist. I try to relax, to unwind, to handle the anxiety of school pressure, the secret of our cohabitation we've kept from our parents, and the pressure to be who I'm supposed to be for him. "

"That is quite a mouthful," she added with a smile. "Let's start with the not telling your parents part. Does the secrecy bother you?"

CANDOR

"We need to tell my mother what we're doing," he said one morning before he left on an appointment. "You need to tell your parents, too. It's just time."

"I know it's time," I said, "I just need to get my courage up. They won't understand; they think I visit you on weekends. They don't even know I've changed schools."

I had to call my parents. The guilt was too much. They still had bills from my first wedding from two years ago, and vivid memories of moving me back from Iowa to Michigan. They had a lot of my previous wedding gifts stored in the front entrance of their small home, many of them never used.

I drink over the guilt, and that is not good. Another reason I drink often is the shame. This is a dangerous combination.

"I'm moving in with him. The guy I've been telling you about all summer. The guy that works for Schlitz and lives in Grand Blanc," I blurted out to my mother on the phone. "We aren't getting married right now. I'm going to go to school in Flint and maybe work part-time."

The silence on the phone was deafening. I finally had to say something.

"He's offered to pay for my classes. Having him pay for my classes is going to be good for me. I want to do this for a lot of reasons. You will like him when you meet him."

"Why are you doing this now? You just moved. Don't you like CMU? my dad asked after taking the phone from my mother. Your sister is going to be there in the fall."

There it was, I didn't measure up. I disappointed. I did not meet their expectations. I was going to fail again.

"Are you engaged, are you getting married?" he asked. "Why not wait until you get married first, that's what people do… or wait until you graduate."

"We have talked about marriage," I reassured. "But, we want to do this now and get to know each other. It is better because it is difficult to commute with his job and my school."

"You'll be with a person you hardly know," my mother said, now back on the phone. "You will have no friends there. He travels around Michigan, doesn't he?"

"We're serious about being together," I add. "I don't want to keep commuting to see him. He doesn't like it either, and wants me at his place when he travels, then I have more study time. It is quiet there."

FRIENDS

We met Jan and Steve walking around the little golf course at Knollwood apartments. They were fun, and we did a lot of things together. They were married for a few years when we met. He was a Japanese

American, so they knew discrimination and had very few friends. They laughed a lot and liked to have cocktails after golf. We were all living a young couple's lifestyle without children or too many cares.

Being together is what we want for us. We have a good time together, and with Jan and Steve. We laugh a lot. He must want to get married, he has pushed for me to be with him almost since the night I met him.

They agreed to be the witnesses for our wedding. It was that simple. The pressure from our families took a toll. Marriage became the decision a few months after I moved in with him. We had no bended knee proposal, just a discussion with the neighbors over cocktails.

Jan agreed I would make her a dress of red-orange silk since we set the date for Thanksgiving weekend, a time workable for our immediate family. Steve agreed because he liked to have a good time. Jan would fashion his mother's and my mother's hair in French twists for the occasion and do ours in big curls. She was a hairdresser and a good one. We would be glamorous, making an occasion of it. Although a second marriage, we would still pull out all the stops.

Jan is very generous. She loves to do things for others. I appreciate her friendship.

PLANS

The drinks list was part of the planning, at the top of the list of things to do. John's local distributor in the Flint area, the Seides, supplied all the Schlitz beer and Gallo wine. We would have plenty for our guest list, which grew quickly to one hundred people. His distributors would handle the delivery and service at the reception at the Knollwood Apartments' Clubhouse in Grand Blanc.

We had a wide assortment of appetizers and a beautiful three-tiered cake ordered from the local Hamady grocery store, another Schlitz outlet. They made sure everything fit around the beverages. The planning happened around us. That was fine with me.

I kept busy making Jan's dress while looking for my own—something that said fun, yet wedding. Mine was finally found in a full-length, fall red-orange satin skirt and cream crepe top adorned with ruffles of the same color. I wore no headpiece with my up-do of big hair, and no jewelry except for pearl earrings, anticipating the little gold band.

My soon-to-be husband wore a brown polyester knit suit and his friend did the same. We all loved their outrageous orange-print ties. We chose orange and cream flowers for our bouquets and boutonnieres.

His parents divorced several years earlier, so his dad did not attend. My parents separated that same month. My mother had no other choice but to drive home with my dad in a snow storm, since all the bus lines were shut down. They did reconcile again after the wedding.

We decorated the party room with fall items but left most of that to the distributors who wanted to handle everything as a gift to us. We had plenty of "cocktail hour" planning sessions before the big day and felt we were putting on quite an event.

The night before, at the rehearsal dinner with our wedding party and immediate family, we celebrated at The Roadhouse. It was a stormy night, but we celebrated with delicious prime rib dinners and a lot of Merlot to wash it down.

His mother paid for the rehearsal dinner. A divorced woman, she traveled alone from Albuquerque to support her son and meet the woman who would become his next wife. She was a high school teacher, and quite shy. It was a big trip for her, but she was eager to meet my family. She also liked her cocktails and fit in well with the rest of us.

We had the dinner at The Roadhouse in downtown Flint... of course, another outlet for Schlitz beer. Always looking to promote business, this had to be the place. The owner paid for a round of drinks to say congratulations. The private dinner for eleven of us was delicious. My parents, his mother, my two younger sisters and their boyfriends, and Jan and Steve were all present.

The rehearsal dinner went well, even with way too much to drink on my part. I loved the way it felt after one glass of wine. Being unhitched some from the stress of the wedding, meeting his mother and trying to impress everyone, I easily spoke out of turn a couple of times. My sisters were used to it and laughed. My parents said nothing.

The next day, the Woodside Church on Court Street in Flint, near the Mott Building, would be our wedding place. It was near where I took classes at the U of M-Flint campus. We chose Woodside because it was a church that spoke its mind, raised questions, and invited unconventional answers. My soon-to-be husband was affiliated with no church, had not been baptized, gone to Sunday School, or attended church camp at any time in his life. Because I had done all of that, and more, it made no difference to him where we got married. He did not care what plans I made, only that it happened.

CELEBRATE

"The weather in southern Michigan at Thanksgiving time is cold, and a chance of snow is imminent," we heard on TV the morning of the wedding. We were going to have fun no matter what the weather. Glasses of champagne flowed early before the ceremony. I made sure everyone knew where the church was, since it was in downtown Flint, but otherwise my morning consisted of getting my hair done and dressing for the occasion.

His mother Ruby, my mother Catherine, and my friend Jan and I assembled at our place for the hair event. We all agreed a bottle of champagne was in order. The crystalline nectar wasted no time in giving me courage. I soon felt happy about my dress, my hair, and getting married… carefree and ready to take on the day.

I no longer drink because I am lonely or anxious, I drink to celebrate and enjoy life. I trust champagne and wine when I am with friends and family. I don't anticipate anything ugly happening at our wedding, but I do see how alcohol is beginning to invade my life.

45

Vows

All our cars pulled in at the handsome, historic Woodside Church about fifteen minutes before we were scheduled to be married. The venue had beckoned us through the tree-lined street adorned with gas lamps in this celebrated historic area of Flint. The whole scene was breathtakingly beautiful as the soft snow began to fall harder. We flashed our lights, and everyone began to file out of their cars and into the chapel as the winds picked up. It was serene and quiet in the chapel, almost somber, but that little bit of the bubbly soon dissipated the serenity as I chatted nervously.

The ceremony was short, sweet, and standard. We did not write our own vows or make it anything special, not even on the advice of Jan and Steve standing next to us. They were another couple who had been married before. We had matching gold wedding bands, beautiful really, with the interlocking "circles of love" symbols around them. Nothing felt wrong about our rushing into marriage after knowing each other less than six months. This was what we wanted to do.

We forged out of the church's luxurious oak door fifteen minutes later, into a blistering snowstorm, to start our life together. It all seemed surreal at the time as we whisked off in our company car to the suburban area of Grand Blanc. The wedding reception was already underway without us.

Our family is cheering and laughing, both with us and at the weather. It is almost symbolic of our whirlwind courtship. We are ready for fun and celebration. I can feel it. My craving alcohol, that need, that wanting above all else. Those psychological factors impair my thinking, make the situation out-of-kilter with life.

The party room soon filled with people. His Schlitz distributors and other clients, the determined hosts, were there setting things up and sampling the spirits. My Godmother Helen, and her daughter Lois, and son-in-law Konrad, who lived in the immediate area, were seated at a back table. Several of John's work friends and their wives arrived, ready to party.

That is what people do when they work for a beer distributor. They party and expect a party, and we were not going to disappoint themselves or anyone else. None of my college or high school friends attended. It was a company affair with some family.

The DJ we hired was already spinning the Seventies' sounds. It was festive. My parents joined my family's table, my sisters Kathy and Roberta, and their boyfriends Frank and Pete, hit the dance floor. My new husband John, and I greeted his friends at the bar. Jan and Steve, who attended for us, were now meeting friends from our other life, his business life. They looked out of place. Steve, the school teacher, and Jan, the hairdresser, seemed to get lost in the shuffle that night. For me, though, it was Gallo red and music, and whirling around in red-orange satin showing off my pretty gold band.

My husband danced with me and his mother, but the painful dance was with my mother. She acted so nervous dancing with my husband, it was difficult to watch. My dad danced with no one, no matter how hard we tried to get him on the dance floor. No amount of disappointment on my face was going to change that scenario for him.

My insecurities come from my mother. I hate admitting that to anyone. I don't want to be like her, I want to be strong and confident every day.

Things I thought would never happen did happen that night. One of John's colleagues cornered me in the hallway near the bathrooms. He was very drunk. He pinned me to the wall and pressed himself against me, almost suffocating me. I was drunk, too, but not drunk enough that I couldn't get away. I slipped under his arm and ran toward the music. I told no one about what happened and returned to the party with a smiling face. I never dreamt of telling my husband for fear of him not believing me.

I realized then my drinking could turn dangerous, but shook it off and went back to my new married life with the beer marketer. At the reception party, with all our friends and family—who were oblivious to my drinking and to what transpired—I opened gifts and kept going all night long. Already being seduced into what marriage should be, I was looking down the rabbit hole of life, wondering what it meant to be a woman who liked to drink with a lot of questions about life. I did not remember the middle of the party moving to the end of the party, or the goodbyes and the final congratulations.

GRAB FOR ALL THE GUSTO

LEAVING ON A JET PLANE

The Sales and Marketing Department for Schlitz Brewing Company, the beer that made Milwaukee famous, took about a thousand of us to Oahu, Hawaii, on chartered stretch jets from Detroit, New York, and Los Angeles in 1972. No matter what part of the country you called home, you ended up in Honolulu for the annual marketing convention, wives included. The number two beer in the country was always plotting to be number one again.

We joined the others at Detroit Metro Airport for our flight to paradise. After Bloody Marys in the bar, we boarded around happy hour to head out toward the Pacific.

A fully stocked open bar nestled at the rear of this plane filled with close to 300 passengers. My husband, and several of his friends in the district manager ranks, bellied up to that bar for the ten-hour flight. Standing most of the way and drinking, they discussed the new company strategies to win back favor with public appeal. The booze flowed, along with all choices of Schlitz beer and Gallo wine. There was no shortage.

We would gain a lot of time from Detroit in EST across to PST at the western coast to another time zone in Hawaii—HST Hawaiian-Aleutian—three hours from PST. With that timeline, it was a long rowdy flight, gaining hours with that open bar. I decided I had better have a few drinks to keep up with the action and join in the fun.

Although I was already exhausted from the rush of getting ready to leave and finishing up with school demands, I headed to the back of the plane for something to relax me. My husband had a Canadian Club and water ready for me.

"Have a drink." He grinned. "Enjoy yourself, you deserve it."

"It's CC and water, what I drink. You'll get sick on a juice mix if we have motion."

"Thanks," I said as I slowly sipped the brown liquid. His control over me was obvious, but in his own way he meant well. The guys around the bar observed us and said nothing.

The taste of this drink he insisted I take… it was hard to get down. As usual, I listened to him and drank it. I was not a beer drinker in this beer-guzzling crowd. Grabbing for the gusto as the Schlitz mantra professed was not for me, at least not in the beer category. With a little encouragement, though, I made up for it with cocktails.

The conversation in the back of the plane stayed on business, the decision Schlitz had made to reformulate their beer to cut costs to meet high demand. The topic eventually turned to football. The two subjects at the time were boring to me, even though we attended college and professional football games on occasion with his Schlitz co-workers and distributors.

I finished the first drink and took a second with me as I headed back to my seat to settle in for the long flight. I was starting to feel better emotionally on the second drink. My husband would be the last man standing in the back, so I read to amuse myself, but was already feeling the drinks on my empty stomach. I did not want to throw up in front of everyone. I needed food. The stewardess saw my look of tension and brought me a snack almost immediately after I hit the buzzer.

Before we landed, I made my way to the back of the plane several more times for another CC and water, and once to the bathroom to throw up. The plane hit turbulence past the halfway point over the Pacific Ocean, which did not let up until we saw the coastal lights. The captain asked for everyone to take their seats but, of course, the party at the rear of the plane was oblivious to the announcements. They considered themselves above the fray of the turbulence.

My husband hardly used his seat the entire flight, so I curled up in both seats by moving the armrest upward. That didn't work. My body clock was out of sync. My head pounded, and I was nauseous. I thought about a sweet drink to keep me awake after we arrived; green crème de menthe would do the trick when we arrived at the hotel.

"I have meetings all day tomorrow," he said after finally returning to his seat for landing. "You're free until the opening dinner at six. Some of the women are planning to have lunch by the pool at eleven thirty. I heard them talking. You should join them."

"I might. I thought I would check out the tennis area. I brought my racket," I commented, asserting myself a bit. "The pool sounds good, too, but why not the beach?"

He didn't answer. He was leaning over me to see Waikiki Beach out the window. The magnificent view of the Royal Hawaiian Hotel with its stunning pink exterior and swooning gas lights was breathtaking. It was just as I thought it would be, the way my dad had described it. "The Pink Palace of the Pacific" had been a rest and relaxation stop for the military during WWII and Vietnam.

The lights of Waikiki sparkled out the window as we came closer and prepared for our landing. I had never flown over the Pacific Ocean. I had been to Puerto Rico, over the Bermuda Triangle, but my travels were limited. This was an adventure.

My dad experienced the Royal Hawaiian from his Navy ship just two days before the Japanese bombings started WWII. The prominent location of the hotel had commanded the beach since the hotel's construction in 1927. It was surreal to think I was now going to vacation here at this same hotel some thirty years after my dad first laid eyes on it. Even the lush lighted tropical gardens rose to the sky as we looked down from the air. It was a poetic moment.

"Beachfront luxury will be ours for a week. I'm excited," I commented.

"Enjoy it. I'll be pretty busy."

WAIKIKI BEACH

Our poolside room was ready but, as anticipated, another drink was in order before we headed upstairs. The green nectar sloshed around in the short wide glass, sweet and sticky, just the way I liked it. I savored it and let it warm my throat. John talked incessantly to somebody from his marketing team about the lost flavor in the beer. I leaned back and watched the waves just outside the open area of the bar. It was heaven here, a beautiful place. My drink cravings intensified. This is what we do on vacation: eat, drink, relax, and party.

Why feel sad in this beautiful place? We love this type of place, the tropics, a beautiful hotel, and company-paid. We have a good life. Be grateful. Why does the drinking come in to play? What is missing in our lives? Why do we not talk about these things, and keep running through life? Enjoy this gorgeous place and take advantage of everything, with him or without him.

The next morning, I scouted out the hotel and decided against tennis. I eventually found the ladies at the pool enjoying Mai Tai's, sunshine, and cabanas providing little sandwiches and fruit bowls. Nervousness washed over me as I ordered a Chardonnay. I didn't mention to them I had already enjoyed a Bloody Mary with my eggs at breakfast.

I was ready for wine and not a fluffy drink. I ordered white wine, Chardonnay, my favorite. I was happy now and looking forward to a day in the sun. It had been a rough winter in Michigan and a January vacation at Waikiki Beach was perfect. Even though some of these women seemed out of my league, the white sweetness made me feel just fine. I fit in enough to add slightly to the conversation.

Pace yourself. Don't be hung over again tomorrow. Don't throw up again today. Barfing is painful. I can't keep retching. I'm ashamed of my behavior, and out of sorts. I don't eat much when I drink, it seems I forget to eat. I eventually throw up bile. This is not me, and not what my husband expects of me. He did not marry me for this. He married a nice Midwestern girl. Where did she go? He loved my innocence in the beginning, what does he love now?

For the next six days, we ate whatever we wanted, we drank any drinks we wanted, and slept very little. We attended functions in the evening that lasted long after dinner. The hotel's outdoor bar was a meeting place. I thought I was invincible and could keep up with not only my husband, who weighed twice what I did, but also his cronies who were experienced drinkers. They all drank for a living and fun. I drank for the fun of it, or so I thought.

I rented a bright yellow Jeep Thing Convertible from the hotel to "rod" around the Island. I invited a couple of the ladies from the pool to join me. They were from Detroit, older than me, and game for some fun. Their husbands were busy, too. We found cocktails at outdoor beach bars, and handsome guys working at these places to entertain us.

I needed to drink just a little around women like these to fit in. They were not my usual friends. They had more money, bigger houses, Ivy League degrees, and came from boarding schools. They sipped their drinks like ladies, not the way I drank. I paid them no mind.

We laughed, listened to music, and drank more than we planned. At least I did. The road back down the hillside was treacherous and almost more than I could handle. I should not have been driving, but no one else knew how to drive a stick-shift Jeep that day.

"Are you sure you're going to be okay to drive?" Margie asked.

"Of course, I am," I commented. "I've only had a few."

Her concern was a bit judging but, with that, the women piled into the Jeep.

I saw my husband each evening for dinner and to meet people for drinks in the bar beforehand, usually a company-planned function. The cocktail parties were lavish, and nobody counted how many drinks anyone had, especially me. My vow of pacing myself had escaped me.

The silk purple floral mini-wrap dress I wore for the awards dinner on that night was already marred with a few drops of wine. They blended into the pattern. I knew where they came from, but I didn't tell my husband, or how much I drank alone before he came back to the room. A couple of glasses of wine to help me get dressed were always in order.

I ate very little at the huge pig roast as the food did not appeal to me, but the drinking did. I talked incessantly to somebody I hardly knew, who seemed more amused by me than interested. All my discomfort at the event came out in my nervousness as I fidgeted with my food, a beautiful meal that just would not go down.

My husband caught my arm as I stood up from the table. He escorted me out the door to the ladies' room. I threw up on the floor in the stall, but not on myself; quite a feat at this point in the evening. He took me back toward our room against my will. I was edgy and still nauseated to the point of dizziness as we left the elevator.

"I won't apologize for you," he said laughing. "You need to be a little less obvious drunk, and not depend on me so much."

This is the way everyone seems to drink. We are around a drinking business. It is our life now. We started our life together with drinks and here we are drinking with others more than with each other. We are a couple in a drinking world, controlled by a drinking company. I feel alone in my marriage and yet, in the beginning, we were so desperate to be together. What happened?

USS ARIZONA

The day before we left the island, I went with three of the same women from the Jeep Thing trip out to the USS Arizona Memorial to tour the scene. I promised my dad I would go for him. Oddly, as a National Park it was eerie, but impressive at the same time. We traveled by bus to see the memorial park honoring the greatest loss of life of any US warship in American history. A lot of Japanese tourists joined us. I felt a huge sense of relief to be there, as I wasn't sure I would make it that morning.

The small, short boat shuttle ride in Pearl Harbor was difficult. I was gagging before we arrived. Any little motion was almost more than I could handle. The sight of the oil slick was startling and not what I needed to see. A sign read, "The Tears of Arizona," and the name caught all of us off-guard.

I had been feeling ill before breakfast. My Bloody Mary with my toast had helped take care of the hair-of-the-dog. Now, though, we were being asked to look down into this historic site through the memorial that straddled the hull of the battleship, while all I wanted was to be invisible.

The memorial did not touch the warship burial of more than 1,100 men. I had to see it. I had to do this no matter how nauseated or how dizzy I was, because this was important. It was a sacred place, and I had promised my dad.

My new friends feel sorry for me and want to help. My embarrassment is minimal, I've been here before. I did not make my dad proud with signs of the shakes. I need to calm down. How am I going to pull myself together for the rest of the day? I want to remember this as a special time, and for it to be peaceful.

LUAU

Our last night in Hawaii featured a Luau on Waikiki Beach with all the usual suspects: sales, marketing, and management all in one place. I had bought a new dress that day, along with new shoes and a handbag.

I wore a soft white knit that blew in the breeze like a well-crafted sail. My long hair was shining, and I had just enough shell jewelry around my neck and ankles to look sassy, swaggering into the event. My husband waited for me in the lobby bar. For a moment I had his attention, upon my entrance.

I decided it had better be a Chardonnay night so if I spilled anything it would not ruin my new dress. The first drink went down easily. I totally forgot I was breaking in new shoes as I began whirling to the music with my new girlfriends. I smiled across the room at my husband, barely focusing on him. A sadness engulfed me as I realized the marriage we had just a year ago survived no longer. We had run it into the ground, we let it go to the wind, we ruined it with alcohol.

I do not remember returning to the room, getting into bed, or taking off my beautiful dress, but there it was the next morning, rolled up into a ball beside the bed. My white patent leather shoes with the shell and gold adornments were on the table on the other side of the room, and my feet hurt terribly. My small white handbag was misplaced.

I suspect I danced or stood up near the bar for a long time and never gave my little puppies a rest. I hate what has become of my glamorous life, yet I crave that social outlet. I feel a rising tide of shame. I can't remember last night. God help me. I love him in my own way, but we are in trouble.

"You need to get up. We have less than an hour to finish packing and get out of here. The cab is going to be downstairs soon and we need to be on time," he said with a stare. Not a hint of the extra stroking of my hair in the morning I knew just a year ago.

"I can't walk, my feet hurt," I said with a wince. "I need to sit in the bathtub. I am serious, this is painful."

"There is no time for that. Take a quick shower and get going. I'm going to check out. I'll be back shortly to help you."

I barely functioned enough to get out of bed. I was frustrated, rushing and throwing things in the suitcase, with no prepacking the day before. I did not know what to ask about last night, and hated that feeling of losing control. He stayed silent and made me ask for the story.

I can't remember how much I drank. He is not volunteering anything. I said no more this morning, and now I am in tears. I feel sick again and my feet are a mess. They are stiff and puffy, unlike anything I have ever seen. Where did my dignity go?

"It's time to go," he yelled from the hallway. "Do you have everything?"

"I'm almost ready, but I can't get my shoes on. My feet are really swollen."

He entered the room. He grabbed my shoes and handed a tip to the bell hop waiting at the room door. All our bags were on the carrier. I took a quick glance at the room; it was a mess, but we were off. I said very little, or a few words in a soft tone, and walked to the elevator, shoeless.

I was okay barefoot in the hotel lobby. The carpet was plush and soft, like a manicured lawn, and the tile felt cool to the touch. But, the pavement outside was hot on my sore feet. I hopped quickly to a shady spot.

"I can't walk in my shoes, or without them. What am I going to do?"

"I don't know. I can't carry you, we have too many carry-on bags."

I tiptoed gingerly to the cab and crawled slowly into the seat. As I positioned myself near the window I looked down at my feet. My toes had blistered together since awakening, and they were swollen shut. They looked like webbed feet. That was only half the problem. They were hot to the touch. I was afraid the blisters would break and knew that was not good. Infection could occur so easily. My first thought was a cold glass of wine would help ease the pain, but would it add to the swelling? Could too much wine have done this?

"Please help me and carry me on the tarmac to the plane," I begged him. "Look at my feet. They are really in bad shape."

He carefully pulled my feet up with his hands to look. He cringed.

"You've had a hell of a trip to Waikiki, and now you're paying for it," was his response. "I know how much you've been drinking. It worries me."

The cab ride was brisk, and I was trying desperately to come up with a comment, but I had none, so said nothing.

The plane was waiting on the runway when we arrived. The cab stopped near the security entrance. I did not move. My husband came around to my side, quickly opened the door, and picked me up in his arms. He motioned for the cab driver to follow us with our carry-on bags from the back seat. The company man designated to help with the suitcases came over immediately. We were quite a spectacle.

We were queried about our trip at security, but they did not ask John to put me down or explain why he was carrying me. The red blistered and swollen feet said volumes. The cab driver handed us our carryon bags and my white sandals. They all passed inspection, only my feet were questionable.

John's carrying me through the gate, but saying nothing. I have my arms around his neck and am lugging my shoes and our bags against his back. We head down the tarmac toward the plane. Nobody says anything, although I hear a few whispers and see a few curious looks. There is comfort in his coming to my aide. It feels for a moment as if we could go back to a more romantic time, a time when we needed each other.

Yes, I had made a mess of things this time, but I just wanted my seat and a glass of wine. I didn't want to explain my feet to anybody, and I surely did not want anybody to explain them to me.

I was grateful for my husband who, for the first time all week, had really noticed me and paid attention to me, even caring enough to help me. It was a rare moment for us when our silence bonded us in our insane behavior. We still had something between us.

The ticket person at the base of the stairs let us on the plane without much chatter. My husband carefully lowered me into the window seat. Though not one of the first ones on the plane, we were one of the first to order a drink. He climbed in next to me and said nothing more about my feet or about abusing myself. He glanced one more time at my feet, smiled, and patted my hand... a gesture I saw infrequently these days.

"Thanks for helping me," I said.

"Forget it," he commented. "Let's just get home uninjured."

The plane took off as scheduled, and beautiful Waikiki Beach pulled away from us quickly. I peered down at it through the window and wondered if I really enjoyed the trip as much as I could have without my husband around most of the time. Or, was I so dependent on him that I had to take his lead to function? Where will we go from here?

What will I remember about this trip? The dinners? The new women friends? The fun? The drinking, the hangovers, or the time alone with my thoughts? Do I have a romantic evening to cling to, or was romance not even remotely in the picture? I am as much at fault as he is, we are letting these times slip by and we do not even recognize them until they are gone. God help me to speak up, to take some control of my life and my marriage.

"Your wine, Miss," she said cheerfully.

The stewardess handed me my drink and broke my thoughts. I was almost in a fog now, dreaming of a trip that should have been, and feeling alone in a place with 300 people, many whom I knew personally.

"Thank you."

"The captain has left the seatbelt sign on, there's some turbulence ahead. Please do not leave your seats," another cheerful voice said from the speaker system.

"Bring us two more," my husband said to the stewardess as she passed by again. "It sounds like we're going to need them tonight."

He finished his drinks and dosed off, but thirty minutes later I woke him up to let me out for the bathroom. The plane had been rocking about in turbulent airspace that came upon us quickly. We were still more than three hours from the mainland. I was not doing well.

My stomach was upset. I had eaten a little, but suffered diarrhea from eating too many things I normally didn't eat. I didn't even consider all the drinking and my lack of sleep. I was getting concerned about how long the queasiness would last.

As soon as he moved slightly, I made a beeline to the small lavatory in the front of the plane, not too far from our seats. I knew the other lavatories in the rear of the plane near the open bar would be standing room only.

The red "take your seat" light was flashing as I locked the door. I was in rough shape, sicker than I imagined, and gagging into the sink. The heaving of the plane kept hurling me forward toward the sink as I threw up. This happened several times before I found the toilet.

This is my punishment for excess this past week, for abusing my body and for a lack of control with my drinking. Why did I do this? Can I stop if I want to? I am not really that bad all the time; this is a vacation. I never wanted to be a drinker and look where I am now. God help me, this is a pathetic way to end ten days in Hawaii.

The pilot kept announcing we were in turbulent airspace and we would be for at least another thirty minutes. He kept insisting everyone return to their seats and fasten their seat belts. My husband came knocking on the lavatory door.

"You need to get back to your seat," he said. "It's going to get pretty rough."

"Not as rough as it is in here," I quipped.

For the next ten minutes, I tried to get back to my seat, to no avail. I was bouncing around in the small space they called a lavatory. I felt trapped and had to figure out a way to slowly return to my seat unnoticed.

Thank God, the plane is quieting down. I can get some sleep. We are gaining hours, so people will sleep over the mainland. They are tired, and I am, too. I need food and another drink. I hope I can hold it down. The next drink will be easier, I will be ready for it after I see the mainland below us, and we are out of this turbulence.

Chicago, Chicago

Transferred

I heard his voice as he entered the recovery room. My throat hurt a lot from the tonsillectomy. I couldn't speak, and was still a little groggy.

"I accepted the transfer to Chicago. They want me there in a week. It's a great promotion, and a fascinating city," John said with his usual big grin. "You'll love tree-lined Lakeshore Drive."

I blinked so he knew I heard him. My not talking didn't make any difference. I had no say in these matters. He took care of things, and I went along pretty much without a fuss.

Our two years together in Michigan involved a lot of this while spending nights out with distributors and people affiliated with Schlitz. Now they were transferring us to a stronger market, a bigger city, and a lot more responsibility for him. The beer business was a social business, and he loved it. Everybody drank. I was not the exception. It would be more of the same, times three.

Was I ready for it?

Socializing

My husband John told me he drank long and hard on business trips, punctuated by some wild tales. I saw that behavior at home, at dinners out with clients, and with the neighbors at our block parties. I blamed him for my drinking too much and too often, but the truth is I liked

61

to drink, too. To take the edge off a stressful day, to calm down. I liked the feeling it gave me, the confidence and the escape from feeling left out of some of the conversations.

We held block parties a couple times each summer, organized by Mary Lou, Loretta, and I. John would order a keg of beer from Schlitz, as well as a lot of extra cases to store in the garage for backup. Each

household donated food. Our street was blocked off at the cul-de-sac of Village Court. Loretta supplied the music from their stereo, as they had the loudest speakers.

A couple of houses had kids, and the rest of us invited a few friends from outside the neighborhood. The total party numbered around thirty-five people. A lot of food, a lot of fun, a lot of laughs filled the day until the guys decided to leap over the food table or win the beer chugging contests. Both met with disasters.

SCHMOOSING

My husband, if you asked him, was paid to "play golf and drink beer" as a district manager for Schlitz, though it amounted to a bit more than that scenario. His responsibilities included schmoozing the distributors and keeping them happy, and serving as the liaison between them and the brewery. I found his work amusing and fun, boring at times, but interesting, and went along with it all willingly. That was what I was supposed to do. The abundance of lounges and nightclubs in the city kept us busy.

I simply needed to look cute, smile, and hold an adult conversation with business associates or clients, often twice my age, on topics I knew very little about, but was willing to learn. I worked part-time as a receptionist in a small sales office near our home and went to community college taking Liberal Arts classes. I had minimal business experience. I was naïve, but eager.

Like a fish out of water, it was often noticeable, but if I had a glass of wine, I did not care so much.

FRIENDSHIPS

We spent time with our neighbors in Michigan, especially Kathy and Phil, after building our home in Grand Blanc. I had school friends there, but his work friends took priority. Would this happen in Chicago, too? Almost from the beginning of our marriage we had separate friends whom I tried to blend, but it never seemed to work out.

Will anything change or get better? It seems whatever and whomever you are looking for, you can find it in Chicago. It is a well-known cross-cultural city. A city of contrasts with an old town and a new town. I do love this place.

SURGERY

With tonsillitis, I had complained about sore throats and sinus and allergy issues for a year. I was anemic most of the time, the B-12 shots did not do much for me. I was often too exhausted and having a hard time getting out of bed in the morning.

My husband played golf regularly with his distributor Leo at the Flint Golf Club, a private club near downtown Flint. They often stayed for drinks at the lavish clubhouse. My husband often commented that it was a "golfer's course," whatever that meant. I was a tennis player and knew all about that game.

One day Leo brought along his neighbor Murray, a doctor, to play with them. In his usual take-charge fashion, John mentioned my ailments to the doctor. Suddenly, I am heading to Flint General Hospital. It was an overnight stay to have my tonsils removed. They decided it was a good idea for me to have the surgery… it would help me feel better and get rid of my persistent sore throat. John did not see a problem with going to Chicago for his promotion interview the day of the surgery. I drove myself to the hospital. Again, I did not question him.

My godmother Helen sent me flowers and called to talk the night before the surgery. She lived near, but couldn't come to see me. Feeling abandoned, but glad she called, I coped and dealt with my time in the hospital, remembering this was only minor surgery.

They set me up in a chair for the surgery, like a dentist's chair, and froze my throat. I was given a Valium just before they wheeled me into the operating room. The doctor who did the surgery was quite the character.

"You have large tonsils for such a little person," he said as he pulled them out with surgical clippers and dropped them in a jar I could see to my right.

He also sang "Wish I was a Rich Man" from the play *Fiddler on the Roof* while he performed the surgery. He was quite good, with a deep voice and the right accent for the part.

"He has the lead next month in the play at the Mott Theatre," explained the head nurse after she checked me into recovery. "You might want to go. It is supposed to be very good."

MOVING

My tonsillectomy succeeded, and after a few days I felt well enough to ask a few questions about Chicago. His new job, the neighborhood, where we would live, and the new people we would associate with were going to be very different.

"What part of Chicago will we live in?" I asked. "I hope we can live in the city. That would be exciting. I would love to be near the Art

Institute and all the public artworks," I blurted out. "Even with the dog, we should be able to find a nice smaller place we can afford near the lake. That would be a great place to walk Casey."

"Are you serious?" he snapped. "I've been looking at houses in the western suburbs. That's where everybody lives. My office and distributors are out there, and it'll be safer to be in DuPage County when I have to travel."

I didn't respond. He made the decisions on the big plans. I took a moment for myself and tried to think of a comment. Usually, I stood back. I could have a glass of wine or two with dinner and forget how little control I had over my life. I chose complacency again.

FOR SALE

"I'll be flying to Chicago each week now," he announced two weeks later. "We need to put the house up for sale after we talk to the guy at First Bank over on Saginaw Street. Remember, he said he wanted to buy it whenever we were ready to sell."

I sipped my wine and listened with one eye on my Irish setter puppy playing in the back yard, my birthday gift a year earlier... a gift I begged for relentlessly. John had come up with so many reasons why he thought I could not take care of a dog.

"You have school and a part-time job," he remarked when I first asked. "Being alone when I travel is too much for you to add in a dog."

That thinking ranked up there with the house decision, but this small victory was finally mine. I named my dog Casey, an Irish name for good luck. He was registered, and I adored him. I used him for stud, a hobby that became a small bit of income and independence for me.

GOODBYE

We had hardly settled into the pretty little ranch house we built on an acre on Riverview Drive when the news of Chicago came up. It stood next to a secluded city park and behind a grade school, separated by a running creek with the street dead-ending at the park. I loved walking there and bicycling with the dog. Saying goodbye to the neighborhood was not easy. It had begun to feel like home. The neighbors, Phil and Kathy, were fun and good to us when we needed them. We had spent time together, even taking them with us for a weekend to Mackinac to meet my parents.

Our yard was showing signs of green and growth after the hard work of laying sod and planting shrubs. The flowerbeds of yellow and white crocus huddled next to a multitude of tulips in all possible colors. Was I going to miss that beauty, too?

What are the neighbors going to think of a real estate sign? He had not told anyone yet, and I was told not to either. They would be offended that their friendship did not mean more, but that was the way he wanted it. The garage sale sign and realty sign posted in the yard the same day. His attitude was, we'll never see these people again. I bought into that way of thinking if I had a glass of wine in my hand to quiet my conscience.

I had no one else to say goodbye too really, so why the guilt? My school friends were a happy-hour bunch on Thursday night after class if John was out of town. Usually, a small group was up for one of the taverns near the campus of U of M-Flint. The Torch Bar and Grill on Buckham Alley was a favorite. I made sure this was not one my husband frequented to promote Schlitz. It was my place with my school friends.

Joe, the "good looking guy" in my Psych class, hung around me at The Torch. I went to his place a few times, but it meant nothing. Too much wine and an extra dose of loneliness got me there. I accepted my poor choice, and blamed alcohol and my husband's frequent absences. It never occurred to me that alcohol was but a symptom of my problems. I saw leaving for Chicago as a chance to wipe the slate clean.

I vow to be more a part of his Schlitz life in Chicago and take a different approach to it all, learning to appreciate his clients in Greek Town, and China Town, and the Italians in Cicero. I will do my share and be more social if we take clients out to someplace like the Drury Lane Theatre for an evening. We hear wonderful things about the place.

I planned to support him further by getting to know these new colleagues, especially the wives. I would stop complaining we were always with other people and never had time alone together. My adventurous suggestion to buy season tickets for the Chicago Symphony and have nights out with his distributors made him happy.

SOLD

"I'll have the contract with me when I get home. The one I told you about, for the tri-level house in the cul-de-sac," he said hurriedly on the phone.

"It's a great buy, a growing area in DuPage County about twenty miles west of downtown Chicago," he continued. "The older couple who owns it are moving to Florida and throwing in their Chicago Bears season tickets for next year. A neighbor has a sailboat off Navy Pier. They share it with the neighbors… you'll like that I'm sure."

"Yes, I would," I agreed and tried to be enthusiastic.

"What does the house look like, how big?" I asked. "You know I prefer a condo downtown since I will eventually be going to school at the University of Chicago."

"I know, but that makes no sense, and we already discussed this. My office is west of downtown a half hour or more, and so is the airport," he continued without missing a beat. "You'll like it. There is a pool area, a clubhouse and tennis courts, about 400 houses."

The house was salmon pink, a good-sized tri-level with cranberry colored shutters, garage door, and front entrance door. A beautiful full oak tree graced the front yard, and a manicured lawn swept up to an array of flower beds. They featured breathtaking white, pink and orange daffodils; white and pink Grecian windflowers; and orange, blue, and purple Dutch iris. The cul-de-sac was impressive, showing off a half-dozen immaculate homes.

The neighbors to our immediate right came out to greet us as we pulled into the driveway. They smiled as they introduced their young boy and girl.

"We're Mary Lou and Lyle. Welcome to the neighborhood," she said in her perky voice. "These are David and Deanna, our children."

"Hi," I said as my Irish setter Casey bounded out of the car toward them.

My husband said hello and began some small talk about our move, while offering a handshake. I listened and pulled the dog back, apologizing for his energy. They didn't mind and were sincerely interested in why we moved there. Mary Lou and Lyle proudly began telling us about the neighborhood amenities and that they had grown up in Chicago and could tell us all about its special attractions.

I appreciated her enthusiasm, but wanted to get inside and settle in for a while. It had been a long drive from Michigan that day, and my exhaustion was beginning to show. We said our goodbyes quickly and unpacked the car. The Mateus Rose wine was packed carefully and I began to search for my favorite little squat bottles.

My husband had stopped for beer the minute we crossed the Cook County line into DuPage County, turning down Plainfield Road toward our new home. He was popping "gusto" open before I found my way to the trunk and the box marked "wine" containing my sweet-tasting libation. It was packed as carefully as my lava lamps.

The moving van had already been there and delivered the furniture and boxes, a perk of our corporate move. We had a lot of work ahead of us, and I hoped it would be as fun as the first house. Maybe an open house like the one we had after the sod was laid at the Michigan house, or the after parties for his baseball team during his summer city league in Flint. My garage projects of decoupage and macramé might happen here, too.

A lot had happened in those two years in Grand Blanc. We had both changed, grown up a little and apart a little. I wasn't the blushing bride anymore. I wasn't sipping wine anymore, I was adding an extra bottle to the pantry for my nights at home alone. I had already been unfaithful and so had he. Were we going to go on like this? Would we try counseling again? Did we even think it would help? Was the lifestyle with Schlitz part of the problem?

I was nervous meeting the other new neighbors, feeling anxiety about needing to meet their expectations. We heard they were all professionals, and that some of the women worked, too. The neighbors, in general, seemed like they would be ready to make plans often and keep things going on our block. That could be good, but our life was already very social with his work and the multitude of things I wanted to see and do. A priority for me was the famous Shed Aquarium. The water of the lake and the sea display there calmed me.

Could we handle more parties? More activities? Could I? Would I have time for them with school and studying, a part-time job, and a half hour commute every day? Did I want the neighbors to know us well, our unconventional marriage of secret affairs and separate lives with our own friends, and of drinking to excess? It was all very exciting but selling ourselves was a lot of work.

HOME

The move happened too quickly for me. I had to slow things down and usually did it with a drink. I often did not know how else to calm myself. It had been a long time since I had written in my diary or said my prayers, even ridden a bicycle. Why did I not take time for those things anymore? Depression had set in, and I could not escape it except in a good book where I did not need to talk to anyone.

I found myself seeking isolation after major events in our lives and this move was one of those times. As usual, I kept my feelings to myself, not mentioning them to my husband. He would laugh at me anyway and tell me I was imaging things, that the life we lived was the envy of our neighbors and I had better start appreciating it

I did appreciate our lovely home, with all the new furniture we purchased to make it quite a showplace. I liked my "new" car, his mother's old sporty Pontiac Le Mans: the turquoise and white gift she gave to me on the first Christmas we visited there from Chicago. We drove it back from New Mexico in style. I loved going to school at one of the best community colleges in the country, College of DuPage in Glen Ellyn. I

69

was living better than ever before, but that did not ease the loneliness or sadness I often felt.

I believed I didn't fit in as the traditional wife like the others in the neighborhood. I was still going to school when everyone around me already had their college degrees. I had no intention of joining a sorority, like most of the wives had, and I hadn't traveled much either. I was often left out of the conversation with his colleagues, especially when their wives were included and college came into the conversation. The day we attended the Museum of History as a group, though, I was in my element. I was home. I was passionate about history, and I knew my history. No alcohol required that day. He expected my smiling face, and he got it.

THE WINDY CITY

Chicago was a great city with a strong mayor in Richard J. Daley, and growing from an industrial city into a financial and transportation city. Moving to the Chicago area worked well for us, as I accepted a starting position in the forklift industry. Though the stockyards and steel mills were closing, the beer business thrived. My husband's position was in full swing.

I found the city an exciting a place in the early 1970s with its up-and-coming fashion center status and an abundance of shopping on Michigan Avenue: the Magnificent Mile. We spent time in the city several nights a month for business dinners with clients, or out to ball games. Chicagoans are hardworking, friendly, busy people-on-the-go, and we were a part of that culture. This ocean seaport was fun and entertaining.

Having fun and entertaining filled our life, too. Drinking and dining found us often at the Playboy Towers or down on Rush Street at the Moulin Rouge, the entertainment center for nightlife in the city. The "swinging discotheque scene" where young couples wanted to be noticed... that's where you found us.

We frequented many of Chicago's finest restaurants to delight our palates and entertain the client: the Cape Cod Room on the Gold Coast at the Drake Hotel that featured fresh fish every night, and Eli's Place for steak and their famous cheesecake along the Gold Coast. Drinks before, during, and after, made for a lot of hangovers for me. I was determined to keep up the pace.

We would take in games at White Sox Park, a Schlitz account, or at Arlington Race Track. The Bulls games were a Schlitz account, too, and sometimes upper management offered great seats. Or, we might attend a Cubs game, a Bears game, or Blackhawks Hockey just for fun. Food or drink could happen at Berghoff's Herman Deli in the Loop before the game.

So much of what we did centered on sports. I learned a lot more about professional sports than I thought possible. All these events had plenty of alcohol flowing from start to finish. That was Chicago, a city that prided itself on patriotism—a way of life there. The St. Patty's Day parade was a religion and, with my birthday on that day, I was happy to be a part of it on more than one occasion. My dog Casey came along sometimes, too.

Life was full of challenges with going to a new school and starting another part-time job, while my husband was busy all day and several evenings a week. I was not grateful for my life, nor did I appreciate the fact that I now drove a new Oldsmobile Starfire, owned a lovely home in the western suburbs, and pretty much consumed whatever I wanted to eat, drink, wear, and enjoy. Sadness lurked behind my big smile. I did not hesitate to down a drink when the opportunity presented itself, which usually added to my depression and problems. Some days I missed our smaller home in Michigan, and my old Le Mans, given to my younger sister when she went off to college.

When making holiday decisions, we had family conflicts with his family in the west in New Mexico and Arizona, and mine in northern Michigan. We often traveled for the holidays and added to our already stressful life decisions on where to go and who we would visit. He usually won out with a trip west. One Christmas, we found ourselves stranded for two days in Nebraska due to bad weather and a diverted flight, but we would do it again the next year.

It was easy for me to get lost in negativity, instead of dwelling on being out of the snow and enjoying the sunshine. I often felt terribly alone and left out. He had his friends and old golf buddies. I spent extra time with his mother, not asking for what I needed or wanted, and we often held a drink early in the day.

Alcoholism is "cunning, baffling, and powerful" and I allowed this disease to creep in and gnaw at me. I tried to focus on my good life, my little world of opportunity and charm, and not to drink so much. I tried to control my drinking, but it was futile.

What fulfilled me? Did I have connections to anyone? I couldn't see it was up to me to change my situation. Alcohol was already beginning to cloud my rational thinking and to disappoint when so much excitement and opportunity lay at hand.

I ran in circles trying to meet my husband's needs and the expectations of our friends, spending more and more time with the neighbors. We often had outings at Alexander's Steakhouse on the South Shore, where a lot of drinking took place. The partying grew out of control with rude behavior on the part of the guys. "Boys will be boys" sufficed as the excuse. If the bar bill was high enough, we usually weren't asked to leave. I rarely confronted my husband about his behavior, laughed it off, and simply drank more when he embarrassed me.

MERRY CHRISTMAS

MY LIFE

"How's the life of the student wife?" my neighbor Mary Lou asked. "Crazy." I laughed. "I started a new part-time job. I'm busy with school at the end of the semester, but I like my classes. Final exams are next week and then time off for the holidays."

"That sounds good. Where are you working?" she asked with curiosity.

"Crown Electric Forklifts, a branch in LaGrange. I work in the sales department three days a week. With school in Glen Ellyn, it is a lot of driving, but I'm glad it is not all in one day, or a drive out on the Kennedy."

She smiled. She had worked in the city for many years and seemed to miss that life. As we talked, I sensed she loved her time at home in the suburbs, too. In some ways, I envied her. She was content and happy, or at least, that is what I always saw.

I feel emotionally inept these days. I cry a lot. School demands are here with year-end papers due. Christmas is always stressful for me. My life is out of control. I'm not handling things very well. I'm drinking alone or with someone from my new job at happy hour, or school friends after classes. I am alone more than I ever thought I would be as a married woman.

CHILDREN

"We've never really discussed kids," I said when asked at our office holiday lunch. "He's gone a lot, and we're both so busy, children wouldn't fit our schedule," I added.

The girls at the office wanted children and looked forward to the holidays with nieces and nephews. That was the farthest thing from my mind. My younger sisters weren't married, so I didn't feel much pressure.

"Won't you regret it someday?" Sandy asked. "Later, I mean when you're older."

"I doubt it," I said, "I can't see it happening; we're not the types. Our life is just not like that with his business schedule and my school plans."

We hardly see each other. He's gone more than I ever thought he would be. I know deep inside this is not a traditional marriage. We should at least talk about kids.

FRIENDSHIP

John and I had lived in the Chicago area for almost four years. The socializing continued with clients and people affiliated with Schlitz. We went on several big trips to Hawaii and Mexico, which he won or his distributors took us on. The marketing department of our district also traveled to conferences in California and Hawaii which, of course, included us. The trips always involved a lot of drinking, and our ski trips to Colorado with the neighbors were no different.

I experience frustration at times for having another life, for finding new friends at the office and at school, but I can't stop it. I like these people, they are fun, and I want to have a good time. The holidays will only add to my loneliness. School is about to end, and the office is closing for several long weekends. My routine will be disrupted. I don't like that idea.

I was afraid if I discussed our situation with my husband he would be lost entirely. I didn't know what to do. He told me once he would not go to counseling, and became defensive when we discussed the way we lived separate lives. He didn't think we needed help; I could go, but he did not wish to talk about our life with strangers.

He accepts our life together and apart. I do not want a divorce, I want to live like our friends Cathy and Phil in Michigan who have a normal life as a couple. Is this what he had in mind when he married me? When he charmed me and convinced me to live with him? When he watched me graduate from a glass of Chardonnay to a double Canadian Club and water, imbibing that drink repeatedly.

This wasn't a healthy marriage, but I didn't know what normal was so I could try to emulate it. I went along for the ride with one more New Year on the horizon. It was 1973. We rolled through another holiday season, putting up the pine tree in the family room. I decorated it alone one night with a half bottle of Chardonnay, under the watchful eye of my faithful dog Casey.

What does Casey know or think of the arguments? Does he sense there is chaos in our home and not love. Dogs are sensitive, he sees we are always coming and going in other directions from each other. Does he not feel loved?

We had bought a few gifts for our families and sent out about fifty photo Christmas cards with the two of us standing in front of the fireplace with the dog; almost a Norman Rockwell moment. There I stood in my green knit blouse and English Christmas plaid full-length skirt. He wore his brown suit. Arriving late for the picture and with a pending client appointment down on Rush Street, he didn't have time to change into his navy sports jacket and tan pants. That outfit lay untouched upstairs.

His grin in the photo told the story. We were hiding things, a lot of things, from each other and our families. We looked like friends and lovers on the outside, but weren't. We tried to cherish our time together and not make things just look good but, in my heart, I knew the truth. This marriage was in trouble, and drinking was adding fuel to the fire.

Tom and Jerry Party

The proverbial neighborhood Christmas party was being held next door this year and heralded as a Tom and Jerry party. Mary Lou's grandmother's famous hot toddy recipe would be on hand and ready to go when we arrived. Being this close to home was good for me, a short walk if I needed it. Not like the summer parties at the clubhouse four blocks away, which had proven a challenge more than once.

I planned my outfit carefully. Red palazzo pants in three layers of satin voile, red patent-leather platform shoes, and a cream-colored crepe blouse adorned with ruffles, with lots of silver jewelry, too. My long hair, hanging to my waist, was slightly curled and bouncing. I did red nails and lips just for this night, not my usual look… but, hell, it was Christmas.

"You look beautiful tonight," John said with a devilish grin. "You'll get noticed. You'll like that attention. Should I be worried?"

"It'll be a big party, I'll blend in," I said laughing slightly. I was nervous about the party and was ready for a pre-party drink.

He opened a bottle of Dom Perignon Brut champagne, a gift from his distributors out of Schaumburg. They usually sent a case of wine or champagne and a case of filet mignon, and this year was no exception. I had no idea the value of the gifts, but guessed they were pricey. They built a successful business starting in the Al Capone era, and still ran it like they did back in the "old days."

We drank in near silence as I walked around the tree in the family room, admiring what few wrapped gifts we had under the boughs. He sat at our black and white, vinyl and chrome bar at the end of the room, watching me. Was he admiring me? Or, was he trying to think of something to say? We had so few quiet times together. I was enjoying it being just the two of us with the glistening lights.

We shared no talk of Christmas Eve Mass or church on Christmas Day. All that had gone away when I met him. He had not grown up in a church and had no interest in pursuing any of it. I did not go to church any more either, caught in the trap of doing what he did, even though I especially missed holiday services. I had stopped going more than five years ago when he asked me to move in with him, back in Michigan.

Why did I so easily walk away from God? Was it to ease the guilt of my life that was not faithful or trustworthy? Why have I not gone to church on my own? Why am I so dependent on him for his approval? Why do I drink at him in anger and with him in fun?

The Tom and Jerry Party was a flurry of happy people donned in festive red and white, or black and green, with gold jewelry glittering everywhere. Lots of holiday cheer accented up-do hairstyles of French twists and sparkling wine glasses. The Tom and Jerry's—made from many egg whites, brandy, and rum—were whipped up in the blender, or simmering in big white mugs with frothy tops and nutmeg caps. The guests enjoyed the light and spicy concoction, knowing full well it was not eggnog and spirits, but Mary Lou's special family recipe.

As we had entered the house, a large dining room table off to the right beckoned us with glorious food: from a duck mousse mold, to a cream cheese pecan yule log, to the ever-popular chocolate fondue. The seventies were a flamboyant time to throw a party, and this group expected just that kind of night for a Christmas gathering. We were not disappointed.

The guests were busy people anxious to get together, despite all they had to do to ready themselves for the holiday season. We were young and energetic and chattering away; laughing and telling stories in mood rings, bell bottoms, leisure suits, and platform shoes. Everyone assembled in this lovely home, from neighbors and work friends to relatives and downtown-Chicago friends.

We shared stories of disco nights in the city or the new wood-paneled station wagon just purchased for the family. It was beef tartar and shrimp canapes, French onion dip with sourdough bread pieces, and pigs-in-a-blanket or sausage-stuffed steak rolls. It was an old-fashioned cocktail party in the western suburbs of Chicago where the up-and-coming had come to play.

It should have been a good night for me, but I feared the experience. I wanted to measure up, to be somebody special. I couldn't blend in well until I found the bar area and ordered a real drink. There was no punch bowl. The drinks were served in real glassware. I liked that... a classy party.

"I'll take a Tom Collins," I said with a smile.

The bartender nodded.

"You look terrific tonight," Mary Lou said as she came up behind me, "but then you always do. You have a real flair."

"Thanks, I like clothes," I said as I took my drink. "Some, I make myself, but John bought this for me at a little shop over in Clarendon Hills. The shop I modeled for last spring for their community charity event."

She smiled. She was a good dresser herself, but a bit flashier than the rest of us that night. All in white and gold with a sheer drape over her flowing pants outfit. She seemed to capture every bit of the room as she moved around her guests.

Why did I go on so much? She only made a small comment about what I am wearing. I am so nervous tonight. You know most of these people and the rest seem harmless. For God's sake, relax!

I finished my drink quickly as I moved around the room. I decided I would drink Canadian Club and water next. My husband always said it would not make me sick like the "pretty drinks." They had stocked the bar well, and the bartender had everything: for a Salty Dog, a Harvey Wallbanger, a Manhattan, or a Martini. Mary Lou was quite the hostess and thought of everything.

My insecure thoughts could easily bring on excessive chatting. I was again trying to justify my existence. That night, I felt invisible instead of noticed, as if I was not interesting enough to warrant a conversation with somebody new. I stayed to myself for a while and made my way to the bar again and again, not counting what I drank. My husband was moving around the room, throwing me a glance on occasion. I started to feel like I didn't matter. The room was buzzing, and nobody was talking to me. My husband was wrong. I wasn't getting attention.

I felt lovely and unlovable. My husband was not introducing me to the people he was so easily meeting. That's what he did all day, talk to people, sell people things, and listen to people he didn't even like. It was easy for him, but not for me. I did not know what to do about it. The drinks helped me feel okay when I wasn't. I observed the party from afar and smiled if somebody looked my way.

"How are you tonight, Patrick?" my neighbor Lyle asked.

He always called me that, so I knew it was him before I turned around. He had his usual twinkle in his eye, a kind man. Lyle made me laugh, and for a moment as we talked my inadequacies fell aside. I felt a bit light-headed, but did okay with the conversation.

Is it them or me? Is it my inability to communicate or are they just into themselves? What is wrong with me? I am an interesting person, too, why do I accept being neglected?

"I need to eat something," I said to Lyle as he began to move on to another conversation.

I headed to the dining room for a plate of food. There was quite an assortment, so I forced myself to fill a plate. I had not eaten since breakfast, and the clock read ten in the evening. I was not steady, feeling queasy and likely to pass out. That was no reason to put the drink down, so I headed to the living room with my food and drink. I found an empty chair to land in and nibbled on my food.

The room, beautifully decorated, glowed for the holidays. The large Christmas tree was a long-needled pine and completely done in white and gold. It looked almost more like one at Marshal Field's department store than a neighborhood home, but it fit this house.

HAIR ON FIRE

After finishing half of the food on the plate, I felt the lightheadedness again and decided to head to the bathroom. I remember entering the room and struggling with my palazzo pants.

The next thing I know I hear banging on the door.

"What the heck is going on in there?" John yelled. "I smell something burning, are you alright? I've been standing out here a long time."

He forced the door open and threw a towel over my head. My hair had caught fire with the candle burning at the back of the toilet. I must have flung my hair back before sitting down and didn't even notice the candle or realize what was happening.

My hair smelled like old burning leaves, and it felt crusty when I reached back to smooth it after removing the towel. I was extremely embarrassed as several people gawked from the hall through the bathroom door. My husband stood in front of me to shield me as best he could, but two guys peeked over his shoulder.

I pulled up my palazzo pants and straightened my blouse. He quickly brushed my hair with Mary Lou's brush lying nearby and put handfuls of my singed auburn hair in the trash. I was ready to cry, but held back my tears.

"I'm sorry," I said. "I didn't see the candle. I'm tired, I need to go home."

"You're drunk again, and tired. And, you're embarrassing us," he snapped. "For God sakes, you could have done something horrific to yourself, or set the place on fire."

As soon as we left the bathroom I headed for the front door for some fresh air, leaving him to explain to the gawkers. On the way, I took a glass of champagne someone was passing around. I staggered down the stairs to the entrance and out the door, while my husband, in his usual style, made light of what happened. He was giving an embellished version to those in the hallway. I hit the cold airspace of a Chicago winter night as if I was a member of the Polar Bear Club heading to Lake Michigan.

BABY, IT'S COLD OUTSIDE

My wanting to leave before doing something else stupid led to something even more stupid. I passed out in the snow about thirty yards from the door of the party house, trying to reach our house. Staggering off the sidewalk, I went into a blackout, not remember a thing once I hit the cold air. I must have lain in a prone position for quite some time in my beautiful silk and crepe outfit. It offered no protection against the elements. I lay face down, as if dead.

Maybe I was dead, or surely depressed, with no idea where I was or for how long. When John picked me up and shook me, I was in a drunken stupor.

"What the hell are you doing out here?" he yelled at me. "You're going to freeze to death, it's below zero wind-chill. Christ, just how much did you drink tonight? You're scaring me now."

"I'm cold, where's my coat?" I asked, not remembering my beautiful raccoon coat left in the neighbor's master bedroom, along with my little black velvet handbag.

"What time is it?" I asked in a groggy voice, "Is the party over?"

"It's over for you," he said as he picked me up and carried me into the house. "You've been out here in the snow fifteen or twenty minutes, and you're drunk. You could have frozen to death. Do you realize that?"

"Please stop yelling," I said.

"The alcohol must have saved you. Jesus, what are we going to do with you?"

"I'm not drunk," I managed to blurt out between sobs

His remarks trigger guilt and shame in me. I am in that vicious cycle where I feel I am wrong repeatedly, and I buy into it. Why don't my feelings matter? Why don't we talk to each other? Why do I always feel so badly? Something's wrong with me. I always feel like I don't measure up.

He took me home to our bathroom and started a hot shower for me. I sat shivering, wrapped in a blanket, waiting for what would happen next.

I don't remember him removing my clothes or saying much. In a daze, I stumbled into the shower, while he put my wet clothes in the laundry room. He dropped me in the bed in warm sleepwear. All within what seemed like minutes of entering the house.

I fell asleep almost immediately, but the next day I had to face the music. He didn't bring my coat or my purse home with him or go back for them. He said he made light of my actions with the neighbors when he called to thank them for the party. I had to face them the next day to get my things, and it wasn't easy.

Why do you judge me? My needs and wants do matter. You've made a lot of mistakes. I feel like I am always being judged by you and made fun of by you. Why is that?

I had expectations of how I wanted him to treat me, but I didn't know how to change things or ask for what I wanted. I did know a glass of wine made this life palpable, so I chose the wine. I obsessed about showing the neighbors and all of our friends what my life should be like, because I deserved that life. It never seemed to work out that way. I sensed they watched me from a new lens now, and I had to ignore them.

ALCOHOL

Alcohol now pulled at my life like a decadent piece of chocolate. Excessive consumption seemed the best way to go. My free-spirited lifestyle was replaced with thoughts of a Bloody Mary necessity in the morning. The taste of the Worcestershire sauce or, even better, the Trader Vic's Bongo Juice from the bartender guidebook my husband too often loved to use to tease me. What happened to our early marriage pleasures: love making and breakfast in bed? I was too naïve to know how to handle it any other way.

Stop losing control when you drink. Stop feel guilty about your behavior. Stop saying never do that again.

My loss of control anguished me, fun was gone, and the marriage was a sham. With my feelings exposed, I shared things with people at work or in a bar, which I had no business talking about. The next day I felt shameful.

"I feel neglected," I told the school nurse psychologist at the beginning of the New Year. "I don't have warm feelings for my husband. We have separate lives. I feel sad a lot of the time." I told her about my holiday drinking as she took copious notes and nodded occasionally.

"I want my marriage to be better than this."

"Emotional neglect is very serious, especially for a young woman," she said after a long pause. "You're feeling alone with the guilt for some of your actions. You feel alienated from your life even though you're living it."

A weight came over me as I took it all in and tried to understand what was going on with me. The shame and guilt of my Christmas vacation were almost more than I could bear.

"Will he go to therapy?" she asked, hoping for a positive response.

"Not now, but he says I can go. That is why I am here. I don't sleep, and I drink too much."

"You'll probably have physical symptoms soon. Do you feel physical pain?"

"I feel angry, and I get nervous. I get headaches and stomachaches, and I don't eat much," I tell her. "That's when I drink, to settle down. I drink alone, too."

"That's shame you are experiencing. You're taking it personally, internally. It can be quite harmful. We will work on it. Things will get better for you, but you must want that to happen for you. You have to find the courage to talk to him, no matter what the outcome."

Patricia L. Brooks

YOU'RE FIRED

"**W**omen respond differently to alcohol," my therapist said as I inched my way closer to her on the couch. "You get drunk faster, you stay drunk longer, and you get sick faster."

"I believe you. I almost killed myself over the holidays," I commented. "I found out the hard way, and now I'm humiliated around the all the neighbors, especially Lyle and Mary Lou. They're good friends."

"You are feeling guilt, and shame means you need counseling. I'm glad you came back to see me," she said as she reached for my hand.

CONTROL

We argued a lot: about late nights, drinking, and money. I was tired of myself and of him, and often went to a bar after work for happy hour when he was on a business trip. I usually drank too much, testing the water for possibly staying behind and not going to Arizona, while pretending to be sorry when he found out. Nobody knew our lives were like this. We had secrets behind closed doors. I was coming unnerved. Accepting the move seemed impossible.

The day before, when I returned from the warehouse to the office, Sandy had said, "Your husband called, he wants a call back right away. He sounds pretty anxious."

"That is odd," I said curiously. "He never calls me at work. Gosh, did somebody die?"

I returned his call, but no one answered, so I quickly returned to the warehouse to work on the inventory. I liked the responsibilities I now had. I felt good about my promotion to middle management in the sales department. I was dressing more professionally now, too: suits and pumps, with my hair up. My mini-skirts and the ribbed sweaters were just for weekends, along with my bell-bottom jeans.

About a half-hour later, the loudspeaker paged me to come back up front to the office. My husband was in the reception area. Sandy raised her eyebrows as I passed her to greet him. He seemed nervous when I came up to him. There was no big grin. I knew something was up.

"You need to take a long lunch break. We need to talk," he said before I could ask a question. "Let's go to the place down on the corner, your hangout. Can you leave now?"

As we slid into the end booth, he ordered hamburgers for us before I could say anything. He did not hesitate and began to tell me what was on his mind. He was on a mission.

"I was fired this morning, simple as that," he said. "I'm not going to beg for my job. I spoke up at the marketing meeting in Milwaukee about the watering down of the beer accusations," he continued. "They are accusing me of being drunk, but I asked a legitimate question of the wrong people. There is something going on with the company. The man has spoken. I no longer work for Schlitz."

I was stunned as I listened to him go on with the story. My thoughts raced to what would happen to us, to our house, the company car, the money we shaved off the expense account for fun. Will we move or stay… does he even want to stay? Then I heard him say Arizona.

He did not want me to give a reason for the move, just my two-week notice. He was putting our house on the market. We would move in a month to Arizona. He wanted to go back home and go into business with a couple of his fraternity brothers.

"Why do you think we can sell the house so quickly?" I asked. "How will we do all of this without company help? The move will be expensive. We can't afford it."

"We have savings, and we'll get a good price for the house. We need a new start," he added. "I'm tired of living here, tired of the snow. We don't have many reasons to stay here."

That was the way it always went. He laid down the rules, made the plans, I asked a few questions, and we did what he wanted to do. I felt alone and frustrated with him sitting directly across from me discussing our future.

This marriage will get worse before it gets better. I know it. I have reasons to stay, my friends, my family.

He went on talking about the big floods we had that spring after the record-breaking snowfall, and how he was tired of it all. He was more negative than I had ever seen before. He was done. In his heart he had moved.

DISCOMFORT

After lunch, we had no discussion about the move or the job offer from one of his distributors—an attractive offer I thought worth considering. His distributor in Schaumburg had proposed the offer to him several times. The first management position in their company for somebody who wasn't family. They loved him, both of us. They had often showered us with gifts and trips. He was a fool not to even consider it. My words of encouragement fell on deaf ears.

How long will this crazy Arizona idea last? Is he serious? He blindsided me. I am distracted with a new promotion at work, and the opportunity to transfer to the University of Chicago in the fall. My dream since we first moved here. God, how is this happening to me?

I felt the discomfort of his stranglehold on me, of a captive animal. Alcohol created problems for me, but I could not resist a good stiff drink from our home bar before returning to work. It felt good to take the first sip.

Okay, don't overreact. There is so much yet unknown. Who's to say this will happen, or that it isn't just one of his grandiose ideas. Let him settle down. That is the best way.

I was not doing well, indigestion set in. I had to get back to the office and keep this quiet, which would not be easy. The office staff knew I hardly ever went to lunch with my husband, or that he rarely called me at work.

Hell, I don't even have a picture of us on my desk.

"My therapist told me the craving for a drink is a warning-sign of needing them. I don't usually have a second drink during the day, but happy hour awaits us," I told my friend Sandy, my trusted confidante, when I returned to the office. "I should have taken that second drink. He had a couple of beers, then told me we are moving, and that he was fired. It is not a transfer this time. Please keep it to yourself for now, I promised him not to say anything just yet."

RESCUED

Do I stay or go to Arizona? We've vacationed there several times, but do people live there? Can I leave Lake Michigan and be far away from my family and friends?

The question… could I make it on my own? Could I depend more and more on myself if I had to? Was I done being so dependent on him? Was this my time for a new start? Would I value my self-worth and do this for me?

Stop complaining, be grateful, exert yourself and be open to this new idea. Am I just being a brat?

"I can end the affair with Barry," I told Sandy at lunch the next day. "It's just one of those crazy office things. I've been going to end it anyway. I suspect John knows, and Barry's wife knows, too. He is a good guy, he deserves more."

"It might be that for you, but I doubt it is that for him," she said looking straight at me in amazement. "Can you leave, knowing nobody else out there in Arizona except John's dad? Will you be able to be happy with him in another big city, making new friends?"

"I don't know. But, I will soon find out, I guess."

"You don't have a choice. He's your husband, he is expecting you to go with him," she said quickly. "I hate to see you go, but look at it as an adventure. You can always come back if it doesn't work out. We'll all be here for you, working together, going out to lunch, to happy hour and an occasional White Sox game."

"Thanks, I appreciate it. We've had some fun times, haven't we?" I said as I drifted off trying to see myself living in the West. "I'll miss you. I know things aren't always the way we want them. My therapist keeps telling me to let go of the illusion of the happy marriage and take a hard look at my life." I managed a slight laugh.

"We will say goodbye here at work, it will be easier for me, not so many tears, but I will have to meet Barry privately for a short goodbye. He deserves that from me. I know it is going to be emotional for him, but I am going to be strong. I want to make a clean break."

So, I began the arduous task of packing our life, selling furniture, giving away plants, and placing newspaper ads to sell the house. He wanted to sell the house himself. I started to believe his grand idea of going into the restaurant business was good for us. With no other frame of reference but to see us pick up the pieces and move forward, I took his instructions.

GRATITUDE

I tried to be grateful for all the fun we had in Chicago, for all the people we met and all the good times with the neighbors—Lyle and Mary Lou, and Dale and Loretta. I tried not to dwell on the time wasted with too much partying. I prayed for some gratitude for my life. My affair in the office with Barry, who was married, too, was a bad decision. The ski trip to Wisconsin with our spouses almost exposed us when the four of us drank too much one day. We were just a little too friendly. Spending a night in Fox Lake complicated things. It was awkward.

I called my therapist and vowed to seek help after we arrived in Arizona. I would need it, we both would, but I would go regardless of his decision. I was grieving the loss of leaving the Midwest and my friends and family. No matter what, I felt abandoned.

"Don't change completely," my therapist said at our last meeting. "You're not hopeless, just weak at times."

"Thank you," I said as we said our goodbyes.

"Don't beat yourself up or berate yourself for the mistakes you made here." She hugged me before I left her forever.

Take care of the tasks at hand. Keep busy. There is a lot to do to move across the country for a new life. When I arrive there, I'll claim my life. It'll be different.

I attempted not to listen to the devil on my shoulder that gnawed at me and made me feel guilty for my past sins. The same voice that could lead me to drinking and sadness, remained vigilant. I tried not to compare myself to others. I sought a fresh start.

"You do not have to measure up to anyone, you just have to show up," my therapist had often said.

I worked that next week to convince myself otherwise with each box I packed, and every day that went by. We didn't totally fail, I told myself, we just made mistakes and now we're heading out for a new adventure.

In Arizona there will be sunshine and no snow. I can be more active outdoors all year long. I'll feel better. I know I will.

My husband was busy ending things with Schlitz and meeting a few of the guys from the marketing department to say goodbye. I gave my notice at the office and had a night out with the old gang. It was short and sweet with the usual conversations. Barry did not make it.

I cancelled school over the phone; it was easier that way.

We had not told the neighbors anything up to this point. They apparently had not seen the ad in the paper; they had not called. It was bittersweet, anticlimactic really, a quiet end to a chaotic and busy life with them.

The house sold almost immediately. I did not get involved. We went into the city one afternoon to sign the papers at our lawyer's office, and it was over in an hour. We celebrated down on Rush Street with happy-hour cocktails, too much hard liquor for me.

I was feeling a bit better about the move. The skinny was that we got a heck of a deal when we bought the house and an even better deal when we sold. He was right again. We did well, and we were going to have money to invest in Arizona.

I consciously chose to give up some of my negative thoughts about Arizona. It was getting me nowhere. I resolved myself to this move and to make the best of it and be open to the Southwest. John was still angry about his firing and the company's possible demise. He was a good salesman, a smart guy, but alcohol ruined things. I embraced the change to survive and did not buy into his attitude.

We left the bar later than planned. I was a spaz, falling near the car as I tried to open my door. The lights, coming up near the waterfront off Michigan Avenue, looked blurry—almost like the northern lights of the Aurora Borealis, a mix of colliding particles.

"Far out, that is beautiful," I said as I tried to point toward the shoreline. "I will miss Lake Michigan and this city."

"Just chill," he said. "You've had too much to drink. I'll miss the lake, too, you know. It's the snow I can live without."

For a moment we connected, going forward in our anxiety and sadness, bound by our new adventure and another phase of our life. We were moving to yet another state.

Exit

The moving van pulled slowly into the yard just as Lyle and Mary Lou left for work. They stood stunned next to their car, unable to wave. We had only told them about the move the day before. They appeared hurt by our nonchalant attitude. It was not the way I wanted it, but it was his way, the way we did things.

We used a non-union truck. The Teamsters were on strike, and we did not want to wait for the strike to end. This move was going to cost us thousands. We had a whole house to move, even with selling a couple of rooms of furniture. I looked at the van, wishing we had sold more, even the antiques, but I was sentimental. John was too impressed with his purchases from farm auctions in Illinois—selling antiques he had bartered for was not going to happen.

"See you on the flip side," Lyle said after he finally waved to us from their driveway.

I could tell he was hurt. Neither one of them came over to make a final goodbye. Somehow, I knew our actions would gnaw at me for a long time. We had thought only of ourselves, and it was wrong.

CRYING TIME

I cried all the way to St. Louis. My dog tried to comfort me. I was afraid of what I was leaving, and more afraid of what I was going to with him, or without him. I allowed myself to be vulnerable again.

Could I be his equal in the restaurant business? Was he serious about all that entailed? Could we work together side-by-side?

We had 2,000 miles to go in my Oldsmobile Starfire. It was exciting, but scary just the same. We would soon be managing a Mexican restaurant in Tempe called Willy & Guillermo's, while buying into it on an installment plan with a hefty down payment. Arizona here we come!

I had not seen the contract and was not in on the negotiations or the phone calls that came to him. I assumed all the details had been worked out. He insisted he knew these guys from school at Arizona State University and it was going to be a good thing.

Somehow, I'll connect to the wonder of living in the West, I'm just not sure how. Will Phoenix improve my insecurity, my attitude? Can I do it with him? Can he do it with me? Will Tempe feel like home?

He had bought a townhouse in Tempe six months earlier, as an investment. We would live there for the time being. It was close to the restaurant site, just a mile from the campus on Apache Trail. Before we ever moved, he had many meetings with these guys to make plans.

"All the details are in place," he said the last time he came home from Arizona. "This restaurant is going to be a success. It's not a typical

Mexican place, it's more designed for the younger crowd in Tempe. You'll like it, and the décor, too."

He kept talking about the place as the car sped along. I tried to hold back tears and watch the ominous sky. Tornado warnings came through the radio as we traveled in the tornado belt of Oklahoma. It grew darker by the minute, as my thoughts about our future kept haunting me. I couldn't seem to share his enthusiasm. I wanted to be a student at ASU, not a waitress. I wanted to be on campus in the classroom, not in a restaurant kitchen.

My tears didn't stop for hours. He would not stop the car as we drove parallel to one of the tornados just across the field along the freeway. We raced with that freight train sound just outside of Tulsa. It was almost synonymous with our life: a train wreck, a runaway train, and a storm out of control.

Why won't he stop? We lived in this weather in Illinois. He knows what it can do. The tornado crossed the field in a heartbeat. I'm scared.

We were not in the motel more than an hour when the hotel's attendant knocked on the door and told us to get in the bathtub or under the bed. The tornado was heading towards us. I had been in this position before once with the dog, in the crawl space below our tri-level house. Her ideas did not sound safe.

I need that bottle of wine I packed for just this occasion. I have had it, and need to relax, I feel like I am coming unglued, this is not funny.

We had no time to look for anything. We could hear that freight train sound we knew to be the tornado. You don't have to live long in the Midwest to recognize that noise. The dog cried, whined, and paced in the room. He knew it, too. Casey needed to be comforted by me, he was family, too.

John went to the bathtub. He could not fit under the bed. I went under the bed with Casey. The sound was horrendous. We waited out the ten minutes for it to pass. It seemed much longer. Then the eerie silence set in, it felt like the coast was clear. We stepped to the center of the room, pulled back the drapes and surveyed the damage.

There were a lot of trees down and things strewn about, but no cars overturned. We noticed damage to our six-month-old car in the form of small punctures from the pelting of the dust and dirt and stones with such a high force of wind. Eventually, it would be taken care of by insurance. I made a desperate attempt to be grateful that was all we had to deal with that day. It could have been much worse.

We left in the morning, as we wanted to arrive on Easter Sunday. The furniture was scheduled to arrive that week, so we had to move on. My anxiety was high. I didn't sleep, and visiting a hotel bar grew old, even though the singer at the last stop in St. Louis did a pretty good rendition of several songs from "Cabaret," which was still a very popular play in 1976.

REAL ESTATE

"The real estate business with my fraternity brothers is the way to go," he said in a matter-of-fact way. "The restaurant deal has fallen through and would have been a lot of work anyway. There was very little profit to be made," he continued.

How can he be so calm talking to me about this after we just moved 2,000 miles? I need time to process this change of plans.

"What happened? I thought it was all settled," I asked, knowing I would get a short answer. He had already made up his mind when he had met the guys for golf the day after we arrived. Maybe he knew before we ever left Illinois.

"They did not have our best interests in mind," he said. "And besides, we can work together, and you can have a real career. We will do well. This is a hot area for real estate, and yes, I did get our deposit back."

I was stunned for a moment, but not surprised. He had bought the house in Chicago without me, the townhouse in Tempe without me, so why wouldn't this venture be all his, too? He had bought cars and evenings gowns for me, too. In fact, sometimes I felt like I could not make any decision ever. And, he wondered why I need to have a glass of wine for anxiety.

When will the chaos slow down? Can we change? How do I justify his moves? He does not always know best. Our working together will only add anxiety. He'll try to control me even more. I'll be drinking way too much.

We fought about this night after night for a week. I stood up to him, but it did no good. I finally quit and drank wine. I cried myself to sleep. I wanted to go to school, to have a degree in psychology, and to work in a field helping people. I didn't want to be in the real estate business.

The only consolation was that we did get our initial investment back and did not have to get an attorney. I did not go with him to pick up the check. I did not want to meet the two men who had given us six months of lies and anxiety. I wanted to move on with my life and to settle in our new home.

His fraternity brother Kenny, who sold us our townhouse, had already recruited him to his real estate office. I suspected they had been talking for some time. The fraternity bond had finally proven to be worth something, though.

John took me with him for the initial interview with his friend Kenny's broker. We paraded around that office with big smiles and lots of palm pressing. They all thought we were the up and coming young couple, the new kind of Realtor for Tempe. We fooled yet another group of people about who we were and what we were about one more time. The wine was close at hand, and I felt powerless.

SCHOOL

As soon as I could, I headed to ASU to apply for school and to check out the campus. I met a couple of people and felt a little more comfortable. ASU was 28,000 students, and bigger than the University of Chicago where I thought I would be attending. It was a different feel, not an urban school, but a nice feel just the same. I also checked out the Human Resources office. I thought if I worked on campus for nine months, it would be all I needed to establish residency. I would get to know my way around, maybe even in the Psychology Department.

"I need you to get your real estate license now," he said without hesitation. "I'm getting too busy, I need your help. We need to be partners."

"You have not talked to me about this. You have told me what *you* want and not asked me what *I* want. I am going to go to school, just as we talked about back in Chicago," I said in one breath, surprising him and myself.

The look on his face scared me. He was emotionally neglectful of me most of our relationship, and certainly psychologically abusive with his controlling nature. But, this time I thought he might turn violent. He seethed because I talked back to him.

"I was at the campus today, and I am ready to go there full-time in January. Nine months is what it will take to have residency. I have talked to a couple of people and I have considered employment there, too." I hoped he would listen.

He said nothing. He stared at me, then walked out the door. He offered no response to what I said. Was he saying no or maybe? Will we ever earn each other's trust or respect again? He did not return until after midnight. I drank a half bottle of wine and went to bed early. He woke me up when he came in. He was drunk.

LICENSED

I passed the real estate exam easily that summer. After about thirty years of being quite predictable, the state real estate exam had been revised. I studied with Sharon, a gal I met in the preparing classes. I fretted over working with John in an office he had been in for six months. The pressure and expectations of what we could do as a couple seemed great. He had sold our townhouse without much conversation or fanfare. I liked living in that townhouse on Dunbar Drive.

We were moving into a golf course property near the office, twice the size of the townhouse and a lot more work for somebody. I set up an office at home, hoping I could do a lot of the paperwork there. I would have my quiet time and my glass of wine when I wanted it and maybe even study for a class or two along the way. I had a plan and was going to see if I could make it work. He had other plans of course, and they were not in agreement with mine.

MARRIAGE ENCOUNTER

"Larry thinks we should do the Marriage Encounter weekend they offer at his church. You're Catholic, you should like it," he said with that usual grin he thinks will punctuate his point and sell me.

"What does your broker have to do with our marriage?" I asked. "Why do we have to do everything with the people in your office?

Our social life was all about that office, and when Larry spoke, John jumped. It was as if he was trying too hard to do the right thing and please Larry, to make up for being fired in Chicago. It was frustrating at best to watch him try to impress people I wasn't sure were even his equal in business.

The office bowling team in their red shirts, which I abhorred, was required. Fortunately, the neighborhood bar was at the bowling alley. The office softball team, sponsored by our broker, was not for me, even though I loved to play softball. The monthly potluck office lunches were a waste of time in my opinion and, since I did not cook, it was hard contributing anything. I was out of place, frustrated, unhappy, and wishing to be anywhere else but in that office.

I avoided daily drinking and challenged myself to work with him. I was going to minimize my stress and leave within a year. I had a plan.

What do I fear about holding on to our marriage or, more importantly, what do I fear about letting it go? I am not happy, I drink too much, and he is not happy either. Is forgiveness an option for me? Why do I keep poisoning myself?

Patricia L. Brooks

SECRETS AND LIES

SECRETS

A re you still keeping secrets?" my new therapist at Arizona State University asked inquisitively.

I nodded.

"Why is that? Don't you feel you're jeopardizing your relationship with your husband?"

"I suppose. But, he demands to know what I do every minute. It's destroyed our relationship. I have no space," I said. "I want some independence, some time for myself with my own friends, my own life."

Moving across the country was a setback for me. I felt alone, sorry for myself with no friends except his friends, and their wives who seemed out of step with me, or was it me, or was it me? We were moving to a smaller city that felt odd to me. I had known before we arrived I was not going to fit in well.

CONFESSION

He spent time with his friends on the golf course and in the local hangouts soon after we arrived. He was all about seeking their advice, bettering himself, but often it seemed like an excuse to be one of the boys again, to go back to the old fraternity days.

My enthusiasm for the move waned early as I realized my chance for full-time school would come slowly. He had pressured me to get a real estate license and join him in the business of selling houses.

That is not what I want to do. What I want to do is go to Arizona State and finish school, and have my own career, maybe my own business. How can I do that? How can I find somebody to help me make that happen?

"Strong couples are usually made up of independent people comfortable being dependent on each other with a clear sense of identity," she offered. "Is that your life?"

"That is not us," I said. "He interrogates me about work, my friends, even school classes I just started at ASU. It is exhausting. He is extremely jealous. I finally gave him something to be jealous about," I said emphatically. "I had a serious affair in Chicago."

SEPARATION

My affair in Chicago started out innocently. Drinks after work with the gang from the sales department, four or six of us at the corner bar and lounge in La Grange on the way home from work. It was dark and sultry in there, and we all felt like we were so grown up. Barry liked me, and I knew it. He paid a lot of attention to me, and I reciprocated. He had a great sense of humor, dressed well, and did well with the company immediately.

The day he was hired, he could not take his eyes off me while he waited in the lobby. I worked the reception area and took him back to his interview.

His resume was impressive and he was quiet but charming. He knew I had wanted them to hire him to add a little class to the sales department. We often had extended conversations in the office that got noticed. My work suffered at times and I had to work late to catch up. I often did extra things for him to help his sales paper flow. I liked him.

"I feel older than my twenty-five years. Old and foolish, lonely, and drinking too often. It hides my feelings, my sadness," I tell Sandy when we had a chance to chat at the office.

"You were easily smitten by his attention, a glass of wine made it all exciting the other night. Be careful," she said as she went about her work.

The happy hours with the sales office crowd moved to the two of us meeting after work in more remote places, then to meeting on the weekends when we could sneak an hour or two. We started taking risks before we hardly knew each other. It was a desperate love relationship. I would have wine before a shopping trip, tell a lie about who I was meeting, and head out. Saturday was golf day at our house, so I was free to roam, and I did.

Two or three hours is turning into four or five. I came home this time after my husband's golf outing, which should be hard to do. My excuses aren't creative, and embarrassing. I weave my tale, but need to be better at it. How did we get to this? Why do I go to all this trouble for a little attention? What is wrong with me?

REASONS

"Your husband's personality appears controlling and demanding. That may be one of the reasons you keep secrets from him," she determined. "But, is that all there is?"

"I feel he's always fishing for something to question. I don't tell him a lot of things anymore. I fear he's going to judge me. He gets angry when I go out with my friends, yet he is often busy or gone."

The affair escalated, it became sexual, risky in parked cars, city parks in the summertime, and motels in the winter. Barry and I were foolishly addicted to each other, and playing a game of secrets and lies we had no business playing. We were married and our spouses suspected. We were fooling nobody but ourselves.

My drinking brain justified my behavior because I was lonely. I thought I deserved to be loved. I never once thought about being open and honest with my husband and suggesting couples counseling again. I had tried that in the beginning and was shot down, so I just kept to myself. We lived separately, but together. I was going inside myself and didn't know it. I could not recognize it. The drinking every day was blinding me into a narrow train of thought and selfishness.

Times spent out to dinner with our mutual friends in Chicago were insane. I would figure out a way to leave the crowd for a while and meet Barry outside the restaurant, or we would spend time talking in front of everyone as if nobody noticed. It was stupid and naïve, like the time my husband came upon us talking in the hallway of the restaurant near the exit doors. We were discussing how we could meet later after our spouses went to sleep. Why did he not question me? Did he not care anymore? Did he have someone else, too?

I lied a lot, but was never a good liar and had no poker face. My husband often sensed when I was guilty, but never pushed it. He realized I had enough pain already, and he had won. It was a sad way to live, and so I drank daily. Wine was my choice, but I never said no to liquor if it was the drink of the moment. I drank heavily at times and often blacked out in the car on the way home, if he was driving. I experienced that lost space in time when you come to, hours later, transported to another place from where you started. I often wondered the next day what I had said or done before the night ended. I would sheepishly fish for clues, while he punished me by giving me none.

EXCUSES

"Why do you feel you have affairs in this marriage?" she asked after we talked awhile.

"It's the excitement, the attention. I don't have that with my husband anymore."

"Do you want to get that back with him?"

"Yes, sometimes, and then I just keep doing what I am doing. Just seems easier, but not really what I want. I am frustrated with our life, my life."

"Things like this often end in a harmful way, to both parties, and to others. But, you know that don't you?"

Several people in the office now knew: Sheila, the sales manager, and Don, the manager of the branch where we worked. They weren't stupid. We had left too many clues. Don commented one day as we all traipsed out to happy hour that we were having too much fun and should be careful. None of us were careful. We drank what we wanted for as long as we wanted. We told personal stories about ourselves and our spouses that should have been kept private. We acted as if we were single and carefree.

I drove home drunk on several occasions, especially the night Barry and I rented a motel suite together. Drinking did that for me, low inhibitions and bravery morphed into risky behavior. Nobody worried about anything. We were friends. We had secrets, and we lived lies. We weren't going to tell on each other. When the next day came, we had to face each other at the office and whisper, "Did I do anything stupid?" and hope the answer was "not any worse than me" and go on for the day. It was a shameful way to live.

ILLUSIONS

"It's an illusion to think you can have both a marriage and an affair. Eventually, you'll be found out. You realize, that don't you?"

"Of course, I do, but I can't resolve the issues alone. We just keep going on the same way, and I keep drinking more and more. I know my secrets are incompatible with commitment," I said. "I know I need to make things right before anything will happen to improve or save our marriage. We both do."

I wasn't in love with this guy who was the pawn in the game I played. He was just the guy from the office who adored me, who convinced me that if we just had fun, nobody would get hurt. Deep inside I knew it was wrong, a lie heading for disaster. Did I want to get caught, or hurt my husband to get his attention? My drinking mind seemed to justify anything and everything with one or two glasses of wine. I was delusional and living in lies as if it was my right and my destiny.

At what point did I cross the line to say that inviting these people to my home was okay? Why did I think hiding his car in our garage after dark was not going to get the attention of one of the neighbors in our cul-de-sac? It seemed exciting at the time, but so dangerous. My husband could have easily come home early from a business trip.

Alcohol did that to me. It made me stupid, selfish, insane, and surely a crazy woman of no common sense. I quickly lost respect for myself and my home. The sad look on my dog's face when we all barged through the garage door and headed for the bar in the den, ignoring his empty dish, said it all. I had no qualms about opening our beautiful home to people from work I hardly knew. Drinking made me a reckless and fearless fool.

Yet, at the office, I was being considered for a promotion while doing well with my classes at community college, ready to graduate in the top ten percent of my class in the spring.

SELF-REFLECTION

"Take time to write to yourself in your journal. Can you do that?" she asked. "Have you kept a diary in the past?"

"I will do that. I loved keeping a diary many years ago. I love to write, I know how good it makes me feel."

I met Barry at a small bar near our house for about twenty minutes to say goodbye. I did not tell him why we were meeting on a Saturday, but he suspected something was up by the tone of my voice. I wasn't emotional, and he was very upset. I could stuff my feelings, having done that all my life. I could be a tough girl if I ordered a glass with of wine and downed it quickly.

My selfish behavior, my excessive drinking, was abusive to him, too. It had been a game for me. The chaos at the office, the misunderstandings and lack of trust at home, were mistakes I now vowed I would not do again. Just like that, I saw this move to Arizona as a chance for a clean slate and a new start. No affairs, less drinking, an adventure. Or, did I?

There was a perennial low level of sadness underneath my big smile. Why did I think now, in my late twenties, I could miraculously change all that? Would I seek deeper professional help? Could I do that? Did I have a healthy enough sense of self to learn about myself? Where would I find that support in Arizona? I only had my husband's aunt and cousin to greet me. Who would I turn to for help?

SPACE

"Writing and quiet time is a space you need," she proposed. "Ask yourself how you're going to find that time for yourself. How you will adjust to his new demands of living in Arizona?"

I looked at myself in my journal and found myself drinking at home alone before heading out for the day. Often leaving hours after he left to golf. I did not work that first summer in Arizona; I moved us in, decorated a little, and did some shopping. I avoided the real estate school classes for months, but finally succumbed. I took them during the evening beginning in late July. Staying to myself pretty much most of the time. I tried to be a good student.

I also spent some time on the Arizona State campus setting up what needed to be done to establish my residency for fall classes and get acclimated to the place. I was a fish out of water since it was a campus twice the size of the community college I had attended in suburban Chicago. I was determined not to give up on that dream, and there were a few campus bars nearby I thought I would check out since I had the time. I had heard Chuy's was a popular jazz club. It soon became a frequent haunt, as jazz was the music I loved and the atmosphere there reminded me of the jazz clubs in Chicago.

FEAR

"Are you acting out in anger because your affair ended abruptly? Are you in fear with your drinking, your time in a bar?" she asked.

"I am not sure."

"Do you get the attention you miss from your husband by doing this?" she asked, point blank. "Secrets are unspoken communication you cannot ignore. Think about that. They are eroding your marriage," she said when our session ended.

My journal writing now is about the real estate office and how much I feel coerced by my husband and the broker into being there, and to going to real estate school to sell houses. I take my husband lunch, with the dog hanging out the window of the El Camino, and somebody invariably asks me when I am coming to work there, when I am going to take the sales licensing classes, and when I will take the test. I cringe at the thought, smile, and don't answer. It is like so much of my life, inevitable.

The day came, as I sat through that first real estate class, angry about being there. It was so boring, so different from my studies in the past. I loved psychology, sociology, political science, and philosophy. How was I going to get excited about learning the laws of the land of a state not truly my home?

I attended classes in Old Town Scottsdale with a large group of people I did not know and, on breaks, kept my ears open or looked around for a club where I could have a glass of wine on the way home. The Glass Door could not be that place as my husband knew the owner. The Cork and Cleaver could not be that place... his friend from ASU football was the bartender. I kept looking until I met Sharon, the wife of an ASU professor, getting her real estate license just for something to do.

We started chatting on the breaks and talked about studying for the exam together. She was not happily married either. I could tell in a heartbeat when she jumped at the idea of going out for a drink one night after class. We settled on the Lobster Trap, a dinner place with a good bar, but a dinner crowd that would leave us alone. We continued with this pattern though our classes and on to exam day. I was feeling better about the real estate business.

LIES

"Lies are false statements to another person with the intention of having them believe them to be true," my therapist stated. "Do you lie often? Could you stop lying? Have you always lied?"

"I do feel guilty about telling lies. It's a bad habit I have had most of my life to protect myself. I lie about when I drink and where I drink. I lie about where I go, what I do. We don't trust each other. He lies to me, too."

The real estate test involved a "new" exam according to the instructor, and he had highly recommended we find a study partner. The State of Arizona had made the exam much more challenging than in the past, trying to make the business more professional.

Sharon and I were smart girls and reliable study partners, we were compatible and worked well together with our study plans. We spent a good part of our time drinking wine and talking about what it would be like to be real estate agents and successful. We drank and dreamed, fantasized, and told each other secrets. It was a relationship I could never have predicted.

I allowed this woman to know me. Was it the drink? The common bonds we had or was it all the frustrations in my life and in hers? We passed the exam with flying colors, the first time, which was not always the case among the many who took it.

She went on to work for a broker who was well known in Tempe, in a family-run business near the campus and their home. I went to work with my husband in a Century 21 office in an upcoming area near the golf course where we now lived.

Not the office I would have picked, nor the neighborhood I would have chosen to live. If I had been able to say how I felt, I certainly would not have been in that career. I was in the middle of a life that did not look like mine, except for the wine and the hangovers and the anger. Those things described me perfectly.

BIAS

"When you find out about one of his lies, his infidelity, do you blame yourself?" she asked. "How do you take it?"

"It's hard emotionally. I feel less than, unworthy to question him, because I lie," I said. "I drink more; it's a vicious cycle, a downward spiral."

I came home late one night after presenting a contract and stopping for a glass of wine, well two, just to let off a little steam from the stress of the negotiations. The contract was one of my first on my own. I was exhausted. He greeted me at the kitchen counter with one of the single women from the office. Marlene had a crush on my husband, but I ignored it. She was not his type, a bit too homegrown for him. But, there she sat, next to him, having a beer with him, laughing with him. He had that grin on his face, too. I didn't ask what they were doing, why she was there, or when she was leaving. I poured myself a glass of wine and went into our bedroom. Was I going to say anything or was it better left alone? Did I even want to say anything? He could be unfaithful.

COVER UP

"Is the cover-up worse than knowing?" she asked.

"Yes. I'm afraid of why he does it, if he wants a divorce. I do not want another divorce, even though I am adding to our problems."

"That's a vicious cycle. A blowup could happen, which might be a good thing, bring it all out in the open," she added. "Do you get angry easily?"

"Yes, I'm jealous. We have a lot of problems, we are both crazy. My life seems so hopeless to me at times, until I throw myself into school and forget it for a while."

"What are the real issues? What are you avoiding? Can you write about them for next time? We will get to the core issues, to the bottom of all of this, and then tackle the idea of a couples' counseling plan."

My resentments grew as the days went on. I couldn't see how to work it out. We were growing so far apart. Sometimes I didn't care anymore. I wrote in my journal about my feelings of frustration and hid it in the extra bedroom in the sewing basket. Why did I vacillate so much between wanting to make our marriage work and wanting to end? How could I think I could make it on my own here? I did not have my education in place, I did not love the real estate business, and I knew very few people who could help me.

I began to see my therapist less and less, making excuses that I had a contract to present or a client to show houses. I said I was doing better and the journal writing was a big help. I was being brought down by the drink, and the sadness and depression it causes.

The bar at The Lakes housing development in Tempe had a beautiful view across the man-made lake that glittered at night from all the gas lights. Their oyster bar, which I began to frequent, allowed a single woman a seat alone without much suspicion. I started to go there often, seeing a few people I knew from the real estate business, but not making a lot of conversation. Usually pretending to be busy with something in a notebook, drinking wine, and eating a small plate of fried zucchini and mushrooms, food that had become my staple.

I was drunk that night when I arrived home, but I decided to let myself in the front door as it would not be as noisy, but he heard me. Before I had all my clothes off in the front bedroom, he was whirling me around the bedroom taking off the rest of my clothes and dragging me to the front door. I could tell he had been drinking, too, by the look in his eyes.

He literally threw me out of the condo in my birthday suit, flying across the slippery grass face down. It was late and still and quiet, maybe two in the morning. I quickly scrambled to my feet and ran to the bushes at the window and hid, shaking, getting chilled, and sobering up quickly.

What was I going to do? Who could I ask for help? We barely knew the neighbors, but they were home, they always were at night. I tapped on their window. In an instant, the man in the condo next to ours was yelling at me.

"What the hell are you doing out there? Are you crazy? Where are your clothes?"

"Please call our condo and talk my husband into letting me inside."

He shut the drapes and for what seemed like forever. I hid behind the shrubs and waited, shivering from fear more than cold. It was a warm, damp night. The sprinklers had just gone off. A few cars passed on the main street a block away, but the cul-de-sac in front of the townhouse was quiet.

Finally, John opened the front door. "Get your ass in here!"

I ran to the door and into the extra bedroom. I stayed in there until I knew he was back in bed, then I took a shower and had another glass of wine. Not much sleep that night, but a lot of time to think about whether we could ever be a happy couple again.

HONESTY

"Trust in a marriage is crucial. Can you verbalize any of this to me so that you might be able to talk to him soon, before it is too late?"

"Not right now. I feel disappointed. I don't know what to say to you."

"Can you find some respect for yourself; appreciate yourself as the good person you are, so he can appreciate you again, too? Will you consider a program for your drinking?"

I nodded and left her office. The session was over, but my long day had only begun. There was so much more waiting for me at home.

"I like our townhouse. It's just enough for us. I don't want to move again. We don't need more room!" I yelled with agony in my voice.

"The house is on a golf course, it's worth a lot more than they're asking for it. Is' only six months old. It's a great investment. I want to do this."

"But I don't, it's going to be a lot of work, and much more money than we can afford. And, it still needs a yard, and a lot of decorating, painting."

"We'll do all that. We'll do well in the real estate business. Why don't you trust me? I know what I'm doing," he continued, relentless as always.

He walked to the kitchen for a beer. I was furious, but stayed in the bedroom even though I wanted a glass of wine. I was not going to join him. Just as it always was, he knew what change was good for us, and I was happy with things the way they were.

The phone rang, and he took his client call on the patio. A client, good, he would be busy for an hour. He seemed to talk forever when it came to houses. I poured a glass of wine and found the dog's leash. I needed a walk, a little quiet time with Casey. That was all I wanted anymore.

We would resolve this tomorrow. There would be another fight before it was over. There always was, and I would try to make my point, as futile as that was for me.

The house he wanted was in Dobson Ranch, on the fourteenth fairway. It had a lovely view, but needed a lot, including decorating. Two ASU professors owned the house, but were in the process of ending their marriage. Bad vibes in the house were inevitable. They wanted a quick sale and a fair price. Even if it was a good deal, it was not a deal for us when we were just starting out in the real estate business.

I kept repeating these thoughts to myself as I trotted along with the dog. Casey loved to keep a good pace, so I had to concentrate or he would pull me head over heels and spill my wine.

Anger and frustration keep welling up inside me like they have so many times. Even the quick pace of my walk is not releasing my stress. I need to make my stand on this. Casey, I am turning us around. We're heading back to deal with this.

When I returned to the kitchen, he was gone. I had another glass of wine and got ready for bed, knowing he may be late and a contract may be pending. I put the dog's food near his bed and settled down to relax.

My husband didn't leave me a note, he never did, he just came and went when he was ready. One more glass of wine and lights out, it would have to be resolved tomorrow. I have no control over any of this, and I knew it. A wave of sadness came crushing over me like a tidal wave of fear. Is this what trauma feels like?

"Wake up, wake up. I need to talk to you," he said while flashing the overhead light. "You need to read something and sign it. It is important."

"What time is it?" With my eyes half shut, I tried to focus on the clock on the night stand. I struggled to comprehend what was about to happen, and afraid to even imagine what he wanted. It could not be good at this hour.

"Why are you bothering me?

"We need to act now. This house has had a lot of activity. We need to move fast. It's a great deal. I'm not going to miss out on it."

"What house? The house you want? I don't feel we should buy that house."

I saw the contract and the paperwork in his hand and recognized that look of determination. There it was... the hard sell, the "you are wrong, I'm right" argument.

"I'm not signing anything. You can't force me. I know you can't!" I screamed. "How could you do all that paperwork when I said no?"

"You're going to sign this. You're not going to ruin it for us to have a great investment. You're not going to hold me back!" he yelled.

The night went on and on like that for hours, but I didn't relent. I held my ground until he stormed out in a rage onto the back patio, and I retreated to the kitchen for my wine. Had I won? Did anything get resolved?

Then I heard it. A scream I had never heard before. I peered out the window at him. He held his hand on his chest with a tremendous look of agony on his face. He had punched his fist through the wooden back gate that leads to the car. Wood splinters stuck out from the fence.

I heard another yell as he swore and paced on the patio. I looked out one more time trying to decide if he needed my help. Should I leave him alone and lock myself in the house? After not moving from the bedroom for quite some time, frozen, I realized not allowing him inside again was the answer.

I quickly moved to the kitchen and locked the back-patio door and shut the drapes before he saw me. He was preoccupied with his hand. His injury must have been quite painful, but he never called out to me or asked for my help. A short time later, his car pulled out of the carport and entered the alley with a squeal.

I was trembling. That fence could have been my face. He had never been so angry before in all our years together.

How did we get to this point? How did material things and wants and greed take over what we need? What is good for us? How did we lose sight of all that's important in a relationship? Did we ever even know what that was?

The bottle of wine was less than half full, and it was the only bottle in the house, but it would do. I sat down at the kitchen counter and poured myself a glass. It was now three in the morning and I was exhausted. Tomorrow was a workday. How was I going to go to the office and work with him, put on a smiling face and move on from this? I had real estate school tomorrow night and studying to do. Maybe I would just stay home and go to school early to avoid him, but that never worked. He always found me.

Exhausted and frustrated all day, my resentment built because he had made a bigger mess of our lives. I was resentful at the idea of being expected to forgive again, just like so many times before. I would do it begrudgingly to make peace.

But this time, it would be different. This time, I would be thinking about when to leave, how to be away from him and when and how to be on my own.

MAKEUP

The next weekend, a few days later, was the office picnic. John wore a large bandage on his hand because he had broken two fingers, set at the emergency room the night of the big fight, the last big fight. He had been telling lies for days about the injury. My favorite: he played basketball with the kids in the neighborhood and fell, trying to do a layup shot that didn't work. He would look over at me to make sure I was going to play along and not tell our dirty little secret. Keeping dirty little secrets like I had for years. What he didn't know was that this little secret was part of a big secret, the beginning of my plans to leave him.

Not knowing how I would do it, or how to live, where to live, or how to take care of myself, still something had to happen.

I would eventually figure it out, and planned to stop going out and drinking, to watch what I did so I could pull myself and my life together. Everything was going to be different and good and wonderful very soon.

MOVING ON, MOVING OUT

SUNRISE

here do I belong? What fulfills me? I wrote in my journal as I
W quietly sat on the back patio of our house. No one was on the
golf course this early in the morning. The dew made it glisten; the green
of the grass was an emerald isle. I heard birds chirping, several different
ones, chickadees for sure. But, it was still the home I didn't want, the
home I was made to agree to live in, even if it was a beautiful place with
an impressive mountain view.

The sunrise and fall air made it even lovelier. It had just rained, an
oddity here in the desert. We had been in the house only six months, but I
knew I was leaving. I had known it from the day we moved in, from the
moment I was forced to sign the contract against my will.

*This must be illegal to force somebody to do things with a
contract they don't want to do. He is forcing me to do things I don't
want to do. How did we get to this point? What happened to the big
smiles and the laughter?*

It never felt like home on Milagro Drive, even when we were the
first ones to lay sod and several neighbors came over to admire it and
welcome us to the neighborhood. Milagro, Spanish for miracle, made me
wish for a miracle for us and our marriage, a new start, improved lives,
more happiness.

It was lonely there, despite the neighbors across the street waving
every time they saw me come or go. I never wanted to live in Mesa. It was
a Mormon stronghold, a family place, and we weren't a family. A big

house on a golf course was never my idea. I was happy with the townhouse we were living in at the time. It seemed golf course life was all he wanted.

I felt more at home in a dark bar, watching the clientele play games, laugh, and drink, out of touch with my husband and my marriage. The couple so many said was a "cute couple," "made for each other," had faded for me. I struggled with the idea of a single life, a second divorce at twenty-seven years old. Reinventing me was what I had to do to grow up and survive, discover who I was and make my own decisions.

AWARENESS

Who am I anyway? What do I want out of life? How do I feel about love and marriage, about commitment? Are those things I can take on again someday?

I was giving up a lot to get my freedom. No more financial security, no more marital status, no more somebody checking on where I am all the time and making decisions for me. Maybe worrying about me, on occasion, even caring, in his own way. I poured my first glass of wine for the day, knowing this move would be saying yes to big changes to be my own person.

I was tired that morning, not hungover really, just weak and weary. I couldn't remember if we even said goodbye when he left that morning for a fishing trip to Mexico with his friends. It was early, and I heard him rummaging around in the kitchen, but I didn't get up. John deserved the trip, he worked hard and told me he was going with no discussion. His friends had been asking him to make the trip for a long time. He packed and went off, telling me very little, not even where they were staying, or who all was going.

I disappeared into my glass of wine early that day: Chardonnay, a special occasion wine in an elegant glass. I went into that black hole called a blackout. I finished the bottle before the afternoon ended, while writing a list of things I wanted to take with me. I managed to start the final packing before I slipped away.

I lost a lot of time that day. That's what happened to me when I started, and couldn't quit until the bottle was empty. I was pretty sure I spent quite a bit of time on the telephone, at least that's what my friend Sharon told me.

"How are things going? Better, I hope, than the day you called me," she said.

"Sorry about that, too much wine again."

"Be careful, your drinking is scaring me."

The darkness of the day took over and, when I sobered up, the house was very still. The dog needed to be fed, and the house closed. I was there alone as my father-in-law Cliff was out. He had moved in with us that week on the insistence of my husband. Again, very little discussion or time for thought on my part.

"He has no one else and no place to go. We have no choice," John said just before Cliff moved in. He said the situation was temporary, but that was my husband's way of getting what he wanted, his soft sell for the hard sell that was actually happening.

Slipping away into my drunken stupor after last night's leftovers from the Chinese restaurant down the street, I thought about our last dinner together. It was nothing romantic, just a stop on the way home from the office with the usual real estate talk.

Another glass of wine from a half empty bottle from the back of the refrigerator would put me to sleep. Tomorrow was a big day.

I thanked God the next morning I had not been out driving or trying to get home, and vowed not to drink myself into a stupor again. But, another bottle of wine sat in a sack on the counter, this one a Pinot. How did I get home from the liquor store? Did I go out last night? I hadn't packed much of anything, and my clothes on the bed were a mess, unkempt, as if I had been in a scuffle.

Why do these episodes not scare me? Why do they only make me curious? Does the alcohol make me that brave, that fearless, or am I just crazy when I drink and not care?

INCIDENTS

This wasn't typical drinking, whatever it was, and I wasn't a heavy drinker like my dad, just a sipper, a continuous sipper. The benchmark was no one got hurt while I blacked out, not anyone but myself. I didn't drink like my husband either, but I did get angry and do stupid things.

Sipping wine was not actually what I did; I just liked to believe that because a lady drinks like that. I tended to gulp wine if I was talking and laughing, or nervous. That fact had been pointed out to me before. I learned to gulp from my husband. He drank beer that way. It wasn't his fault I emulated him, drinking and eating fast, out of fear I would not get my share.

In my frustration with his Mexico trip, I too was transported, but not to the beach as he was, but to the wrong part of my thoughts with a few too many glasses of wine. I lost time, a lot of time. While reminiscing in my journal about all we had and lost, and what we could have tried or done but never attempted, I cried more than I had ever cried. I was not a crier. Why now? Was it because nobody was looking? Or was it the wine or a sense of failure?

RECKONING

Is this my life or somebody else's life I am living? Why don't I recognize it? How the hell did I get to such a state? Who is this man I am married to? Why am I talking to men in a bar when I should be home? Why don't I just go home?

Do you need anything Cliff?" I asked early in the morning. "I'm going to be pretty busy today."

He never answered and headed out the back door, as he usually did, to find solace in our yard. He was not happy living with us, and knew I was not in agreement with the whole idea. I liked the old man well enough. He had never said anything hurtful to me. But, he was indeed coming to live with us at the worst possible time. Or, was it? Did it really matter; did we hide what was going on from him? I doubt it.

As a handyman, he was supposed to help us fix up the house, maintain it and keep it clean, but he wasn't quite working out that way. He was not very motivated to do any of that. He liked his privacy and was a loner, and was not capable of helping as much as I hoped. Plus, we had the unfortunate situation when he was fixing the air conditioner on the roof. A golf ball hit him in the chest on a dog-leg, as the golfer's say, when it veers off the course. This happened often, our yard was always full of golf balls.

"He is going to be okay, even though he has a pacemaker in place, "the paramedics confirmed.

It was scary, though. He now had a reason to do less around the house, and I had plenty of guilt for asking him to check on the air conditioner that day. I heard later from John that the City of Mesa did put in trees along a section of the course to get the golfers to go the other way and stop the barrage of golf balls into the yard. The trees solved the problem and the dog no longer carried golf balls around in his mouth.

Cliff often seemed to be in the way, especially when I came home late and found him waiting up when my husband was out. He was a drinker, too, and didn't say much. He lived under our roof, he could easily see the situation. Maybe he didn't know what to say. His wife had asked him to leave a long time ago, so he did not meddle with our lives.

EXCUSES

Society looks down on and strongly judges women who drink. Does my father-in-law judge me, too? He knows we have alcohol in the house and drink daily, and that we go out to bars separately. Does he disapprove of our lifestyle or care?

This is wine, a classy socially accepted drink, I thought, as I watched him watching me out of the corner of his eye. 'Tis the conversation drink, the "let down your hair," you-can-now-be-friendly-witty-and-fun drink. Ladies drink it in the movies. Audrey Hepburn drank wine, and so did Ingrid Bergman, as the "I'm not uptight," glamour-girl

119

drink. It was not the drunken woman drink portrayed by Elizabeth Taylor in *Who's Afraid of Virginia Wolff.*

It was the natural drink to bring to a party, the thank you gift they would open immediately and offer to you. Wine had pluses on so many levels, and it was sweet or tart, but always soothing, sensual. And oh, those pretty glasses.

The 1970s gave me a new spirit of equal opportunity drinking. Women drank as often as men and caused quite a stir. I always tried to keep up with my husband, even though he was twice my size, but now the challenge would be over. I could drink at my own pace, fast or slow, hard or easy, and with whom I wished.

Alcohol consumption appeared to be peaking in the 1970s, after the Vietnam War, it was as prevalent as Coca-Cola, and seen as legal, adult, and acceptable. It became legal to drink at age eighteen in 1971. We could vote, and we could drink. That year, since I had turned twenty-one, I qualified to drink either way, although drinking for quite some time. Age had never stopped me, as I had spent years around men older than me, who bought me drinks while the bartender or waitress turned a blind eye. I was a young and independent barfly. It was almost a status symbol.

I spent most evenings in a bar, even if my husband was in town. I often stopped for a quick glass of wine to unwind after leaving the office, with or without a client or colleague. He would be out presenting a real estate contract, or bowling with the team from the office, or with his guy friends at a bar shooting pool, but not where I wanted to go.

We no more needed the big house he insisted we own than fish need a sandbox. We did not cook there or eat there, and rarely entertained there. It was a shell with furniture in it and it felt like it… a big storage unit with an attached garage housing a boat we rarely used. It was a lonely place. Just as it was for the ASU professor and his wife who built it and lived there only six months before divorcing. Was this house jinxed? What was in the walls to make the love go away and the anger and hurt reside?

I drank too much, spent time in dangerous places, blacked out, and got sick. With no husband or a father-in-law reminding me or questioning me enough about my drinking, things progressed. My husband had given up, and maybe didn't even care anymore. Did I want him to care, to nag me? I was slowly being left alone now to my own devices, to be free to live my life.

DECISION TIME

"Cliff, I'm hiring the neighbor's two high-school boys to help me move. I've borrowed a truck for the day. I'm leaving him tomorrow," I told Cliff as he walked outside one more time to tend the flowers. "It's what I've planned for a long time. John won't be surprised."

He said nothing in response to my news, just put his head down to water the plants on the patio, pretending he was busy. I could see his large hands trembling, hands that had known a lot of manual labor with his handyman business. Hands that also toiled away hours in a bar and ruined his marriage to John's mother.

I didn't tell Cliff how hung over I was, or how sick I had been earlier that morning. Our bedrooms were on opposite sides of the house, so he couldn't hear me gagging into the bowl, aching and coughing. He was a late sleeper.

I wasn't sure if he was nervous, or hung over himself and needed a drink. Maybe he was waiting for me to go out, so he could have a drink and forget what he just heard. As a loner all his life, I am sure it was hard for him to live with us at this stage in life.

"I am moving into one of our listings. A lovely townhouse in Tempe, just a few miles away, and west of the house on Baseline Road. It's a few miles south of the ASU Campus, convenient for me to get to my classes," I continued, even though he would not look up.

I kept talking, my nervousness increasing. "It's been vacant for a while and with the owners in New York, they are happy to have me move in to help them show off the place and sell it."

"He doesn't want you to go," Cliff finally said in his deep voice. "You need to stay here and wait for him to come home, you need to talk to him about this."

The sting of that first glass of wine arrived early that day. It had been poured before I had even started talking to Cliff. I couldn't answer him or defend my decision, and walked back into the house with the dog following me. My Casey knew there was more sadness in the air. He stayed close to me all morning.

I packed quickly. The neighbor's boys were ready to help me at noon. I was taking only my clothes and my personal things, plus my sewing machine, my books, my bicycle, and my stereo. Things I hardly had time to use anymore, but they made me feel like a real person, and I wanted them with me.

I didn't need much. I would be working and going to school, and out all the time. I wanted to travel light, to have as little responsibility as possible. For the first time in my life, I would pay my own way: my own bills, my own rent, my own car payment. It was going to be a challenge.

"I will be leaving my Casey, a hard thing to do since he was my twenty-first birthday present back in Michigan when we were first married," I commented to Cliff as I went back out to the patio again to let the dog out.

His beautiful red Irish setter coat glistened in the sun. Cliff did not comment.

"I spent a lot of time with him, training him and loving him. He loves me back, too, but there is no place for him in a townhouse. I have to trust he will be okay left behind, and that you will help take care of him," I continued.

Cliff shook his head and continued to puff his cigarette and watch the sun hit the mountains. Something told me it would be hard on Casey, and I would regret it for a long time. My heart ached.

The bedroom set would go, too, not because I liked it, but out of necessity. Everything else was left from our four-bedroom home, things we had brought out from Chicago, and a few things purchased in Arizona. Nothing felt like it belonged to me anymore. The excitement of a move and a new place had just enough fire for me to stick to my plan.

GOODBYE

Alcohol dulled my senses, and I needed it that day to walk out on my second husband of seven years while he was in Mexico fishing. Even though the office called to tell me the guys had spent a night in jail in Rocky Pointe for disturbing the peace, I did not find it amusing like the others did, or change my mind. I was not going to be frightened or concerned by any of it. Those days were over. I was beginning to feel free.

I'm ready to be on my own. I'll manage on my own... somehow, I'll do it. I'm scared but will be better off. I'm sure of it.

I was feeling strong and defiant because he wasn't there to defeat me. The alcohol gave me courage, and my father-in-law stayed mute all the rest of the day, staying clear of me as much as he could. He sat on the patio with the dog, who peered through the screen door most of the afternoon. I had to ignore them and keep moving. Eventually, Cliff left and did not return, and I put the dog in the garage, it was too hard to watch his sad face. I hugged him and cried into his beautiful red fur feeling him tremble as much as I was, for what seemed like a long time. A sadness came over me that I did not expect. I went inside and poured myself a glass of wine.

The move was uneventful, most of the neighbors stayed away, afraid probably to ask what was going on at our house. The truck rental company was on time, the boys in the neighborhood worked hard, and I was all moved in by six that evening. I paid them even more than planned and, feeling satisfied, delivered the truck back in time to pick up a bottle of wine to celebrate before the sunset.

Don't drink too much tonight, don't allow yourself to be vulnerable to danger tonight when he returns and finds you are gone. If he goes into a rage, be strong.

I was tired of years of altering my behavior to please him. I had loved him once, maybe still did, but alcohol had changed so much for us. Things were going to be different. They had to be. They had to change for me, for both of us.

It was tiring sitting amongst the boxes on the floor in the middle of the room. The room was beginning to spin, and I felt sleepy. I had no couch to crawl upon, and the bed was not assembled in the other room; the guys left it in a heap. It was not a difficult task for me, but too much for now. The living room had no lamps or tables, and the kitchen was full of boxes. Only the overhead light in the kitchen was on, and it was too bright. I shut it off and sat in the dark.

There I sat, amongst what was my life, all packaged up neatly, ready to open. But, I could not move. Maybe tomorrow, maybe the next day. It would keep. Nothing in my life was perishable except my marriage.

I began to cry. All of what I had left behind he had picked out, even the comforter. I was going to get all new things, colorful things; things that would make me feel good. Not all those earth tones. I would do that as soon as I had my first commission check on my own. I sobbed uncontrollably for some time. Sad. Angry. Alone again. But, I wanted this, I had left.

Why did I not feel happy and excited? Why did I have an ache in my heart and a deep sense of loss?

The wine went down easily, that smooth warm sensation I knew so well. I felt myself relax a little and begin to accept that barging through life, never apologizing for anything, was really me. My life had been powerless and shameful, full of secrets. Now I was angry, feeling more like a tough girl trying to get out. Alcohol was helping me feel safe from judgment. I would do whatever I wanted to do, regardless of when he came to get me and insist I come home.

HOLD OUT

The bottle was almost empty, the room dark. I needed protection against drinking too fast or too much, but who would provide it? I needed protection, too, from myself to not go home, to go back to what I knew as my comfort zone, even if it was not comfortable.

The pounding on the door startled me. He must have pounded a while, because now he was yelling. I must have blacked out a little when that sound brought me around.

"I know you're in there, open up. What the hell is this?"

"You can't come in. I'm in bed. Go away!" I yelled

"Open the damn door or I'll break it down."

The pounding continued at the door and in my head. The wine wasn't working, and he wasn't going away. I held on to a box to stand, and made my way to the door. I saw a man who must have been a neighbor coming toward him as he turned, and I let him into the townhouse. I shut the door quickly and stared at him.

"You took the damn bed. What the hell were you thinking?"

"I'm not coming back. I'm going to live here. I don't want our life anymore." I tried to explain and not be intimidated or cry.

"You'll regret this. You'll be sorry. How could you do this while I was gone? You have no idea how to take care of yourself," he said as he turned and walked out the door.

I heard the car speed out of the drive and out of my life. The neighbor's lights were still on, and a police car drove by slowly as I closed the door on that marriage.

How do I drink and keep a job and make a new life? How do I survive with two divorces under my belt at age twenty-seven? What will people think? How will I tell my sisters? How do I stay confident I can do this?

When you drink every day, you find the right job, the right career, and make the right life to work with all your drinking and crazy behavior. That was what I did, and the real estate business perfectly fit a drinking life. Being single in my twenties helped, too. This was the right life, the drinking life in the 1970s in the Phoenix area. It seemed everyone was single.

I slept in, worked late, made later appointments, worked when I wanted to work, was out late where I wanted to go, and drank when I felt like it. I liked my life until, when sobering up one morning, the excruciating headache, heartache, and stomachaches began.

SETTLE IN

At times, I was in fear due to the pressure to support myself for the first time in my life. Or angry, when hearing he had a girlfriend or was doing well with business, or not agreeing to what I wanted in the divorce settlement. I was defiant about my drinking when called on it, and that was happening now, both by people in the office and my close friends.

Troubling episodes were accumulating with my money management skills, like being in negative cash flow due to the too-quick accumulation of rental properties. Lacking business expertise in certain areas, such as setting a budget, I made bad decisions and investments. I was still learning the real estate business, my first career. My choice of questionable men was collecting scrutiny along the way, too, and beginning to worry my friends. The divorce had not yet happened.

When happy with a home sale, I celebrated and drank. When sad and talking about my divorce and my financial situation, I drank. When angry because life was unfair to me, more drinking took place. My mode of operation was thinking about a drink all the time.

Why have I been unfulfilled for so long? Why is there this hole in me that cannot seem to be filled? Why am I so hard to please when I so desperately want to be happy? What is missing in my life? Am I willing to do more therapy?

Dealing Divorce

Money

"**A**re you sleeping any better this week?" my therapist asked at the first sight of me.

"No. Not really. It's been quite an adjustment, harder than I thought," I said as I snuggled into her soft blue couch and grabbed a pillow for my head.

For the first time in my life, I was living on my own, at twenty-seven years old. In a matter of eight years, I had gone from my parents' home to a dormitory, to a husband in Iowa, back to a dormitory in Michigan, to another husband, to finally living on my own in Arizona. It was a pace no normal woman should try to keep.

I was now paying my own rent, managing a checkbook, paying a car payment, and trying to stay on a budget for the first time in my life. Working on full-commission sales was difficult, to say the least, but I loved the freedom.

"There was emotional abuse in your second marriage and you were tied closely to financial abuse," my therapist commented.

"Yes, our joint finances involved him managing everything concerning money, controlling our spending, our savings and our investments. It's a new life for me."

I was oblivious to how much our mortgage or car payment was, or what our monthly expenses were, having never seen our budget. He gave me a cash allowance on Friday for my basic needs. When we needed to buy groceries, my husband estimated what the total would be by the list I wrote, and gave me that amount in cash for shopping. I returned the change and the receipt to him. He knew about every purchase, except a bottle of wine or two I snuck into the house.

This arrangement caused serious problems for me later. How to write a check or balance a checkbook had to be learned. I lacked the confidence needed to make good financial decisions, and made poor ones for a long time. I paid too much, too often, for basic things like food and clothing, and had no credit references.

In our marriage, I was completely dependent on him financially. Even though I often had a part-time job, my income was insignificant. He had no problem monitoring the money I spent. Yet I, in turn, had no idea what he spent.

"I'm stressed all the time about finances, even though I have money coming in and money in the bank," I confessed to her. "I am afraid things could change quickly as they have so many times in my life. And, I have not slowed down on the drinking even though I keep saying I'm going to do that now that I have my new life."

"Why do you think that is? Can you visualize yourself not drinking so much?"

"Sometimes, but it's hard, it's so much of my life now, so routine. Not sure when it became every day, but it has. I want to turn my life into something positive, and not drink at every little twist or turn."

I tried to drink only one glass of wine, but it never worked out that way. When I went out with girlfriends, I tried to drink like them, to savor it. The wine sustained me until it was gone. I usually was ahead of them, ordering another before they finished their first.

"I drink to calm myself at the end of a busy day," I said with a smile.

Even though I had promised I wouldn't drink anything before coming to therapy, she could sense it.

"The next time you come here under the influence, you'll be asked to leave."

I was a bit embarrassed but shrugged it off.

"I wasn't feeling well, I'm sorry."

My session that day ended abruptly with an assignment.

"Start logging in every cent you spend for business, personal, and household. Look at your expenses and your budget and stay positive about your progress," she instructed. "Be kind to yourself about the drinking, and remember everyone is fighting their own battles."

I will be kinder to me and to others, get more sleep, and enjoy quiet time in the townhouse. I will keep my home clean and neat, so it will feel inviting. When I walk through the door and drop my purse and my briefcase in the middle of the room, I will read something positive. I will discipline myself to kick off my shoes, shower, and relax with my journal.

PROPOSITION

"Have you filed for divorce?" she asked at our next therapy session. "You'll bear the guilt if you do the filing, you know that don't you? It just happens that way, it's part of feeling failure despite the circumstances."

"Yes, I filed with the first one, and felt some guilt but, this time, it will be greater. I already feel we could have tried harder; we could have done better for each other. We just couldn't make this marriage work alone, and we were so alone most of the time. We didn't try. We kept doing our same selfish behaviors repeatedly. I just gave up."

A few glasses of wine before therapy took me to that space of regret, of sadness, of depression, of failure, of guilt. It was futile. Being ashamed of my drinking habits, and being asked to leave my session, was not enough to quit.

"What are you doing?" my friend Wanda rushed to ask after I answered the phone.

"Nothing, just home from therapy. What's on your mind?" I was ready for a Friday night out, even though I was showing property all day on Saturday, and Wanda was a get-out girl.

I originally met Wanda in Phoenix a year earlier, while delivering escrow instructions to a client at a telemarketing company. She was working there and, for some odd reason, we started up a conversation. She was older than me, a mother of a young boy, never married. She had short bleached hair, and the first woman I knew who had enlarged her breasts. They cost all her savings. She was funny and full of energy. I liked her immediately. We became fast friends.

"Let's go to TGIF in Phoenix. It's not too far for you from Tempe. It's a fun place," she said in her usual party girl voice. "I was there last weekend when you were working. Meet me at five o'clock or it'll be too crowded to get in."

I hurried back to my townhouse from the office. Being within biking distance to the Arizona State campus, I always had to be careful, especially at night on those warm nights, after drinks, heading home with one eye open. I was a bike rider, too, and I prayed many times a student wouldn't lunge out in front of me.

I entered the door in a rush to change quickly into my new sundress. While in the kitchen opening mail, listening to the phone recorder, and eating a piece of cheese for dinner, I gulped my first glass of wine. Nothing in my life seemed to be peaceful anymore.

It was a beautiful evening, but warm. June in Phoenix was like that, not stifling, with no humidity. Warm enough to dress for summer, I picked the orange one, the dress the lady in the store said made me stand out. My tan glowed across my shoulders since this was the strapless one. The attention would be nice—even attention I didn't want, but sought.

I caught myself in the hall mirror and admired the way I looked, cool and comfortable, not too sexy, but just enough. I slipped into my black sandals and found my black hoop earrings. I was ready. No time for a shawl or to change my purse, it was a thirty-minute drive to the Colonnade Mall on Friday night and Camelback Road would be busy. With another big swig of my wine, I was on the road.

The new freeway now came to the corner of Baseline and Price roads, close to me and accessible for a shorter way to Phoenix. So, I entered quickly and headed west. One glass of wine was hardly a start, but I wanted to beat the traffic and get a strategic place at the bar. Wanda was probably already there on her perch, looking dramatic in a tight dress, overly sexy, flashy, and with plenty of jewelry. We didn't match on the outside, but we did on the inside, every time we talked she sounded like me, a wild hare trying to find a place to land.

I exited the I-10 to go north on 24th Street to the Biltmore Corridor, maybe my neighborhood someday. Right now, though, Tempe was where I lived and worked. I didn't need another move until I was divorced and had money to make a buying decision. Anyway, who knows if I would even stay in Arizona? It still didn't feel like home.

The white Chevy Nova my husband bought me to use for my real estate business had another year of payments. It was a good car, but not me, not what I would have ever bought for myself. He just came home one day with the car.

"I bought you a new car for real estate, a solid four-door car. It has a lot of extras on it. It will be good for you," he announced one night at dinner, handing me the keys unexpectantly. I fumbled with them, trying to decide what to say… a scene we had played out so many times.

It is a nice-enough car with a red vinyl interior and a lot of extras, but it is too traditional. It has no flair. It is white, like about eighty percent of the cars on the road in Arizona. I love color. It's not my choice, like our houses weren't my choice either. I do not feel any attachment to the car or care about it in the least. A white four-door sedan is somebody else's car. I will park it at the end of the parking lot. It doesn't match my pretty dress!

TGIF

TGIF's was crowded and loud. The red and white décor was familiar; tacky, but fun. I had been there before and knew the layout. The raised bar in the middle was full of people three deep, and it pulled me in. I saw Wanda waving at me from the far side. Two men in pin-striped suits sat next to her, like book ends, with curious looks on their faces.

"Hi, I'm Jerry, this is Ron," the guy on Wanda's right said as I sat down next to her. He offered his seat to me and stood behind us, leaning in. Jerry and Ron were older and, as they talked, I learned they were lawyers. Not surprising as TGIF was a businessman's bar, and a lot of lawyers from the Biltmore Corridor hung out there. They seemed to fit the "in crowd" well.

After a glass of wine, I felt comfortable enough to chat with Jerry. Wanda was already entertaining Ron with her stories about growing up on the mean streets of Phoenix. He seemed amused. I wasn't quite there, so I gulped my wine, to Jerry's amusement, and ordered another Chardonnay while he talked about his law practice.

It had been another busy week of unhappy clients, an escrow gone south, a pending lawsuit with the Veterans Administration on a questionable loan for a client I could not control, and my pending divorce. I had no money to proceed, or was there another excuse? Was I hesitating? Maybe another glass of wine would get me an answer. Jerry seemed to be having a good time. He kept telling me how pretty I was and about his plans for his law firm.

"Jerry is a lawyer; he does divorces," Wanda blurted out in the middle of his story. "Maybe he can help you out." She never did mince words.

"Are you going through a divorce?" he asked with curiosity. "I might be able to help; maybe we could have lunch sometime and talk about it."

"Thanks, but I am not sure what to do, my husband has all the money. He would have to approve this, and he probably has already picked a lawyer for us."

Jerry laughed. "I have never heard of two parties divorcing and sharing a lawyer, but it can be done."

I wanted to put it on the back burner, but he would not let it go. Not much seemed to work to get him to talk about something else. He pressed me further.

"How long have you been married? Are there any children?"

I ordered wine again, because I felt pinned to the wall to talk about my second failed marriage. To admit defeat, to admit my part and add to my guilt was difficult. I was talking about it, to a lawyer I didn't know, in a bar for God's sake! My impulsive drinking during the week was now planned and calculated. I was thirty minutes from home, and going to just have one or two, or was it three by now?

"Your friend says you're a real estate agent and a pretty good one at that. Is that true?" he asked looking me intensely in the eye like a lawyer would do.

"Yes, I am an agent, and I do well," I said with a grin.

"How is the real estate business these days? I hear it is a hot market here in Phoenix, everybody wants to move here, is that a good thing?"

"I suppose so, good for my pocket. Not sure the natives like it. My husband is a native. His family is not thrilled with the growth, but they are old-time ranchers."

I took another sip of wine. Then I hesitated.

Why am I telling my husband's story to a lawyer? He could be a plant by my husband. I'm feeling funny, partially because of the wine, and partially because I'm running off at the mouth, which is what I do when I drink too much.

"I've been in the business two years. It has its moments, but usually, I like it alright. The money is good. I'm working on my business degree at Arizona State," I added as I watched him watch me. "I don't know what else I would do. My husband suggested this career for me while I finish school. I can't afford to go to school full-time. It is going to take years of night school."

The next thing I know, he's buying me dinner, and we are discussing exchanging services, a divorce for a real estate contract negotiation. I find the land, put it in escrow for him, and he handles the divorce paperwork. Simple as that, what could go wrong?

As the wine continued, he became a nicer, more attractive man and the whole idea just couldn't be more perfect. He made it sound so easy. Things are always better at closing time.

I did not feel I owed him because he was a nice guy or bought me dinner. He was a professional, and he wanted to help me and help himself. I kept it there and kept my wits about me—no blackout, no after-dinner drink. I was good. I didn't want or need his attention, but it felt good. He sincerely believed I could help him, that I was smart enough and knowledgeable enough to solve his commercial land needs. He was going to erect an office building for two attorneys, him and his friend Ron.

THE OFFER

I spent the next several weeks researching land on commercial corners in the Phoenix Country Club area, the vicinity he requested. I traveled to Phoenix several times a week to do a visual of these properties. After a month of visits, I was sure I had the one to make an offer on for his proposed office.

"It sounds good," he said without hesitation. "I know the corner. I was unaware it was available. Good detective work."

"The woman who owns it is in a nursing home in California, but the executor of her estate says she is ready to sell, and to go ahead and make her an offer," I explained with a little excitement. I was treading on new ground.

He gave me a number and I wrote it up. We made plans to meet that evening at Phoenix County Club where he was a member; in the bar of course. One glass of wine I told myself, this was business, not happy hour. My first commercial deal was about to happen. I would be noticed at the office. It could lead to more, this was a great opportunity for me.

I ordered a second glass of wine without hesitation as we finished up the details of the contract. I asked myself how I had convinced any client to use me for such a big decision. What did I say that assured him he could trust me to handle it for him? Did he like the idea that this was my first land deal?

I was clumsy as I picked up the paperwork when we left the club. I felt the two glasses of wine, and saw myself as drinking too much again. I had not had much sleep that week and no dinner again that night, either. But, I was proud I was not still sitting at the bar with him, even if on the edge of making a fool of myself. I would be ready to present this contract by phone in the morning.

We shook hands and, as we parted ways, I said, "I'll call you as soon as I know anything. It's a good offer."

"Thank you, I feel it is, too!" he yelled back at me as he waved and headed to his car.

He must be happy. He gave all indications that he was, and left with a smile.

I pretended to be steady as I moved to my car under the watchful eye of the doorman who had helped us with the heavy doors at the entrance. I knew it was illegal to sign real estate contracts under the influence, but was it illegal to write one in Arizona, or present it, while feeling your drinks?

I'll remember this night, so it must be okay.

NEGOTIATIONS

I met with my broker early the next morning to have the offer reviewed, as it was my first land contract. I had to be careful to protect myself and my client.

"The seller is in a retirement home in California and has a representative and a Realtor," I told him quickly, hoping he would give it only a glance, and I could make my call. I was nervous about the transaction and eager to get it done. "I have not met any of them," I continued as he read. "Just phone calls. I learned this morning I am to deliver the contract to an office in Phoenix."

My broker read it twice and approved what I wrote, made a few suggestions about what I would say, and wished me luck.

"You can page me if you need me," he said.

"I will, I am heading to the other lawyer's office in Phoenix right now."

It was down on Central Avenue, and I had instructions to deliver the contract before noon. The receptionist received it and receipted me. I went immediately to John's Green Gables at 24th Street and Thomas for a glass of wine and lunch. The knight in armor on the white horse out front greeted me.

Since I was alone, I ate at the bar. I immediately ordered my glass of Chardonnay along with the trout special. This was a popular place for business people. It was dark inside after the bright sunlight, well decorated in dark wood and red velvet, and full of businessmen for lunch. Some other women sat at the bar, so the bartender chatted a little, but I kept to myself. I was preoccupied with my new client, and the possibility of a signed agreement that should come quickly.

It was land, no move-out or moves-in, no mortgage needed. My lawyer-client had the cash. It was a clean deal. He would take it as it was, and not demand any inspections. I ordered another glass of the house Chardonnay. It was pretty good. I had an hour to kill and keep busy. This law office nearby was the go-between on the deal, they would contact me with a response, question, or comment; or I was to call the agent back at two if they had not paged me. They were faxing my contract to California on the seller's behalf, and on her family's behalf. They assured me she wanted to sell and hoped for an immediate answer.

The bartender noticed when I paid how I fumbled with my purse and my Day-Timer. I had been writing in it for some time. I tipped him and headed to the lobby, checking my pager on the way.

It's almost two. I'm going to make that call. I'm anxious, even with two glasses of wine. I want to know something. How long can this take, one little lady to say yes or no? I am being watched. The others at the bar seem to be wondering what I am doing. I'll use the private phone booth to make the call. I am alone as usual, there's no one to share this exciting moment.

"The owner's representative has just informed me her children have gotten an injunction and are not allowing the sale of the property. They're declaring their mother mentally incompetent to sell the land," the female voice said from the other end of the line.

I am stunned to be having a conversation with a lawyer I have never met, about an unrecognizable transaction. I have no idea how to respond, or even if my client has a recourse. My mind has gone blank.

"What are we going to do now?" I am out of ideas. "What do you suggest I tell my client, as he will want a plan?"

I have now turned around in the phone booth and see a lineup of people waiting to make a call. I need to hang-up, have a drink, and call my client later. I must think this situation through, before calling my broker and redoing my morning plan.

"I'll call you in twenty-four hours. This response is not acceptable. I'll do some investigating." I hung up before she could tell me the deal was dead. I believe she thought it was at that moment.

"Don't drink too much," I heard that voice in my head say as I walked past the crowd in the lobby waiting for the phone. I headed back to the bar to take time to think, to prepare, to sound like a professional before I called Jerry.

"I'll have another Chardonnay," I told the bartender. He slowly handed me the glass. I tried to appear clearheaded as I reached for it, recognizing my drunkenness.

My drinking haunts me like a lonely ship in the night. My day is far from over and certainly has changed quickly. I am learning a lot about the commercial real estate business in one small transaction. Or, is it small?

COLLABORATE

"This changes things, but as a lawyer, I can represent myself in court, maybe better than you can," Jerry offered immediately. "I just need the phone number and the address of the lawyer's office in California. I will handle it with paperwork and take them to court. They have not been aboveboard and fair, or disclosing. I think we have something here."

For the next year, the transaction was in limbo. Jerry continued to pursue the woman's property, with all the lawyers and representatives he could throw at them. I, on the other hand, went back to selling houses in the East Valley. Oh yes, and getting divorced.

Jerry went through with his end of the bargain. He not only handled the divorce for me, he even agreed to do the paperwork for my husband. John told me, "If you want this divorce, you handle it. You found a lawyer, have him do it all. I'm not paying for a lawyer." And so, that is just what happened. I got two-for-one—or we did—something like that.

137

Within about six weeks after Jerry took over the land deal, I became officially divorced.

I feel guilty about divorcing him so quickly, about not trying harder to make the marriage work. I feel guilty about using Jerry and not holding up my half of the bargain and closing his escrow, and about moving on with my life. Have I really moved on? There are a lot of loose ends, and I spent plenty of time over a glass of wine thinking about them. I am not perfect, but I will do better.

"Is it over?" my husband asked on the phone just about a year after we had moved to Arizona.

"Yes, it recorded today," I answered.

"Well, good luck to you," he said and hung up on seven years of chaos, wild fun, and missed opportunities.

It was a Friday night. I didn't go out. I drank at home alone. I cried a lot that weekend, mostly for the loss I felt for what could have been. If only so much had been different, or we had been different. But, it was not meant to be. The "enemy within," that demon guilt, had to be stricken from me. I did not know how to do it. I had my divorce, I had my freedom, Jerry was representing himself in the land deal, and happy to do it. What was it going to take for me to move on and be happy?

MASQUERADE

CHANGES

"I'm thinking seriously about interviewing for a new home sales position with Pulte Homes," I told my friend Gloria at lunch. "They're hiring, and I've always wanted to try that end of the business."

"Really?" she blurted out, "that's a very different way of selling, it seems so confining. I can't see you doing it," she added as we finished up to get back to the office.

The 9th and Ash, a busy lunch place in downtown Tempe, served good food. A quick getaway a lot of people liked. It was an old house located in a quaint neighborhood by the campus. It took you away from business for a while.

She is right about one thing, I am not one for a lot of rules. Just the same, the structure of new home sales appeals to me. The buyers coming to me is more my style than driving people around.

Although not the top sales person in the office, or rookie of the year, I did well. Even though I tried very hard to win awards, it was frustrating. I was good at what I did, but ready for a change… and restless, my usual state these days.

I was wrestling with depression again, feeling sad often and drinking too much. It now interfered with my work. A career change seemed to be just what I needed. My ex-husband had picked this career for me. I would pick the next one with new-home sales.

The wine soothed me at night when my clients caused me frustration. Or, was it me who caused the frustration with unrealistic expectations of people? The wine helped me with my anxiety, too. It was my friend, my helper.

I wasn't enjoying the whole single life as much as I thought I would, either. It was fun to be on my own, making my own decisions, but it was lonely, too. The buffer from pervasive loneliness was the drinking— my lover, my confidante.

How do I feel about alcohol? Do I love it or hate it? Some days I answer one way and some days the other. But, one thing is for sure, it is a big part of my life.

THE INTERVIEW

"You've been on the resale end of the business two years, why do you want to sell new homes?" the Pulte sales manager asked me in a cautious tone.

Photo: Norm Strafford, Tempe, AZ

"I prefer new homes and the idea of working in the construction industry," I answered without hesitation. "The building of a new home is more my style."

"We are hiring two new people for our Chandler subdivision. That area is the fastest growing area in the Valley. Do you know anything about Chandler?" he asked.

"I've been out there many times to show property since it is just south of Tempe, close to my office, and less expensive. I am aware of the growth. It is exciting to watch and a good place to take clients. They see the expansion."

We talked quite a while, and he asked me to wait to speak to the company's Arizona president. That went well, too. I liked the man and he liked me. He moved me along to the second interview for the next day. After two more hours of interviewing, I became the first woman Pulte Homes ever hired to sell for them. It was 1981, and it was time. It was my time.

I am not going to sell decorating as initially proposed to me, but actual homes, in a subdivision, just like the other ten guys on the sales team. I am in, making small strides on my own! New-home sales is dominated by men, but I am going to help change all that tomorrow.

I left, weary from the strain of the long afternoon with them, but excited about the potential of a new position. I still had questions, but I would make a list and call back to get them answered. My next stop was the Windjammer Bar at the Lakes. My celebration spot had a seat for me near somebody happy to see me

It was a big day. I could sense it. I made my first career decision and it felt good. A celebration was in order. I would no longer be working where my ex thought I should be working, but doing what I wanted to do. This moment felt motivating.

THE GIFT

"Are you available for lunch this week?" my ex-husband's aunt asked politely over the phone. "I have something to tell you and something to give you. You know how special you are to me.""

"Sure, I've something to tell you, too," I said, "It's been a long time since we've talked, I look forward to seeing you again."

The Fiesta Inn was busy, but I saw her immediately. His widowed Aunt Mary still had her classic good looks despite her years. Her wavy gray hair was cropped close to her head and she wore no makeup. Her Arizona tan and silver and turquoise jewelry declared: "I've lived here all my life, this is who I am."

She greeted me with a hug, and we engaged in small talk before we ordered. She was her usual curious self, asking a lot of questions about my work and my friends. She always cared about me, and took me under her wing early on when I first entered the family.

141

I told her about the Pulte Homes offer. She was genuinely pleased for me. She always supported me whenever she could.

At one point, she took a deep breath and looked at me intensely.

"John's getting married soon. Her name is Sue. She is in the real estate business, too, and has a son. They are moving into your house this weekend," she said in one fell swoop.

I wasn't surprised it happened so soon, but still found it unnerving. He liked being married, maybe even *had* to be married. I knew Sue, we had mutual tennis friends.

"I still have things at the house. I should go there," I said, feeling uneasy. "Do you mind if I order a glass of wine?" I asked sheepishly.

"Of course, not dear. I'll have a beer," she said as she waved the waiter over.

"You'll want to call ahead and plan on taking everything in one trip," she advised.

"I will," I said slowly, remembering my beautiful Lenox Moonspun china set for twelve, with matching silverware and crystal.

I would need to bring boxes and wrapping paper with me, and plan for at least an hour. She would want me to do that for sure. She valued her lovely things, even though she lived frugally for her financial situation.

Dear God, what am I going to do with it all? I don't entertain, never have used it much. It's from my first marriage. I will keep it for another time and place, or sell it.

"What about my dog Casey?" I asked her, almost unconsciously. "Does she have a dog?

"I don't know, dear," she answered quietly. "You'll have to decide that, too."

I was only half available as the chitchat continued, thinking about having to call my ex-husband and make plans to go to the house when they weren't there. Getting my beautiful things and saying goodbye to Casey for the last time would not be easy. I felt sad and angry at the same time. The reality of the divorce settled in just then.

Our lunch lasted about an hour. I needed another glass of wine, but I didn't order it. My mind raced as I anticipated the many times our mutual friends would tell me he had remarried. Why so soon? We had married soon after our first marriages, so why not do it again? We had both failed terribly at our marriage, but this felt like a slap in the face.

"The last thing is, I have five thousand dollars for you, to do with as you please," she said as she paid the bill for lunch and passed me a small envelope. "I hope you keep it for a rainy day. They will come, they always do. I don't want you to come on hard times because you lack the money you need to help you."

I was stunned. I looked at her for a moment and thought about how generous it was, and whether she had told anyone else, especially my ex-husband. John would not approve and would certainly be jealous. He would not be getting any more money from her. He had squandered some of her money in the past, and she knew it. That was unfortunate, she had a lot of money to share, having had no children. She had always been caring toward me, but this was quite a surprise, a true gift.

"Thank you so much," I said, "I will spend the money wisely, investing in my future. You can be sure of that and, yes, there is a rainy day ahead. That is life."

We parted with a hug and a wave, and I watched her walk briskly to her car, defying her age. I always liked this woman, but wondered if I would ever see her again. She liked me, too. This felt like our final goodbye. It was closure for her and had to be for me, too. She needed to move on and be his aunt first. I could hear it in her voice as she said goodbye. I needed to let her do that as well.

HALLOWEEN

"Your ex and Sue moved down the street to a bigger house. Did you know?" Gloria asked on the phone early one morning.

"No, I didn't."

"They're having a Halloween Party and house warming this weekend. Rick's going so we can go with him as long as we disguise ourselves, especially you."

"He's one of John's friends. Is this a practical joke?" I asked.

"It is, but why not?" she asked with a grin.

"I'll need a bottle of wine for this," I laughed. "What's the plan?"

"I'm Jane, Rick is Tarzan, Randy is Dr. Livingston, and you are an Ubangi African woman from the Congo. What do you think?"

"That's pretty good."

I agreed instantly, and started planning my costume with no thought of how insane it was only a year after our divorce. It felt mischievous, and I liked that part immediately.

"They have a Gong Show planned. Rick and Randy will have bongo drums, and you and I will do the dancing," she added before hanging up. "Talk to you later."

My costume consisted of Rick's friend's black afro wig, my black leotard top and tights, a grass skirt from an old luau party, red plastic lips from the costume store, a large brown wooden necklace and even larger silver hoop earrings. The topper was taking the large pink rubber tips from the end of a pair of deflated beach balls and attaching them to the front of my leotard with safety pins. They looked as much like saggy breasts as I could muster. The black theater makeup I applied to my face, hands, and feet came from the neighbors. They did community theatre and loved the idea.

How can I do this, pull this off? Nobody will ever suspect I'm crazy enough to do it. I'm disguised enough that a house full of partiers will never recognize me, including my ex-husband and his new wife, and a dozen others who know me, I'm prepared for the big night.

I had several glasses of wine to add to my encouragement along with some spitefulness for his marriage. I was going to show him he could not get the best of me. Feeling strong and over our marriage, I had moved on.

How do I really feel about doing this party? Am I jealous? How do I feel about his new wife? What else will I have to lose before I give up trying to prove my independence to him?

This maladaptive behavior certainly didn't show I was coping. It was immature. I told no one. This was going to be a crazy night, and too much fun to turn back now.

As I dressed and sipped my wine, I contemplated what was about to happen and what I was doing. The defeat of another divorce was one of the toughest things I had to accept. Had I not really accepted it? I was addicted to him, but no longer in love with him.

The drinking before the party numbed me to a point. My drinking was taking me farther into my sadness, but when I heard Gloria's van outside I jumped into action. Alcohol was my uninhibition driver. My true self went away. I often did crazy things like this evening.

Gloria was thrilled with my costume and was sure nobody would know me. She parked several blocks from the house party. We finalized our plans for the night as Rick walked toward us. Randy, her faithful husband, had been patiently observing everything in the back seat, waiting for us to tell him what to do.

"Nobody talks to Pat. Pat, you speak to no one," Rick said quickly. "We all stick together and avoid a lot of questions."

"How long will we do our dancing?" Gloria asked.

"We get five minutes for the Gong Show," he answered, "and then the Gong goes off.

"Okay, let's go and have fun," Gloria said as she led the way in her sexy leopard print Jane outfit with Randy and Rick following her and me pulling up the rear.

The party was loud and crowded. A lot of food and even more bottles of liquor and wine lined the kitchen island. Most of the guests congregated inside, so we passed through quickly to the backyard. The beer keg was there and had a good crowd around it. The suds flowed. People looked at us and laughed, but nobody stopped us or asked any questions. The night was young.

I was sure there were drugs, but I could not tell at this early stage. Rumors reported drugs showed up at their parties. I condoned marijuana, but I wasn't looking for any. I could get in enough trouble with my bottle of wine.

"Hi, how are you?" asked a guy I recognized from last week's realty meeting. I didn't answer, I just smiled. He smiled and moved on. He must have figured I was going incognito for the night.

"I know who you are," another guy said behind me. I startled. I recognized him, too, but did not know his name. I said nothing. He was just fishing. There was no way he recognized me. When I would not speak, he laughed, and moved on.

The night went on like that for more than an hour, until I heard Rick's voice. "Let's go. The Gong Show is about to happen, and we drew the number three spot," he said.

I approached him and Gloria. Randy was nearby talking to a young woman. We were on a mission.

"Dance close to me," Gloria said. "I'll take the lead."

Without hesitation, the four of us assembled to do our Congo dance routine. By that time of night, I had put a real dent in my bottle, downing at least five glasses of wine. I was feeling no reservations about our soon-to-be debut performance.

The audience included almost all the guests from inside and outside the house… about 200 people. They yelled and cheered for the group ahead of us, who were doing a rock and roll routine.

When we were called to step onto the makeshift stage, the crowd filling that large back yard laughed, whispered, and applauded. Rick introduced us.

"This is Jane, Tarzan, Dr. Livingston, and our Ubangi Queen. We will do a traditional Congo spiritual dance for you."

With more laughs, Gloria and I began to whirl around the yard to the beats of the bongo drums. We kept shaking to the sound and dancing faster. I could feel my head spinning as the gas patio lights flew by me with each twirl. I was lost in the beats and the drunkenness. The drums stopped, the applause erupted, and I heard a loud voice from the crowd yell, "Winner! Winner!"

Not as concerned with winning as much as I was with my disguise, I heard a man's voice, loud and familiar.

"Who is she? I want to know. It's my house."

"It's your ex-wife," yelled another guy. The crowd erupted again with laughter.

The four of us hurried off the stage and headed to the side of the house to regroup. I was exhausted from the dancing, the wine, and the stress of wondering if my ex knew the truth. For almost two hours, I had not said a word.

"I'm feeling my drinks. I'm hot in the wig, and I'm suspicious we'll be found out."

"Do you think they know, or just guessing?" Gloria asked Rick.

"No, they're guessing," Rick said. "How could they know?"

"Let's go," Randy said directly to Gloria. "We've had our fun. Let's not push it."

Does my ex know what is happening? Is he in on the secret? Does his wife know, too? Is this a house burning with rage or one that can take a joke? Is the joke on me?

I underestimated what could happen next. We had crashed the party, won their Gong Show, ate their food, and almost fooled them. It was time to go. I finished my glass of wine with a deep sense of foreboding, just as I heard that familiar voice again.

"Take her home, Rick, the joke's over. You shouldn't have brought her here."

He stood there only a moment, then turned and left us at the front of the house. Since the night's alcohol had seduced me to numb the pain of our failed marriage and his hurried remarriage, I was in no mood to argue or even comment.

"We're leaving," Rick said. "Fun's over. We won, so the jokes on them."

We all agreed and headed toward the long walkway. I took one last swig of wine before looking back outside at the partiers to catch his smile. He was amused.

As Gloria and I passed the front yard fountain, I took the wig and nylon lining off my head and shook out my long hair. Then I stuck my head in the fresh flowing water. It was cool. A feeling of rebelliousness came over me as my long hair fell into the water.

"Get the hell out of my fountain," yelled a woman's voice from inside the house.

Laughing hysterically, I pulled back from the fountain and ran ahead of Gloria, who was doubled over in laughter. Carrying my wet wig, with my soggy hair trailing behind me, I sprinted the couple blocks to the van in my bare feet.

Is this the beginning or the end of my relationship with my ex? Am I done with him? Is my fun over? Will I move on?

HAPPINESS

"Are you bringing yourself down by staying so connected to him?" my therapist asked after I told her the story of the party night.

"I'm trying to be happy and free, but it's hard work. I feel I can't let go. I don't know why," I said slowly. I was hung over, and had dragged myself to her office on a Saturday.

"Did you really want this divorce, or were you allowing your drinking to act for you?"

"I'm not sure, but do know I feel angry with myself for leaving."

"What are you afraid of if you sever all ties with him?"

"That I've made a big mistake I'll regret for a long time. That I'll drink more than I do because I'm sad."

"What if everything turns out okay, can you visualize that for yourself?" she continued.

"Maybe, but it's so like me to be overwhelmed after I've decided something. I spent so many years having all my decisions made for me, I hesitate."

I expect to behave a certain way, and then get disappointed when I don't, and I drink over it. Why do I think we will have a friendly divorce? Most couples don't. Why can't I see their point? They don't want me in their life. I left. I moved out and filed for divorce. I got what I wanted. They don't have to do what I want.

"Maybe you should be open to the idea that when your friends urge you to join them, and you have had a little wine, you can be selfish or insensitive," she began again.

"I'll think about it. That's probably true."

I need a drink. That one hurt me. She thinks I am a brat and immature. I don't like that.

"For the next week, stop asking why you can't have something your way," she instructed.

"I can do that. I'll write about it. Thanks for today, I need to run."

I felt frustrated at being given another assignment, but it seemed simple enough. Asking myself why he behaved the way he did only frustrated me and caused me to drink. This had to stop. If anyone asked me why I drank or crashed his Halloween party, I got defensive, bringing out the cat claws with green eyes glaring.

"It's not for you to ask why of him or anyone else. Can you accept that?" she asked again before she walked me out of her office.

"I'll try. I'm feeling really tired and sad today," I said sheepishly. "I know I made a fool of myself at the party, but what's done is done."

"Instead of asking why when you think of him or his new wife, try focusing on 'what now,'" she suggested. "Take a realistic look at your life. What's going to be your next move?"

"I will, I promise. I know I must do this. Goodbye."

Who can I call to meet for a drink or dinner? Should I start going back to church to meet new people or join a singles group? Can I truly move on? Do I have the courage to manage the situation, handle the divorce, and take hold of my life and my career?

Affirmations each morning could have helped me to be stronger. Words I spoke to myself were critical to me; I learned all that in sales training. Slowing down the drinking and take better care of myself was on my agenda.

I was not afraid the alcohol would kill me, but that I would get in serious trouble next time, and things would get a lot worse before they got better. If I slowed down, I could avoid tragedies potentially on the horizon, embarrassments could be avoided. I was not sure I was willing to do that. These thoughts continued as I arrived home and poured a glass of wine.

Patricia L. Brooks

NAKED AND UNAFRAID

MR. COWBOY

What is he doing here? Damn, I don't remember him from last night. He must have come back here with Kay. This is just like her to take off in the night. Does he even know where he is?

I had descended the stairs in the nude, looking for orange juice. Lightheaded, my throat was sore, my mouth dry, and I couldn't talk. The weather was warm.

My mind raced about what to do next. I had to start feeling better fast as my work day started at noon on Saturday, and there was nobody else to cover for me. It was a holiday weekend. I didn't celebrate Thanksgiving these days.

How the hell did he get in here? Drinking is dangerous!

I drank the orange juice, but decided a Bloody Mary mix and a vodka chaser was needed, too. I felt lousy at this point, tired and achy with a headache and nausea.

Damn, I did it again. I blacked out for a couple of hours last night. Chuy's Jazz Club is so busy and loud, but a "blackout" from alcohol tunes it all out for me. I function, but I don't know it. I remember nothing hours later.

I took my drink upstairs to find my full-length robe before trying to wake the stranger. I had to find out who he was and get him out of the house. Things you think will never happen, do—good and bad.

What if he resists me? What if he fights me?

I hurried back downstairs, robed and ready.

"You have to leave," I said nudging his nude body sprawled face-down on my single bed in the downstairs bedroom. Alcohol was my shock absorber, so the Bloody Mary was helping.

My beautiful rust-colored custom-made comforter was strewn everywhere. The morning sun came through the window off the courtyard, but he wasn't visible to the neighbors. The queen palm blocked the view from the walkway. His turquoise and silver watchband glistened in the rays. It was all he wore. His large black Tony Lama's sat near the bed next to a heap of clothes on the floor.

"You need to get up," I said, trying again. "I have to go to work. You can't stay here." I continued pushing harder on his big shoulders.

"Who are you, beautiful?" he asked with a grin, rubbing his eyes and rolling over, much to my chagrin. "What time is it?" he asked squinting at his watch.

"Better question… who are you?" I said impatiently, hoping for much-needed information.

"I'm Darren, I ended up here with your friend Kay. She left early this morning, hours ago. She said she had to feed and run her horses."

I turned away as he moved to get dressed, wondering how Kay, at five feet ten inches, and this big guy got together in my single bed. Though the thought amused me, I headed back to the kitchen, hoping he would dress quickly and leave with not much fanfare.

"How about breakfast, honey? I'm starving, my treat. Then you can drive me back to my car," he quipped, as if asking for a date. "What do you say, darling?" He pulled on his boots and straightened his shirt.

"I'm not going anywhere with you, or taking you back to your car," I said in a curt voice. Alcohol had caught up with me that morning, and it was not glamourous. He had tried to outfox me. "You can call a cab. I must get ready for work. I don't have time for breakfast. Please, I need you to leave," I added, "The party is over."

"Okay, okay, you don't need to be mad at me. I'm willing to leave. Can I use your phone? We took a cab here, and I have a number."

Alcohol makes everything better, and then it makes everything worse. I hate being in my skin today. Please God, move this day along.

I was furious with Kay, more than with Mr. Cowboy, and certainly with myself for being so drunk I didn't even realize they were here when I arrived home. I was hung over and had a strange two-hundred-pound man in my house. I desperately needed to get rid of him and make use of what little time I had left to get to feeling well enough to deal with the public for the next eight hours.

What happened to me last night? It was the usual Friday night at Chuy's Jazz Club on Mill Avenue, with sisters Margo and Francine Reed singing. Guys were hitting on women, with the smell of marijuana everywhere. One glass of wine after another put me away early; the drink of inebriation made me vulnerable. But, I'm resilient. I survived again.

I had met Kay there about nine o'clock. We planned to stay awhile and move on to the Windjammer at The Lakes. Apparently, we never left. Her husband was at a conference. He often left for periods of time, being a full professor was demanding. Kay took advantage of her full-time freedom and called me as soon as she knew his schedule. She had a key to my condo near the campus since she lived in south Tempe, a long drive on a party night.

Leaving a guy in my downstairs bedroom unannounced is unacceptable, even for this drunk. This guy could have been a dangerous character. She has some explaining to do. Bad things could have happened. We have known each other a long time, but this move tops it all.

"Thanks for the bed for the night. The breakfast offer still stands, maybe another time," he said as he headed out the door.

The cab came, he left, and I took a lot of aspirin and dressed quickly for the day. Nothing seemed to change from one crazy weekend to another, just the names, faces and places. The feelings were always the same: anger disgust, regret, followed by me swearing off drinking too much one more time and wondering how I got there. I made a note to call Kay.

NAKED MAN

My day involved two written contracts and a lot of traffic through the models. It culminated with a trip to my friend Jim's house in Mesa after closing. I was switching my car for his truck to move some furniture on Monday, my day off. It would take ten minutes to make the exchange. I planned to go directly home. I was beat and still hung over from the night before. He would understand. We were usually on the same page.

"What's going on?" I asked as I came through the back door. "Are you having a party?"

"No, just some friends over," Jim said as he motioned me to the pool area. "They're leaving soon, been here awhile. Have a glass of wine with us. We're in the Jacuzzi."

I was only there to pick up his truck. I had used it before. I had to be at work again Sunday morning and needed rest to move furniture on Monday. My days off were always like that, busy "doing." I filled every minute as if I didn't want to see myself. With no free nights, I worked all week and was often tired. My nightly compulsion for wine kicked in.

"Come on in," said one of the girls as she stepped out of the Jacuzzi in the nude. "I'm heading home soon, just ready for one more glass of wine."

Oh boy, here we go again, more nude bodies. That was the way it was at this house, casual and loose. I poured myself a glass of wine and sat near them on the side of the pool, dangling my feet in the water thinking I should smile more.

"Come on, get in," one of the guys yelled, "you're not shy, are you?"

Is he kidding? I've already been nude once today with a stranger. Shy is not an adjective to describe me this weekend. I can keep up with these guys.

I don't know if it was tiredness, the second glass of wine, or the heat of the Jacuzzi, but I felt weak within minutes of stepping into that bath of 105 degrees. All I could think about was getting home to sleep, to be ready for work tomorrow, and my plans for Monday.

154

"I need to go," I said abruptly as I pulled my red, hot, naked body from the steaming water. I was wobbly, but figured I'd shake it off. I had to, I was leaving my car and taking his truck with me, regardless.

"I'll leave my car in your driveway. My keys are in your kitchen by the phone," I said with a shortness of breath as I reached for my clothes and headed for the house.

"You know where my keys are, good luck. The truck is in the street," he yelled, and turned back to his friends.

Jim had done some work for me on my rental properties. He was reliable, and I liked that about him. A rare quality in the men I knew. We kept it simple as far as our relationship, I liked it that way. Too many men didn't accept my aggressive, hardworking demeanor, but Jim did.

I dressed quickly and headed for the street. Although tipsier, I felt well enough to drive. Besides, nobody was leaving here to help me. Jim's truck was one I had driven before, yet it seemed larger that night. I struggled to open the door, then threw my purse on the passenger seat with my wet sandals that had gotten caught in the sprinklers.

I tried desperately to pull the seat up. It wouldn't move, it was stuck. Getting out of the truck to try again didn't work. I fidgeted more with the handle, but no luck. I heard voices over the fence to my right, but decided not to ask for help.

Oh hell, just leap up there and drive the damn thing. You can reach your toes on the pedal. You'll be fine. It's only ten minutes back to Tempe.

I slowly pulled out onto the street and began to maneuver my way to Route 60 and Tempe. My toes kept slipping off the pedal and I became frustrated. It was quiet as I moved along, passing only a dog walker leaving his neighborhood. I leaned onto the steering wheel since I couldn't lean back on the seat. While weaving a bit on the road, I was sure it was because of my position in the truck and not my tipsiness from the wine.

MR. POLICEMAN

Before entering Route 60 at Dobson Road, the lights of a police car flashed in my rear window. I panicked. Too much to drink, and no lunch or dinner that day. This was trouble. The mirror was blinding my eyes with each flicker.

I slowly pulled off to the shoulder of the road, knowing I had better get my sandals on quickly before the officer approached me. It was against the law to drive barefoot in Arizona, let alone tipsy and on the steering wheel.

Good grief this has been a hell of a day... stupid me, and my crazy ideas. Why was I so easily bullied into a drink? Or was I? God help me.

I pulled past the overpass and parked the car at the side of the road on the shoulder, as carefully as I could. The officer approached me cautiously.

"Your driver's license please," he asked, "and the truck registration."

"Here's my license," I said after struggling with my wallet. "But, the truck is not mine, it's borrowed. I'm not sure about the registration." I searched the glove box.

"You were swerving over the center line repeatedly for the last mile or so, and you have a taillight out," he began, "I'm going to need to have you step out of the truck."

Damn it, a tail light, too! Okay, put on your sandals, hope for the best. Shoot, they're still wet. This is not good. Stay calm. Please God, not a ticket. I just like to drink.

"Please get out of the truck," he said again with a stronger tone as I jumped down to the street from the cab. "Walk with one foot in front of the other until I tell you to stop," he said with his voice getting even sterner.

"Put your right finger to your nose slowly, right hand then left," he continued.

I was failing miserably, I was nervous, nauseated, and had to go to the bathroom. I was in deep trouble, scared and ashamed.

156

"Have you ever taken a breathalyzer test before?" he asked.

"No, I haven't, but I know what it is," I said as I watched him prepare to give me the test.

Maybe dumb luck will intervene. Maybe he will only give me a ticket for no registration or no tail light ticket? Using alcohol to cope is a joke. I hide behind it, but no hiding here.

I was sobering up. My head cleared a little bit as the evening breeze had cooled. My stomach growled. It had been a long time since breakfast. One more glass of wine would calm my nerves.

"Your blood level is 1.5. That is legally drunk under Arizona law," he said in a voice of authority. "Please get in the squad car and give me your keys. I'm calling for a backup to help me take care of the truck. You'll be coming with me."

Oh damn, he's taking me to the station, maybe to jail. How the hell did this happen? I drink because I am lonely, or anxious. Who can help me get out of this? I'm going to throw up.

The other officer showed up to assist almost immediately. The new laws were there to protect the public from drunk drivers. I was grateful for not killing somebody or myself. These laws were changed that year because too little was done about drunk drivers in the past. Too many people had not walked away from drunk-driving accidents.

Drinking and driving is a serious offense. A judge will decide my fate, not the police. Wine makes me do stupid things. Trouble seems to find me when I drink, but I love the way wine works on me.

The second police officer pulled the truck into the hotel parking lot across from the intersection as we pulled away. I was sheepish, but I listened to the police officer inform me of what to expect. He told me I would see a judge in the early morning, even though it was Sunday, and I would spend the night in the Mesa jail.

"We will process your ticket and fingerprint you tonight, and enter information on the breathalyzer to be ready for the judge," he said in a matter-of-fact voice. "Do you have any questions?"

JAILBIRD

No questions, but exhausted and cold, and wishing to be anyplace but at the Mesa jail. I would call somebody in the morning, but who would that be? Maybe my casual boyfriend Scott. No, he was not one to handle something like this. He was a bit naïve about my lifestyle. I needed to end it with him anyway… I was using him.

What else do I have to lose now? Myself? My heart? My soul?

"Do you have someone you can call in the morning? After you meet with the judge we will release you," the clerk at the desk said. She seemed anxious to finish with me and move on.

"I need to think about that, can I tell you in the morning?" I asked, hoping she would not press me. My head hurt. My hands trembled. Thoughts of who I would call or how I would get home raced through my head. I had disappeared for years in my drinking, and my list of friends had dwindled.

I guess I can call a cab to get to the truck. Should I tell anyone? I've made a real mess of things this time. I need somebody to help me. It's so embarrassing. I'm so ashamed. I'm so mad at myself. I've fallen so low, down the trap door.

"Okay, but we won't drive you anywhere," she said emphatically and moved on to the fingerprinting. Since I had a real estate license, I had been fingerprinted before.

How will this affect my license? Will I have to disclose this to the broker at the office or the Real Estate department downtown? Oh God, what a mess.

"May I have a cup of coffee or hot tea?" I asked the woman at the desk after she handed me over to the security guard.

"No coffee or tea allowed to those spending the night in the jail," she answered. "I'll bring you a glass of water."

Wow. How weird. I'm really a serious inmate now.

There were two older women in the jail cell sleeping. I kept to myself, thinking about all my years of drinking and crazy behavior. I couldn't sleep, yet had no idea of time. My new watch was reluctantly given up at the front desk. I reminded myself this would end, despite the consequences, but my nervousness didn't go away.

"You're free to go, the judge will see you next week," the officer announced very early the next morning. He startled me. I must have dozed off a bit, even though I was sitting up in a huddled position. The other women were now awake, looking at me curiously.

"Are you ready to make your phone call?" the woman at the desk asked.

"Yes, I am. What time is it?" I asked as I tried to feel presentable.

"It's seven o'clock," she said with an impatient tone. She probably answered the same questions at every release. "Here are your things, be sure to check them over before signing the release. You can use the phone through that door, only a five-minute call, please."

"It's all here," I said and signed for my jewelry, putting it back on to gain some courage. I called Gloria, my oldest Arizona friend. She lived nearby in Mesa and, although a late sleeper, she would come to help me. Gloria could keep this story a secret, even though she would complain about the hour. She had her crazy stories, too, but I would have to beg for her to help me.

"What the heck time is it?" she asked in a sleepy voice. "Where are you?"

"The Mesa Jail, please come. I'll explain in the car."

My DUI processed under the new law. I survived the night in jail, and a court-ordered thirty days without a driver's license.

How do I drive and get to work and my meetings with no license? This is insane. Who am I to defy the law?

LAWYER LADY

Upon my release from jail, I immediately called a woman attorney in Mesa who had bought a house from me a couple of years earlier. She practiced criminal law and had a good reputation, and I believed she would be able to help me.

"You know there's not much I can do for you," she said when I met her the next week at her office. "The new law is pretty strict, and for good reason."

"Can you look at things and see if they'll bend on the thirty days without a license?" I asked. "That's going to be a hardship for me. I have no husband or family here and my friends are busy."

"I'll try, but no promises," she said reluctantly. "I would suggest you start making plans to deal with it, maybe a driver service. That is what people must do in these situations," she added as she indicated it was time for me to go.

I left her office and decided if I couldn't get out of the lost license I would drive anyway. I was a good driver, and I wouldn't be drinking, but going to those meetings. It would be easy for thirty days to get that card signed and appease the court.

It will all be over before I know it. Thirty days is nothing. I'm not a real alcoholic; I just need to drink less, and only wine. It's the hard stuff and crazy behavior that gets me in trouble.

I drove every day I had no license, to and from work, for errands on the way home and to recovery meetings at night and on my days off. I was nervous about it, continuously looking in the rear-view mirror. I told no one and counted the days on my calendar, checking them off daily.

The recovery meetings were friendly enough, many close to work and home. They were interesting to me in many ways. I took notes, something the police psychologist suggested. I met a lot of good, kind people but, after thirty days of asking for a signature on that court card, it was time to move on, to get back to my life. It was odd not to drink. Abstinence was okay for a while, but not for me. At least not now, barely into my thirties.

It was as simple as that; I missed drinking. It was not easy resisting the temptation. The nice woman who ran one meeting I regularly attended at St. Tim's church in Mesa gave me her phone number. I gave her mine, too, and we talked a little on the phone when she called me. I never seemed to have time to call her.

"Call me anytime if you want to talk," she said the last time I attended. I saw on her face she knew I would not be back. It was obvious.

"It's important in the beginning to have someone to call," she said as I thanked her.

"I'm good," I said. "I'm just here for the court, but thank you."

As I walked away, I recognized sadness on her face, too. She told me she believed I had made a bad decision. I ignored her and headed for the parking lot, wondering why I needed to give up drinking anyway, after paying my dues and planning to drink only wine anyway.

I paid a two-hundred-dollar fine to the court and attended three sessions with a police psychologist. I had done thirty days of recovery meetings with a court-ordered card signed by the meeting leader. I appeared in court sixty days after completing these requirements to show proof I had met all of them.

What the hell did all that mean anyway? I can't afford a chauffeur. I'm not a loser. I just have problems I need to solve.

LADYLIKE

Things eventually went back to normal, well, my, normal… a crazy work schedule of evenings and weekends, with a social life that made no sense. I began drinking only wine and in smaller amounts. No more hard liquor. Wine went down easier, was cheaper, and more ladylike. It fit me, it soothed me, calmed me.

My life took a turn when I was seduced to go to Wood Brothers Homes to open a new subdivision in Chandler. They offered me a chance to manage two developments and be part of the ground-floor plans, to have the complete run of the place. They wanted a successful woman, and I had earned a reputation in the industry as a hard worker, a producer, and a go-getter. My ego was getting the best of me with the awards and recognition accumulated in a short couple of years. Women catching up to men made me tick, with selling and with drinking.

I resigned from Pulte Homes on short notice for this position, with no discussion with anyone, leaving the people who gave me my first chance at new-home sales. Those who trained me, supported me and encouraged me to go after what proved to be the best move for me. I left people who cared for me because a chance at more money was waving in front of me.

Why didn't I research who worked here before making the move? The management is crazy. The lead guy is a dictator and the sales team ruthless. What have I gotten myself into?

Before the subdivision broke ground, I took deposits on lots, and home orders off blueprints sprawled out on the hood of my car. I sold houses sight unseen. I came to work in blue jeans and cowboy boots, because of the unfinished streets, often muddy. Along with plenty of dust and dirt, a lot of urgency stirred up. The models were unique, the price was right, the location desirable. It was my time to shine.

Eventually, I worked by candlelight in the models, due to a glitch in the electrical hookup to completely decorated rooms, including a sales office. The subdivision had no power or water. The City of Chandler fought us on several aspects of the plans, but that did not stop me. I was going to be the star. I felt it in my bones, and became obsessed with the idea that women could have it all.

I was willing to work like a crazy person. I loved that it was my project and I was making a lot of the decisions. Whatever it took, I kept going, not wanting to share sales with anyone. With wine stored in the back of the refrigerator in the office, and a change of clothes in the closet, I slept the night there more than once to numb the pain of going home to an empty house.

I was living up to my reputation as a hard worker, and the sales manager who hired me loved it. My ego ran amuck when he placed an article in the company's national newsletter about my project and success. He had his star. This male-dominated environment only added to my motivation.

I was on top of the world with the DUI experience in a distant past. The development came together, and the City of Chandler cooperated, and I was asked to speak at a City Council meeting regarding the single-car garages on the townhomes. It went well. The Council Chambers filled with neighbors who showed up in the rain to fight what they thought would take down the neighborhood. Their protests fell on deaf ears and, at the end of the night, we won. Sales continued in a tidal wave. I celebrated with my customers by holding a happy hour in the sales office.

I wrote contracts at the rate of ten to twelve a weekend by getting to work earlier and earlier, and leaving later and later. I was all things to all people: sales person, customer service person, negotiator and all-around fire putter-outer. My life was perfect, but I had no life. By often working seven to ten days straight without relief, I drank on the job.

With a lot of sales, plenty of wine, and more than my share of pats on the back at the Monday morning sales meetings, a star was born. It felt great. I could drink the night before, and the day after, and feel a part of the world of business success.

While drinking to cope, and release stress and anxiety, I was often extremely lonely with a lot of people in my life. No badge of honor there. I did not have it all, it just looked like it to others.

Patricia L. Brooks

QUITTING TIME

PLANS

"I'm thinking about quitting drinking," I blurted out as we pushed away from the dock. "I'm seriously considering going back to recovery meetings, too."

"That's going to make you a lot of fun," Joe said with a laugh as he lifted a beer from the cooler. "Anybody want a beer?"

"Not me," I said. "Maybe a little wine later, I brought a jug of wine coolers with me."

"You're serious!" Dave took his shirt off and stretched out with a joint, the sun shining on his already tanned body.

Robin said nothing, with her long thin legs curled across the front of the boat and her head resting on her special pillow. She did not come to drink or talk. She wanted quiet time in the sun. She wouldn't risk the calories in alcohol, so the cooler jug was mine.

The guys would drink the beer, and the three of them would share the marijuana. I would pass on it. I did not like the effect or the smell. Wine was all I wanted, with a little sun and some attention from Joe.

I drink to forget, to not feel, to be somebody else for a while. Drinking is an escape from my life, the life I didn't intend for me.

We planned to float on Black Canyon Lake for three or four hours before driving back to the Valley, forgetting our customers and the headaches of selling new homes. It was a weekday, so it wasn't busy, we liked it that way. With the lake sparsely populated, the smell of Mary

Jane was not going to be an issue. The water was calm and a beautiful azure blue.

We were all in the same career of new-home sales—no couples, just friends and co-workers. That was how to describe us. On occasion, our days off were spent together. Robin and I worked together at Wood Brothers Homes. Dave and Joe worked for Continental Homes, two of the most productive homebuilders at the time. We all did quite well.

A little shop talk while gliding over the water that day worked for me. Mostly, though, the conversation was about the latest restaurant or bar in Scottsdale, movies we liked, or other trivial things happening around town. Eventually, we started fading off to nap in the sun.

The guys took turns managing the boat. That seemed to work out the best. Robin and I were happy to oversee the coolers and sunscreen. Nobody had expectations of anybody. I had been with Dave for a while, but lately, with Joe. They knew it, but it didn't seem to matter. Just friends. All four of us were divorced many years now. Our friendships were bigger than jealousy, we had been there for each other and we could do it again.

Robin had a boyfriend in California.

We all knew a lot about each other, but some things weren't discussed, just accepted. Our friendships lasted several years with only a few mishaps, even after too much drinking. This arrangement was not going to change. It was a strange bond, but compatible. Only too much alcohol caused the riffs. We all needed to quit.

"If you go to recovery meetings again, I'll go, too," Dave threw out after we had been on the lake for about an hour. "I went for quite a while when I lived in Vegas, when I was dealing, and had some trouble up there. I'll go again. I want to quit, too."

I hide my drinking well. I'm good at what I do, but it's wearing on me. I have bouts of depression. I don't feel in step anymore, not even with myself!

"Sounds good," I said with a slight smile. "Maybe the buddy system will work."

We all laughed, but nobody put down their drink just yet.

"I'll go, too," Joe said surprisingly as he got to his feet. We had been floating now for a couple of hours with not a lot of talk, the alcohol and marijuana had taken over. "I've never been to meetings, but this damn alcohol killed my old man and made my mom's life a living hell."

As usual, Robin said nothing. She kept quiet about a lot of things, including the fact that she didn't eat enough for a bird. We were quite a team as we packed the Bronco to start our trek back down the mountain. Nobody discussed her thinness. It was what she did.

"Anyone want to stop for one more before we call it a night?" Joe asked with a twinkle in his eye. "We can quit tomorrow."

Nobody commented. Quitting and staying quit was not going to be easy, maybe impossible.

Drinking causes me to lose my morals. It feels like another world to me. I do things I regret. I want that to change. If I don't drink, that may change.

CELEBRATING

I closed the subdivision at eight o'clock in the evening. It was dark, a typical Sunday night in October, windy and chilly, but a clear night. I was exhausted from a busy three-day weekend. I'd started out tired from having too much sun and wine at Black Canyon Lake, and too little sleep.

With five contracts to turn in for the Monday morning sales meeting, it would be the usual roll call, with me probably having the most sales. Being on top was fun, having won the Salesperson of the Month title about six times that year.

I changed my clothes quickly at the office, a navy and cream striped sundress, one of my favorites. It didn't take me long. I'd been ready for hours with the right shoes and jewelry. I just needed to see the last of the customers and say goodbye for the night.

I pulled out of the sales office driveway in Chandler by eight thirty and headed for the Scottsdale Radisson Resort. They featured a live band on Sunday nights, so dancing was possible even though you would usually find me sitting at the end of the bar. That was my choice... drink to forget.

167

Would I quit drinking that day, or would depression hover nearby and the wine flow?

The place was busy and the music loud, maybe just what I needed. Having driven more than thirty minutes to get there, spending the night in the hotel could happen. I had done that before as they knew me there. Just a couple of glasses of wine tonight though, so it shouldn't be necessary.

"Good night," I said to the bartender, after what seemed like two or three glasses of wine and one dance with an insistent patron from New York City.

"Are you okay? Do you need a room tonight or a cab?" he asked.

"No, I'll be fine," I said, even though I didn't feel very steady. Finding my car after wandering around the parking lot for what seemed like a long time, I cautiously headed down Scottsdale Road. It was going to be okay and a safe drive to my condo in Tempe.

I drink more than I expect. The evening surprises me. I am very tired. I don't leave when I should. I'm not witty, but sloppy, not the way I like to be.

RED LIGHTS

"You were driving on the wrong side of the road. Did you realize that?" the police officer asked in a stern voice.

"No, I didn't," I said as I tried to clear my thoughts. Not remembering how I got to the side of the road after he stopped me, or what else had been said and done.

I vaguely remembered him stopping me when the flashing red lights in my rearview mirror started obstructing my view. Nothing from that night resonated with me as he began a litany of questions about the evening, my destination, and how much I drank. I felt weak, at times seeing he was talking to me, but not hearing him. It felt very strange, as if something bad was about to happen.

"We're keeping you here tonight, please leave your jewelry and purse with me," said the woman at the desk. "You've failed the sobriety tests at the scene," she went on, "We can't' release you. You've been ticketed for DUI. Do you understand what is happening to you?"

"Yes, I think so," I said sheepishly. "I don't remember everything."

"Most people don't," she said as she went about her business, not even looking up at me.

My heart started to pound. I began to feel anxiety like I had never known.

How did this happen again? It had only been two years. I'm quitting tomorrow. How did I get to the jail? Was I in a blackout? God help me.

They ushered me off to a cold cell for the night. It was quiet. I needed that peace, just not there. Not being able to sleep, I started to sober up and contemplate what was happening to me. How much trouble I was in this time.

Drinking is a habit I can no longer deny. Suddenly, when I least expect it. I'm drinking too much, drinking alone. I don't know how I got to where I am. Just like tonight!

HOMECOMING

My cleaning gal was there when I arrived home that morning. The last person I wanted to see or explain anything to, but there she was anyway.

"I need my privacy today. You don't need to finish. I'll pay you for today," I said and led her out to her van that smelled of alcohol. Often, visible bottles of booze rattled in her van, but I never said anything. She needed the money, and she worked hard. Possibly she understood, but I was not in the mood to confide in her.

"Okay, I'll be going then," she said, not really looking at me as I handed her a check. It was almost as if she was saying she knew, and it was okay with her.

Working hard and drinking is the pleasure part of my day. Trying to disguise it into being chic doesn't seem to work anymore.

169

I immediately called the main office of Wood Brothers Homes and left a message for my sales manager.

"I can't make to the sales meeting, I'm not well. I will have my contracts delivered by messenger this morning. Thank you."

Somebody would be suspicious, nobody used messengers in this company, not even me. It was a first. Even though I was the top sales person, I was pushing it thinking I could get away with that one.

I called my long-time friend and co-worker Gloria, but she was out. I left a message, then regretted it. She came knocking at the door, and peeked through my stained-glass window.

"I came as soon as I heard your message," she said. "I had an early appointment." She shoved a handful of Valium into my hand. She always had Valium in her purse.

"Take these, they will calm you down. You look terrible. What the hell happened this time?"

She listened to my woes while I showered. Covering the DUI, the jail time, and the possible loss of my license, it all blurted out quickly. No Valium for me. They would knock me out.

"I'm going to quit for good. It's over. Made a real mess of my life this time," I said in a flurry, while dressing for a day that I never planned.

"You should just do pot, like me," she said emphatically, as if that was the answer. "I've told you that for years," she added as she headed to the door. "Call me later."

I'm on the treadmill at work. I bust my ass, sell, sell, sell. I'm exhausted at the end of the day, running in a vicious circle with stress and loneliness close behind.

WORKDAY

I opened the subdivision late that day, fought a hangover, and felt the stress from the last twenty-four hours. My whole body ached as if it had been physically beaten. Fearing the wrath of my sales manager, who expected my smiling face at the sales meeting in Scottsdale, I kept looking over my shoulder and acting guilty.

The woman lawyer in Mesa, who had handled my first DUI case two years earlier, answered the phone.

"I need your help again. I have another DUI," I blurted out.

"What is it with you people?" she said immediately in a heart-piercing voice I had not heard in the past. "Why do you keep doing this to yourself and expect lawyers like me to bail you out?"

Numb and angry, I knew our conversation was over. She would not help me, and didn't want to help me.

"Sorry I called," I said and hung up with a short goodbye. That was not good.

I am aware I drink too much. It's just so hard to admit it to anyone. I run from myself and others. I lie about my drinking, where I go, and what I do. God help me.

My next call was to a real estate lawyer I had been having an affair with for some time. He was in the Phoenix Thunderbirds, a local men's fraternity that did a lot of charitable work. He socialized with a lot of people, especially other successful lawyers, and he liked me a lot. He would help me if he could.

"Please have John call me as soon as he can," I told the receptionist at his office when she said he was in court.

"He's very busy on Mondays. I'll do my best," she said reluctantly.

Although cordial, she was impatient with me. She often saw me asking John for something, using him, and that he used me, too. She condoned our relationship, covered for him, and was paid well to do so.

Two days went by before I heard from him. A lot of questions on his part, and tears on mine, but eventually he gave me the name of a DUI lawyer in Phoenix.

Drinking makes me more gregarious, more social. I'm awkward without it. Life will be very different not drinking. Having an affair will seem wrong; I'll end it with John once things settle down. He may not want to be around me anymore.

171

"He's tough, he's expensive, and he gets the job done," John said with some trepidation in his voice. "You're dealing with some strict new laws you know."

"Yes, I know that."

"Call me tomorrow. Give me a chance to prepare him for your call. He'll help you if I ask him to do it. We went to law school together at ASU. He's good at what he does."

"Thank you, I appreciate it a lot."

MY LAWYER

My first meeting with Roger, the DUI lawyer, was good and bad. While draining my savings to pay his retainer, he prepared paperwork to put off my court day for a year. If I went to recovery meetings and documented going, he could possibly convince the judge to give me leniency and lessen the sentence. I agreed to his plan. There was no other choice.

He took me to lunch several times to discuss my case. I ordered a salad and a Diet Coke, and he ordered a double Scotch on the rocks, shuffled my papers and took notes. Although a big guy with a gruff voice, he was smart and knew his stuff, just as John had said. I felt confident about working with him and that, despite his rugged good looks, this was all business.

We talked about my case and what needed to be done. Quite a pair though, both unwilling to talk about alcoholism and excessive drinking. There was a job to do, and that was to try to keep me out of jail, and minimize the license loss time and the fine charges.

He explained to me the new DUI laws meant the loss of my driver's license for a year and up to two months in jail at the 35th Avenue and Durango facility in south Phoenix. I had never heard of the place, but it sounded very scary to me. The court cost estimate was five hundred dollars. He guaranteed me nothing.

"If you go to a recovery program and document those meetings with signatures from the leaders, we might be able to fall in favor with the judge," he suggested. "I cannot promise much more than a slow-down of the process, so you can get comfortable with what is happening to you."

"This is so scary to me, but I trust you on the new law. This is my second time. I cannot believe I made this mistake again."

I feel sad, life has taken another negative turn. I have a long way to go to be well. I must never give up hope. I can find a happier life than this. I can find my way.

"You need to move on now and mentally prepare yourself for the jail part," he said as he ordered another drink and I finished my salad. "They've only recently started sending women with DUIs to that facility; it's quite a place. A lot of the women in there are in for prostitution, theft, drug sales, or bad checks. Find a woman in your recovery program who has been there and can tell you about jail."

My mind trailed off, trying to comprehend even having this conversation.

WORKPLACE

"We need to talk, I'll be out to see you today," my sales manager said as he made a couple of other comments in a matter-of-fact voice. "Plan on seeing me before you leave today."

Denny showed up at six o'clock, just as I was closing the models and feeling exhausted. I could hardly breathe, and he was not his usual laughing self. I knew something was up.

"We've had one too many complaints from potential buyers who have been in here. They are saying you don't take care of them," he started. "What is going on with you? Last year you were our top sales person, the first woman to win that award. Now, I have a pile of complaint letters on you."

He's right. I'm a high achiever, but I want to escape. I can't understand my behavior. I feel like drinking alone, yet I feel so guilty too because alcohol transforms me. I'm self-destructive. Why is that?

"I'm having some personal problems. I know what I need to do," I began. "I am so sorry... another DUI last weekend. Maybe some time

173

off for therapy and to meet with my lawyer. I'm going to go to recovery meetings, I just haven't set it all up," I blurted out.

He looked stunned, but relieved in some way. He was not angry or upset. He softened his stance and sat down. His voice changed immediately, and he continued in a conversational tone that I was more used to when we talked.

"The marketing guy Chuck, at the Landall Ad Agency—the one we use here for our home promotion—is in a recovery program. He'll take you to a meeting; I will talk to him for you," he offered. "I will call him today. You have met him, but when you get to know him, you'll like him even more. Chuck is a good guy. Trust him to help you. He's been a friend for a long time," Denny said with a compassion I had never heard before.

"Two of our upper management guys don't drink. They'll be receptive to paying for your therapy or a treatment program. Human Resources will investigate what the insurance will cover. We have done this before for others. Do you want the company to do that for you?" he asked easily

I stared at him in amazement at how this meeting had changed in a heartbeat.

I only need one person to help me when times get tough. Is he going to be my person now? Is he going to support me? I told him I've been reckless, but will I survive this whole thing? I will be strong.

REHAB-IT

Within a week, I found myself in an eight-week program for outpatient treatment at Desert Samaritan Hospital in Mesa from seven to eleven every morning before I went to work. Held four days a week, the group involved twenty-two people with every addiction recovery from alcohol to food to gambling to drugs. We were quite a group, yet we were supportive of one another. I enjoyed going from the very beginning.

The therapist who led the group was tough, but gentle and kind. She tightly enforced her rules, and we liked her for it. We were ready for discipline, at least I was. With impressive credentials from the University of Michigan, she won me over, since I had attended the U of M-Flint branch. I liked the Go Blue banners in her office. They gave me a sense of home when I walked in. She was good enough for me.

I met Chuck at my first meeting for my second round with recovery. Ironically, we met at St. Barnabas Church in Scottsdale, just down the street from where our sales meetings were held, and a mile from the hotel where I had my last drunk.

I want to stay sober, and not drink. I want to ask God for help. I know a recovery program is the answer.

The meeting, at seven thirty on Thursday night, was full of laughing, smiling people enjoying each other. He immediately spotted the woman he wanted me to meet, and we headed over to her. Rusty radiated energy, and wore great clothes and beautiful turquoise jewelry. Chuck told me she was a successful Realtor in town with a good sense of humor, and that she sponsored a lot of women and had agreed to be my sponsor. I liked her right away because she had a strong handshake and a mischievous smile.

She had a hearty laugh and was confident about herself. She appeared sincere and genuinely happy to meet me, but like someone who had paid her dues, too. I knew she would be honest with me if I was honest with her.

That night began my recovery journey toward my nondrinking life, toward solving my emotional problems and living a spiritual life. It was only the beginning, though. I had a lot of work to do, a lot of soul-searching, and a lot of honesty and trust to add to my daily life.

I will start fresh. It's risky, but my friends believe in me. I'll patch together a plan. I like doing that. I will finish the puzzle and find those missing pieces that make me drink.

The meetings took on meaning for me. I met people, made friends, and found a social life in recovery. I attended four to five times a week while attending my rehab program at the hospital. The first couple months of my sober life were very busy. My career became secondary for the first time in my life. The craving and need to drink began to dissipate. It was a miracle. I began to feel hopeful, even though the jail part and the loss of my license always loomed.

"Give it to God," my sponsor said. "Let go of expectations and work the program. Things happen for a reason."

All the slogans and concepts were hard for me to handle. I was big on motivation and positive thinking, but these concepts were beyond what I was used to doing. I was fearful in a lot of ways.

My lawyer called just before I headed to the Los Angeles Olympics that August, with friends from Michigan. They drank, but knew my situation.

"Your trial is set for September. I'll try to have a date for you soon," Roger said. "Go, have a good time, we'll handle it when you get back. Just don't do anything you'll regret."

He laughed and hung up.

Be open, everyone has something to teach me, even this scotch-drinking lawyer. I can't let alcohol in. It's always looking for that open door to bust into my life. I'll make peace with my quitting and commit to recovery, it's my only chance. Go USA!

I FOUND GOD IN JAIL

OLYMPICS

I headed to the Los Angeles Olympics in August of 1984, having made plans for this trip a year before. I bought several event tickets through the Sears ticket lottery. I wasn't going to stay home and sell them just because of my DUI. My friend Kyle, her sister Jane, and their dad Bud agreed to meet me in LA. A good idea, except they were drinkers. They knew I wasn't drinking and had another DUI to deal with, although no details except that I might be heading to jail in September.

"We'll meet you at the Coliseum on Thursday," Kyle said in her usual cheery voice. "We'll do track and field events that day. See Carl Lewis for sure."

"Sounds good," I said. "I'm going over a few days earlier for the diving finals."

"Good for you," she added. "Going with someone?"

"Yes, a friend I met in San Diego last year at the Toastmasters International convention. He doesn't drink, and he's harmless, should be fun and safe," I said with a laugh.

Greg Louganis won his gold my first day at the Olympics. My anxiety about attending dissipated quickly. Mark and I had a leisurely day at the MacDonald's aquatic center watching hours of diving. After dinner, I retreated to my room at the Sheraton near the Forum. The bar at the Sheraton was noisy with international revelers, Asians, Germans,

Spaniards, celebrating their Olympians. I peered in to see what was going on. Laughter and storytelling in loud voices permeated the air. I then went immediately to my room, there were many long days ahead, and rest was required. Bars were dangerous places for me. It took my new-found strength to peer in and then leave.

COLISEUM

The Coliseum on the USC campus was breathtaking as I arrived that morning in August of 1984 to meet Kyle, Jane, and Bud. Mary Decker was tripped up by Australian Zola Budd and her hopes for gold were shattered just as we took our seats. We sat near the media, so there was quite a frenzy when she went down in her red suit directly across the field from us. Her loss made me realize how fortunate I was to get another chance to start again, even if it meant jail time. She may never have another chance at the Olympics, or even to run, depending on her injuries.

It is a challenge to deal with my friends celebrating at the Olympic Village with beer and wine being served. Laughter is now my medicine, my juice, not the wine that is flowing freely. I also can't be tempted by the attention we receive from the international men who are everywhere, especially the Germans who are so outgoing and flirtatious.

I was heading to jail and on borrowed time, but resolved to some degree to be playful and enjoy myself. My life had changed drastically in a short period of time and abstinence was now my resolve. I didn't plan to attend a recovery meeting while in LA. For the first time in almost a year, I relied on the voice of my sponsor on the phone and my daily meditation book to be connected to my resolve. Often feeling like the odd one out with my friends, even though I had known them for many years. When you don't drink, you're different, and when you quit, drinkers fear you'll judge them.

Kyle and I also attended the men's volleyball finals in Long Beach, a favorite sport of mine. We stayed in Huntington Beach at my friend Rick's condo. He was in Japan on business for IBM, so we had the run of the place.

"The bar's full, help yourself," he said as he called with last-minute items. "I'm gone for two weeks, stay as long as you like, enjoy the beach."

I didn't tell Rick too much. I decided to keep it brief and just say thanks. Alcohol used to be a comfort to me, but now it represented heartache. The less I said about it with those who did not understand alcoholism the better I felt about myself. Kyle didn't drink any of his liquor either.

The men were victorious at volleyball and Tom Selleck showed up to support them as their mascot. I enjoyed the volleyball, but track and field were my favorite sports. As a runner, I could relate to the high, the endorphins; it was more real to me. The swimming and diving were beautiful, as was the dressage with the horses, but my mind came back to the Coliseum when thoughts of the Olympics surfaced near the end of the trip.

"Thanks for a great week," Kyle said as I hugged her goodbye the next morning. "Good luck. I wish you the best, you deserve a break." She waved as she sped off in a cab.

Did I deserve a break? I had broken the law. Would I do it again if I did not have to pay for it? Times were stressful, but I was ready for my day in court. My vacation, my fun was enjoyable, but now it was time to pay the piper, whatever that meant.

I headed to the airport later that day, hoping to catch the closing ceremonies on TV before boarding the plane. Lionel Richie was the headliner. I loved his music and heard him before I approached the airport bar near my gate at the Southwest terminal. I pulled myself up to the last seat.

"What would you like young lady?" the bartender asked in a friendly voice.

"Ginger ale, no ice," I said, "Verner's if you have it."

"Canada Dry okay?" he asked.

"Yes, yes, of course," I said, as if I had decided on some exotic drink with expensive rum. Lionel Richie smiled back at me from the TV screen, singing beautifully in his husky warble, and I smiled back.

179

That night was a good night. I would go to bed without alcohol and be sober tomorrow to practice more self-care with prayer and meditation. Alcoholism had been a disease of secrecy in drinking alone, but no more, now it was teaching me about myself.

Now Directly to Jail

The women in the Maricopa County jail system and I are equal in the eyes of the law. They are me, and I am them. Status means nothing, education and income aren't relevant. We are doing time together under the same rules and might as well be shipwrecked on a remote island.

My maximum two-month sentence had not changed after all my lawyer's efforts. Within a month after returning from the Olympics, I would be an hour from home in a medium-security facility. Surviving my jail time and staying sober was my focus. Having found strength over the past year in a recovery program, there was no choice, I put my anger and frustration into God's hands. I trusted the faith I had known since childhood but lost along the way.

As a Christian, the God element in my recovery program worked for me, and served as an important message. I attended church on occasion and often wanted to go more, but held back since I worked Sundays. I still had the Bible my hometown church gave me at high school graduation. That must mean something. I also found carrying a cross in my purse was a good idea.

I had not stopped drinking on my own in the past, through my many attempts, but my faith grew stronger now. Jail served as a blessing in disguise.

Home Away from Home

Even though I have food to eat, a bunk to sleep in, and air conditioning that works most of the time, it is still a dismal place to learn hard lessons. I reach deep for gratitude for my life being the way it is in my first year of sobriety.

"Do you know any women going to jail?" I asked my sponsor Diane before I went to jail.

"No, but I know a guy named Mal going in soon. He'll be at the Towers, next door to the jail where you will be. Maybe he can help. At least you'll know someone in the same situation," Diane offered in her business networking voice. "I'll have him call you. He's a successful business man, you will like him. This is a big deal for him, too."

Mal became my DUI jailbird buddy for a month before we both had to go to jail. We shared stories of what we had heard about the Estrella Jail facilities. We both knew jails, but only for a night or two in Scottsdale's City Jail, not for months in the Sheriff's County system—the place you went for DUI crimes, the place for criminal activity.

We prepared with God and shared our thoughts in meetings. We learned from a few others that incarceration was a life changer. Several men shared their stories with Mal in his men's stag meeting, and he shared them with me, such as ones about losing simple freedoms you take for granted.

My Al-Anon friend Ellen and my recovery program boyfriend Raul drove me down to the Estrella jail in my new yellow Chrysler New Yorker before loaning it to my hairdresser Judy. She was also watching my condo and caring for my little dog Goldie. None of them judged me. They did the best they could, and it was enough, maybe more than I expected. Our goodbyes the morning I went to jail were brief.

Raul had a big hug for me and a kiss, Ellen shared a hug, too. I had said a quick goodbye to Goldie, too, it seemed easier that way. I was in shock about what was happening and could not cry. Ellen seemed teary eyed. Raul watched me as I stepped away from them. It was surreal, as I did not know precisely how long the system would keep me.

The women guards strip-searched me immediately after the scary sound of that huge metal door slamming behind me. My heart ached to be in another place as I entered the world of incarceration. A gray, dimly lit room with no windows was my first stop. I was humiliated even before the first order was given, and sheepish at best about the entire process. My head was down, out of character for me, and I waited.

"Bend over and spread your cheeks," the guard said as I reluctantly took off my clothes.

Humiliation came over me like a rush of heat from a hot summer afternoon. I was fingerprinted and photographed. The orange pajamas were too large, and the flip flops, a men's pair cut off at the back to fit smaller feet. My self-esteem fell to an all-time low. I prayed for the strength gained in my recovery meetings, but it was fleeting as I went through the motions.

I discovered only a couple of the women were there for DUI. Most were there for prostitution, petty theft, embezzlement, bad checks, and aiding in another crime such as helping a boyfriend sell drugs. I was wary of trusting any of them.

My cellmate used drugs. She made that obvious the first night when I walked in on her putting away her hypodermic needle. I wondered how she got drug paraphernalia into jail, but there were no immediate answers, especially because fear kept me from asking questions. I eventually learned the guards would help you smuggle them in if you had money and help from the outside.

Even in such close quarters, my cellmate and I talked very little and trusted each other even less. I kept to myself and slept only a few hours a night. In the top bunk, I suffered with the sensation the ceiling was closing in on me. The guards locked us in our cells at night. Keeping at bay dark thoughts about my cellmate and the guards was not easy. I shuddered every time the rattle of the guard's keys played out, and prayed God would keep me safe. I did not want to be isolated from the others, for fear of being taken aside by a guard and asked to do things against my will. There were stories.

The security in our area was heavy. The guards roamed the facility all night, yet I was still afraid. My nervousness led to restlessness, waking up often in a sweat. The women argued or fought during the night. I heard crying, too, which did not support good rest for any of us. Outside the cells, the guard station was always busy with activity and muffled laughter.

"Statistics show every time someone drives drunk and gets a DUI, they have driven while intoxicated another two hundred times," my lawyer told me on the phone while I was in jail.

"I will not be a part of another statistic for a third DUI. I know that would mean prison for a year or more."

We were allowed one five-minute phone call a week. Some of us fought for the phone, trying to not get pushed out of the line during phone-call hour. My first phone call was to my parents, with ten women listening in on the brief conversation.

"You're strong. You can do this," my dad said with sadness in his voice.

"I hope so. This is not a fun place. I'm so sorry I ended up here."

"You can't be an alcoholic. You were a cheerleader. You didn't drink in high school," my mother commented.

I did not respond. I let it go and said goodbye, hanging up the phone determined to make the best of things. I accepted my situation. Jail life was my reality, and my fears of abuse had to be reckoned with daily. I kept my wits about me, not by choice, but by necessity. Jail was my new normal.

DO THE TIME

Serving time with the State of Arizona Department of Corrections in 1984, just shy of my first recovery program anniversary, was extremely stressful. Recovery slogans repeated in my head. "Live and Let Live, Let Go and Let God." I prayed about receiving my one-year anniversary chip at my home-group, but was not sure how that was going to happen. If a miracle happened, I would be out of jail in time, but that was in God's hands.

My lawyer came by with good news about a week after I arrived at the jail. He was more encouraging than in the past about early release.

He had found a glitch in my first DUI from 1981 and believed it would help support a shorter stay.

"Very few women serve time for DUI. You are one of the first to be in here under the new law. Lay low, do what is expected. I am working on a technicality," he said.

"I am trying, but it is not easy," I said quietly. "I want to get a job in here, to work off some of my time. I sleep very little and eat even less. The food is horrendous."

At this initial consultation, he tried to be helpful, but also reminded me the new Arizona DUI laws were designed to be harsh. He had told me before to play the game with cigarettes and food as barter, to stay safe from the tough girls.

I reported how this worked. "I found that my milk or dessert has bargaining power, so I am left alone. Cigarettes work, too, but I am not a smoker and it is obvious if I have them with me. It is a game."

"Hang in there," he said with some comfort. "You're going to be okay."

WORK IT OFF

My journey to accepting my situation began with my job in the laundry room alongside a young prostitute named Princess. This decision helped me carve off some jail time. The laundry room became more than it appeared, and Princess much more than a friend, someone to care about me. I told her little about myself, not trusting her completely. My other life had to be kept private to keep me safe. She was a young black woman with street smarts, and she had been in jail several times before this time. Yet, I felt some sense of camaraderie with her.

With this small act of taking a work assignment, I discovered I could adjust to this life.

"Folding towels provides a schedule and a structure. I look forward to it and talking to my new friend Princess. Time seems to go by more quickly as she has a lot of stories and tells them with wit and humor."

"Keep to yourself," my lawyer reminded me. "Be careful."

The bits and pieces of our conversations over warm towels helped me feel somewhat human again. God was everywhere, even in the laundry room. This young woman was a kind person. Her hard life on the street was all she knew, but it had not broken her. She watched out for me, giving me tips on how to handle the guards, especially the female guards who tempted us with soda and chocolate when they wanted our attention or affection.

"You keep your eyes open, girl," Princess said early on. "They are here for themselves and look for ways to make money or enjoy themselves.

We were given thirty minutes of exercise out in the yard each day. Armed guards paced around the twenty-foot perimeter wall above us... an eerie sight. Anything could happen: an accident, a fight. Gunfire sounded only in my head. I prayed nobody made trouble.

"The recreation here is far from relaxing, but I take it. It's a chance to be outside. Even if it is a hot day, I do it," I told my friend Ellen when she came to visit with my boyfriend Raul.

"Be careful. Just be careful," she said.

The meeting was brief. We were not allowed to touch each other. No hugs, no handholding. Humbled by their effort to visit me, I mostly cried while they did the talking. It was a long drive down and back to the jail, and an hour to be processed to get into the visitor's center. They were special people to do this for me.

My lawyer, Michael, kept working for me, even while I was in jail, to make it easier for an early release. I grabbed for anything and trusted him. He now had all my savings, but was all I had in the legal arena. Though somewhat sympathetic at our weekly visits, he became clearly amused when I told him the place scared me.

"Jail is designed to be a deterrent, a punishment. There is nothing rehabilitative about it," he said. "Accept it and move forward. This will end."

"It is the end of alcohol for me. I am truly committed to my recovery. I cannot go on to prison with a third DUI. I know that would mean prison, not jail, and a whole lot more fear, with a tougher bunch of women, a longer sentence, and a more secure and stricter facility."

"It would be maximum security. A one-year sentence would be mandatory," he added.

"Dear God, please no next time," I whispered.

"You will survive. Just keep your head down and don't get noticed."

While I was in jail, Michael did get the first DUI from Mesa squelched, due to incomplete records resulting from a fire at the Mesa courthouse months earlier. I was saved by the fire, as a lot of the records were destroyed, including mine. My first DUI file was gone, so there was no proof I had been read the Miranda rights. My two-month sentence became two weeks, and my gratitude cemented when I learned the good news.

When I entered jail, I was given the option of work furlough, which meant I would go in and out every day to an outside job, with more strip searches when I returned. I chose to be inside the jail all day and night until my release, making my time go faster with that extra eight hours served.

If I opt for the work furlough, the huge chore will be to find someone willing to make the forty-five-minute drive each way to pick me up and bring me back. I'm afraid of not going back if they let me out... of lapsing back to my old habit of running away in fear. My sentence will be doubled, and I'd be arrested again for sure. That is not the way of recovery. I need to pay the price for my actions.

Before my jail time started, I made the decision to tell my employer—whose upper management had changed—I had a family emergency in Michigan and needed to be home for a while. It worked. Ellen said there were no questions asked when she saw one of our co-workers at a meeting.

"I want it to be over as soon as possible, and to do the right thing in the eyes of God," I told my sponsor on the phone. "I have a job in here."

Finding God in Jail

My recovery meetings saved my life while I prepared to go to jail. It gave me time to deal with the withdrawal from alcohol and the stress of living without a mood-altering substance. I found God again and my spirituality in those meetings but, behind bars, I became truly convinced, without my faith, my life would end.

Even with that year of recovery behind me, I didn't go crazy, but I did experience a panic attack during my remaining incarceration. I asked for a priest or a nun to visit me. My lawyer told me it was possible and to take advantage of everything positive I could.

The guards sent a nun over to talk to me. She was about my age, and from St. Mary's Basilica. Her visit bound me even more to my faith. She was a gentle soul who nurtured me at my low point. She was kind and listened to me. God was present in that small room that day as we talked for an hour and prayed together, too.

"Ask for forgiveness," she said plainly. "God forgives those who ask."

"I know, Sister. I'm just so angry with myself for making such a mess of my life."

There were no scheduled recovery meetings in jail, so the next day I asked if one could be scheduled, explaining what was involved. The guard agreed to check into it, which surprised me, since nothing moved very quickly in the jail system. It did this time, though, and I was grateful.

My sponsor Diane and a few other women from my home group at the Franciscan Renewal Center—Vickie, Ellen, and Marcia—came without hesitation. It took a lot of effort to get into the jail due to background checks. If any of them had a warrant, they would have been kept there under suspicion, possibly for a long time.

They were fingerprinted, but not strip searched and, I am sure, afraid at times. They were beautiful to see when I spotted their smiling faces through the dividing window. I huddled in a corner, covered in a blanket waiting for their entry. I was cold. Not because they had fixed the air-conditioning, but because I feared they would be turned away for some frivolous reason.

We held the meeting on the old linoleum floor of the lunchroom. A few others in my cell area attended. They may have just wanted to get out of the double-locked pod, but it didn't matter, it was all good. We talked about God and recovery, and agreed there was an end in sight. My homegroup friends reminded me that day to be grateful. After about an hour, the guards escorted them out with only a wave goodbye, and I found it hard to say farewell to them without the traditional recovery program hug.

I spent that evening thinking about our meeting and my time at the Olympics, focusing on positive thoughts, happier times. I chose to say no to alcohol at the Olympics, instead choosing fun with my friends, and happiness for the winning athletes. I was a winner, too. This jail time was just a bump in the road.

GOING HOME

My heart pounded in my chest while I waited in the holding cell. Relieved to be going home, but still feeling anxious, I kept wringing my hands. The guard approached with the key, stopping my breath. *Click.* She motioned for me, and a sense of relief I had not known for a long time came over me. The end was in sight. Both Ellen and Raul returned to pick me up at the jail. They were happy to see me, and I was certainly happy to see them. They looked beautiful.

"Thanks so much for being here," I said to them, letting the sun hit my face. "It's good to be out of there. I appreciate you two so much."

"You're welcome. We're glad it's over, too," Ellen said, a little choked up.

Raul hugged me, and we left. I was truly grateful for them, my freedom, and no glitches that day.

My young friend Princess, from the laundry room, was released at the same time. My friends agreed to give her a ride to a motel on Van

Buren Street. We said a quick goodbye, and she disappeared into the crowd in front of the motel as if we hardly knew each other.

Ellen, Raul, and I talked a little on the way back, but mostly sat in silence. There was a lot to tell them, but I wasn't ready to talk. Hanging my head out the window and enjoying the scenery of life on the outside—people walking on the street, cars going by us—was a better idea. The ride was like a parade for me. I breathed in the fresh air, a pleasant breeze even in the heat of September as we drove along an older dusty Phoenix road.

Diane had told me before jail that God gives us only what we can handle. At the correctional facility, I endured enough to keep me sober for a long time. With the principles of my recovery program, and my friends who were waiting to see me, I felt stronger. With much gratitude, I forgave myself and found hope that morning. God had long forgiven me.

My release came only days away from my being sober for a year. What a blessing. It could have been so easy to get caught up in my old life, and back into trouble, as many do after release. No longer in denial about what being an alcoholic really meant, I accepted that alcoholism fit me, even as I welcomed the sight of my condo and my dog Goldie with great appreciation.

After jail time at Estrella, the memory of keeping the bigger, badder girls at bay did not soon leave me. Hearing those eerie cries in the night, and not being able to shave or take a shower alone without the guards watching, stayed vivid in my mind each morning. Sleeping in fear in a locked cell with a woman using heroin led me closer to God with each memory of those days. I was serious about sobriety. This was the end and the beginning.

GRATEFUL

God's grace allowed me to feel gratitude when released from jail, just days shy of my first recovery program birthday. A new life awaited me. My meeting friends, and Raul and Diane, were still there with open arms to support me. These characters in my story would always be remembered for their kindness at this time, despite how my relationship went with them later in life.

"I thank God the court sentenced me to jail to get my attention," I told Diane on the phone a few days later, as we planned my "birthday" celebration. "Jail will keep me from killing myself, or somebody else, while driving drunk. Jail will encourage me to continue recovery meetings, too. I am ready for God's plan. I crave a better way of life."

MY WAY

FIRST YEAR

"Your recovery birthday is in a few days," my sponsor reminded me. "I'm excited for you."

"Hard to believe I'm out of jail in time. God's in charge. It's been a heck of a year."

I allowed myself to feel my emotions today, good and bad. Prayed to not relapse and get complacent like I did with the first DUI. I see recovering people go back out. That is not for me. God help me.

Although dealing with the stress of no driver's license for a year, I decided to drive cautiously to meetings and to work, despite the possible consequences. It was too expensive for me to hire a driver. My work schedule with new home sales was at odds with my friends' work schedules, and public transportation was limited.

While looking further at my past and confronting my demons with my sponsor in year two of sobriety, I approached the Twelve Step program. It required a long way to go to find peace. They were designed to help me clear away the debris on my journey. The rubble in my past held the DUIs, abuse, trauma, jail, anger and resentment, and so much more.

"I don't want any more trouble, police, courts, and jail. I want mind, body, and spirit; healing, and positive choices," I told my sponsor at our lunch meeting at Tokyo Express. We had only a quick hour to spend there, but made the best of it. "I'm going to be driving without a license for the next year and am asking God to go with me."

"Are you sure about this?" she questioned immediately. "It's dangerous, let alone illegal, and not the sober way. I suggest you pray about this and give it some thought. God's in charge now. Be respectful of your situation, be grateful."

My anxiety is high. I keep trying to project an image of holding it all together, but I am showing signs of fatigue. I'm jumpy and not my lively self. People notice in meetings.

"Are you okay?" Rusty asked me one night when we went out for coffee. "You look like you need more sleep."

"I do. I'm still stressed about jail, and the sentencing. It is just all too new."

I didn't tell her the whole story, which added more stress for me. That's not the recovery way.

LOVE IN RECOVERY

My second addiction, love addiction, is raising its ugly head. My relationship with Raul is in question. He is my boyfriend but, new to sobriety, not a good combination. His sponsor is pushing for him to end our relationship. My neediness with him, my wanting to control our relationship, is not healthy.

We had met through my tennis friends in Tempe at the Arizona Athletic Club just six months earlier, and were in a relationship when he came to his first recovery meeting with me. Even so, his sponsor still said no way. The philosophy of the recovery program, when practiced, meant no dating or relationships the first year. My sponsor was a little more liberal, but Raul's sponsor was adamant about this idea. Raul broke it off with me on a phone call with little warning. He was very matter-of-fact about it being completely over.

I went crazy, which was not the recovery way for someone a couple years into sobriety. I acted like a teenager breaking up after the prom, crying on the phone to my friends about my anger at his sponsor. My abandonment issues, from childhood and other relationships, surfaced immediately. I felt depressed and angry, and acted out by stalking him, going to his home and pounding on the door on more than one occasion.

"I'm losing sleep over this," I told my friend Ellen. "He doesn't call me back or answer his door when I go by to see him."

"You're wasting valuable time on him and making a fool of yourself," she said without hesitation. "You are expecting something that won't happen. You need to accept this is not going to change, it is bigger than you."

"I agree with his sponsor Charlie," Diane said when I finally called her and admitted to my stalking him. "Charlie is long-time, old-school recovery. You will just have to accept that about the situation and the way he sponsors. The two of you need to work on your own programs apart from each other. If your being together is meant to be, it will happen."

Diane was not as tough a sponsor, we were friends through other friends, and shared the real estate business as a common thread. She did not make too many demands on me, but was adamant about going to meetings and staying in touch. I liked it that way.

I want to turn things off in my head, dim the lights, and I don't want to drink. I want to start again, feel reborn, and celebrate my year of sobriety. I don't know how to do any of it.

The only way to have a fresh start was to let go of the things I couldn't control and move on. It was a painful time. I forced myself to go to meetings and to Coco's for coffee with friends after the Friday-night speaker meeting. My feelings were raw, with nothing to numb the pain but prayer. I listened for what I was supposed to hear and doubled up on meetings. After about a month, I stopped obsessing about him, stopped looking for him, and stopped wondering who he was with and what he was doing.

My shame for being so co-dependent, so love addicted, was visible to those who knew me. I started going to co-dependency meetings, too, but I always came back strong to my original recovery program. The CODA meetings were good for my emotional neediness. I learned alcohol was but a symptom of my real problem, love addiction, and codependency was there, too. I needed attention and to be with someone. I was not comfortable alone in my own skin.

My recovery program is home. That is where I will find myself. I am an alcoholic first and, once I get a handle on that to some degree, I will take on the others. I share about my obsession in women's meetings and find out repeatedly I am not alone.

DANCE WITH ME

It was awkward to be in a social situation after going to jail. I felt different, singled out, and needed to move past the stigma for myself. I had always had alcohol to help me feel like I fit in, was having fun and part of the party. Drinking for me had so much romance associated with it. I felt awkward and out of sorts until a young guy asked me to dance, flirting with me the whole time. I acted like a school girl soaking it all up.

Vickie, my new woman friend in recovery, who was to meet me at the dance, had not yet shown up. She had a demanding job at the hospital and studied at ASU, so things could come up in her life. I wasn't willing to wait for her, I was going to have fun.

"What meetings do you go to?" he asked as he pulled me closer for the slow dance. "I've never seen you around, my name is James."

"I'm Pat. I go to meetings in Scottsdale mostly, a couple off Lincoln Drive, and a few women's meetings," I answered as if to justify my recovery. "I've been going over a year now."

"You've been around awhile," he said. "Most of the women who come to these dances are new to the meetings, and pretty young. Good to meet you, I like experience," he said with a wicked laugh and a smile to match. His well-built body was obvious in his tight clothes.

"How long have you been going to the meetings?" I asked, hoping he wasn't too new and I would have to walk away.

"Almost a year, well, about nine months this time. I'm what you call a retread," he said with a cockiness I liked, but also scared me.

As soon as I heard that, I should have backed off from a second dance, but I didn't. I took my old attitude of I'm not hurting anyone and I deserve a good time. That was dangerous thinking. I could hear my sponsor's voice in my head: "Is this the recovery way?"

Celebrating was always associated with drinking for me, and there I was with another one of the "beautiful people" talking about celebrating recovery. Thank God Vickie finally showed up to interrupt what might have happened next. My social angst was waning, and I was about to move closer to him. To another dance, maybe a dance right out the door.

"I live in Tempe," I heard him say as Vickie gave me a firm "don't you dare" look. "I usually go to meetings over there. Moved back from Flagstaff a few years ago, things didn't work out for me at NAU. I had a football scholarship, but blew it with alcohol and drugs."

This is one of those occasions that should turn me off. I want life to be different, and not what it was with drinking. I can't ignore the red flags. He is new to recovery, too young, too cocky, and looks like trouble.

"I had two DUIs. Alcohol was my drug of choice, and I did too much, too often," I said as we walked to the food table, pretending we were discussing the weather at a garden party. He was not a great conversationalist, perhaps because of his young age. It was awkward, I felt like I was in high school again, not in my thirties.

Vickie joined us at the food table, but kept venturing off to find others to talk to and have her own fun.

"I can't just have one drink anymore, it is impossible. I actually knew that for a long time," I added. "I didn't have to end up in the gutter to know I was an alcoholic, a 'high bottom' drunk as we say in 'the rooms.' I did not have to drink all day every day to know it was alcoholism, and to hit 'rock bottom' and lose it all. I accept it, with every day and every meeting."

That is what alcohol and drugs do to you, halt your emotional growth.

The dance ended at midnight, and it was now eleven o'clock... time to go. Vickie was chatting with others, and I felt he was about to put his big move on me. I was in East Phoenix, thirty minutes from my condo in Old Town Scottsdale, chatting with somebody new and different.

Don't let it get complicated or let your guard down.

At thirty-four years old, I still needed help to live. I had probably always needed that help. For a long time, alcohol was my friend and confidante. At that moment, I needed to talk to my sponsor, but it was too late to call her. I prepared to leave and not be afraid to ask her for help… to admit I still did not know what the hell I was doing without a crutch. I didn't feel like a big girl in high heels anymore. I didn't have my wine. I crumbled inside as I watched the others laughing and having fun, assuming they were all comfortable in their own skins. They probably weren't. They were new to recovery, too.

At six in the morning, after a not-so-restful sleep, I called my sponsor Diane. As usual, she answered the phone when she saw my number on her caller ID. She was always up early anyway, often heading to a seven o'clock meeting. I told her about the night in a sweeping announcement. She listened and let me talk it out.

"Alcohol helped me out in so many ways. It worked until it didn't work anymore," I told her as I finished my tirade and my coffee. "Alcohol smoothed me out and helped me cruise along like an old Buick, until it couldn't anymore. I was not comfortable at the Crossroads dance last night, and I have almost two years around my recovery program. Why is that?"

"Drinking is progressive," she said, "You know that. You fell in love with it; you wanted it, and you befriended it. You didn't feel alone when you had it with you all the time. Alcohol is a physical and an emotional withdrawal. Now, you are experiencing the emotional withdrawal. Try to remember your DUIs, when alcohol betrayed you and hurt you, and you walked away with a little help from the law and God. You are still grieving this loss. It was distrustful."

"It is a loss. I feel it as easily as if experiencing a death in my life."

"Be good to yourself or you'll feel that hole and ache again—like deserving a treat—and ease that pain with a man. It's easy to do in early sobriety, anytime actually. We've all done it."

James was my escape for about three months, my slowdown of the stress of losing my license and going to jail. My second year had been hectic with cleaning up things I made a mess of for years, such as my finances and relationships. I focused on my priority: financial difficulties that were getting worse. My heart was not in my work. I had no drive to move my career forward in another company. I needed help in making decisions, but wasn't asking for it. I hid out with James, my recovery friends, and our socializing.

Meeting him at a recovery program dance did not make me see him in the program's light. He had just left a half-way house and was new to an apartment. I was not completely honest with my sponsor about his status, or how it was affecting me. I was isolating emotionally.

This relationship with James is flawed. I am not as important to him as I insist on making him to me. I want to believe the fantasy, especially after he introduced me to his mother and sister, but they seem quite surprised I am with him. His mother alluded to a couple of things about his past, but I do not want to go back there.

I was good at keeping my distance from friends and family when I wanted things to be the way I wanted them to be. Life was hard for me, and without alcohol, even harder. This was truly not the way, the "being open and honest with another person in recovery" way.

I began to confide in my sponsor, Diane, and saw how he could put me in a dangerous situation when he did things erratically. He threatened my sobriety and my sanity. He attended fewer meetings and often changed his story. I obsessed over all of it.

He showed me many indications he was using or selling drugs by his secretive phone calls and trips to Phoenix in a taxi. He was getting caught in his lies, especially when his mother called me. He was rarely where he said he was.

One day at a meeting, a guy we both knew told me to be careful. Nothing else, just be careful, plain and simple. That was the day I insisted on driving him to "an appointment." When it took us to South Phoenix, almost to South Mountain Park and Central Avenue, I knew I had helped him do a drug pickup.

Terrified I was with a drug dealer, and he'd brought drugs into my car, we headed back from Phoenix. With no driver's license, and with two DUIs under my belt, out of jail about six months, my heart raced as we sped down Baseline Road. He asked me to take him to his mother's house just west of Tempe High School, off of Mill Avenue. I hardly spoke, sure the words would not leave my throat anyway. I never saw him again after that day.

CHANGE IS GOOD

"I'm in a dark place," I told Sydney, my new sponsor. "I ended up in a relationship a few months ago that was bad for me, it could have destroyed my sobriety. I don't feel well."

"You are three years into a long journey," she said. "It's not always going to be an easy ride. Drinking, or your old ways, are not an option. Keep the faith. God will take care of you, but you need to do the legwork."

"I asked you to be my sponsor because I heard you were tough on the Twelve Steps. I need to do them again."

I needed more guidance. So, I told Diane I had asked Sydney, a flight attendant ready to retire from Pan Am, to sponsor me. Sydney was about to graduate from college at Arizona State, and would be busy, but she agreed. Diane was okay with it. She was very busy with her sons' many activities in school. She had not been enough for me lately.

Syd is encouraging to me. She's witty and enjoyable to be around. I want her good attitude and happy life for myself. Not a perfect life, just a better life with some emotional stability. She is strong and committed in her convictions and her program. She will not go easy on me, but she will be fair. I like meeting with her.

"There's no indispensable manual for life," she said early in our sponsorship. "I'll tell you what I know, what I have learned in recovery. You take what works with you and leave the rest or put it on a shelf. It is all good. Hopefully, some of my experience will resonate with you, and you will hear God's message."

198

I left her that day to go home and think about what it was that made me feel so sad. I journaled about it for a better analysis, which worked well.

I had a job and friends, family who cared, and I was healthy. I decided I needed to work more on the Twelve Steps; especially the Third Step of turning my will and my life over to the care of God. My faith was being tested, and now was the time to live it.

"The past cannot be kept silent, we need to talk about it, all of it," Syd said on our next visit. "I want you to work your Fourth Step again, write it all down like it shows you in *The Big Book*, our Bible. That is where you take a hard look at your part and all the resentments you have toward other people. All the anger you have been harboring toward others can be let go. I know you have done this before, but we need to do it again, to set you free from whatever burden you still carry."

"I will do that. I want to live this program and reap the benefits. I don't want to be on the outside looking in. I have done that all my life."

My body trembled, representing a physical need for me to release the anger and resentments. I was more than emotionally and spiritually bankrupt. I was physically sick, getting headaches and feeling very tired often, even with a good night's sleep.

We began meeting weekly, at Sydney's small condo north of Chaparral Lake. We worked diligently to follow the recommendations of *The Big Book*. I read to her what I had written, and we discussed it and prayed. Sometimes we drove down the street to Randy's Ice Cream Parlor, to treat ourselves to a chocolate sundae, and talked further. I was preparing myself to make amends to those I had injured, even though I feared doing this act of forgiveness. I was compelled to do it for my sanity.

"I'm patching together my recovery, finding the missing pieces. It feels good," I told Syd. "My resentments from how I was abused emotionally by neglect have shown me I need to ask for what I want in life."

She smiled and nodded, and we went on with our evening of good conversation.

BRUCE

Bruce came out of nowhere, bigger than life, almost clown-like in his behavior. Too charming really, everyone knew he stretched the truth. He was older than me by twenty years, entertaining, and almost too brash for me, so I watched from the sidelines. He spoke at the Friday night meeting at Valley Presbyterian Church in Scottsdale, a big meeting, attended by a lot of people I knew, including Sydney.

"How are you tonight?" he asked in the same booming voice he used when speaking earlier.

He found me pouring coffee at the back of the room. Nobody noticed us talking at first, but a couple of double-takes made it exciting for me.

"So, what do you think? Am I your guy?" he asked with a grin that should have made me run, but instead it made me laugh. That turned a few heads, and I was embarrassed. There I was, acting like a school girl again… somebody was paying attention to me.

I laughed again at something else this dapper witty man said, and stepped back a little. Though amused at his comment, I tried not to be interested in a conversation. I noticed he wore a herringbone tweed coat, a bow tie, and saddle shoes. He told me he was a retired stockbroker, who once drank late in the day at the Pink Pony after the market closed back East.

"Hi, Syd, come and join us. I was just going to ask this lovely lady to go for coffee," he said as I turned to see my sponsor walking toward me.

"Not tonight, Bruce, maybe another time. I have early morning plans, and so does Pat, we are volunteering at the Andre House in Phoenix, serving the homeless. Remember, it's Easter weekend."

According to Sydney, Bruce had been quite a successful stockbroker, and a womanizer. He was known around town, and now in the recovery program. I should beware of him. He had an ex-wife and two boys in recovery, so it was best I did not get mixed up in all that family drama. Apparently, there was plenty of it. Syd also admitted to an affair with him before her sobriety. She was not proud of those days. Just like me, with the many days I needed to forgive myself for, too.

He called early Sunday morning to go to breakfast. I said yes, as if nothing Syd had said made any difference. We met at the Safari Hotel for a long talk over eggs and toast. We discussed the people we knew in recovery, and our stories of how we got sober. He had been in the program ten years.

I was glad we were there in the morning and not after the meeting. The Safari Hotel was a hangout for recovery types after evening meetings. It would have been too much for me to handle, explain and defend. With him, it was not going to be easy.

I spent six months with Bruce, without the blessing of Syd, my friends, or my old sponsor Rusty. I learned both Syd and Rusty had dated him at the same time. They were closer to his age, and a lot of fun in their drinking days. He was estranged from his boys often, before and after recovery, which was well known.

Bruce gets close to me and pulls away, hovers over me, and disappears for days and days. Then, he appears at my door or calls as if nothing happened. He brings me gifts, sometimes a teddy bear, sometimes jewelry, but this time an expensive black leather jacket. A high-fashion style jacket, almost more than I can wear with my other clothes. It is gorgeous. I will wear it sometime, somewhere.

If we had plans, and he forgot or just did not show up, he said he was sorry with a gift. Once it was a pair of gorgeous red knee-high boots in the softest suede possible. I loved those boots. Then, there was the white cashmere sweater and the black leather boots with the silver tassels. His fear of intimacy, of getting close to anyone, of trusting in a relationship exceeded mine, but his eye for quality and fashion was endless. He had a real flair for it, and used it when he could not emotionally cope. It made him a snappy dresser.

We were not healthy together, co-dependent for emotional needs, secretive in why we were together, not working our program together, but we did not drink. We had other things to ease the pain, such as giving and taking. What I needed was more meetings and more time with my sponsor.

That became apparent when an older woman ran a red light and almost killed me, hitting my car broadside at the intersection of McDowell and Pima Roads. Thank God, I had my license back and was in good graces with the police. It was not my fault, but the stress was still there just being interviewed by the police, both from Scottsdale and the Indian reservation.

Instead of talking to God or calling my sponsor, I called Bruce to come and help me. He did not answer my message on his machine, so I headed in the ambulance to the emergency room alone. I called Syd after I arrived at the hospital. I had nothing broken, but needed a brace on my neck. With a head injury, too, I needed a lot of rest. It was exhausting to be there.

"I'm disappointed. I left him a message two days ago. He still hasn't called or come by. I need help, another car, and to get to the chiropractor," I began in a crazy voice.

"That relationship is a classic recovery mismatch. It always has been with him, but you are dependent on each other for something. I'm not sure what it is, but it is there. It will take what it takes for you to see that. Can you accept what it is?" Syd asked point blank. "God is trying to teach you something about yourself. Listen. You have friends in recovery who will be there for you."

HOGAN'S HEROES

My home group, Hogan's Heroes, met at the Franciscan Renewal Center in Paradise Valley at five o'clock on Sunday nights. By then, I had chaired the meeting several times, spoken there, and been secretary for a year. I felt accepted by the group, a part of the program. I was coming up on my fifth year in recovery. I was living almost exclusively in the program's world.

I go to three meetings a week in Scottsdale. I live in Old Town Scottsdale. I sold my condo in Tempe to my tenants for almost nothing. I am ready for a change, a better life.

I was going out for coffee often with recovering friends, and to Mass at the Franciscan Renewal Center after my Hogan's Heroes home group. A good schedule on Sunday night. My temptation to drink, to isolate, or to seek relief with fantasy love had paled. I was beginning to feel healed from my abandonment issues, although on occasion anxious. That was normal for me.

"I'm not comfortable in my own skin, and tired of the career path I've been on for so long. It's not even a career for me anymore," I told Sydney one night. "The real estate and mortgage business do not fit me, they never did. I'm more of a right-brain creative type, a helping person. To write and speak, do workshops for others… that is what I love."

"Pray about this, give it to God, and visualize yourself in those roles. You will know when it is right to make a change or go back to school," she offered. "Be ready for the answer because, once you give it to the universe, it will come to you."

She always gave me the God answer, especially when I was anxious. I always fought it, at least for a while, but she was right. I was allowing financial pressure to run my life, and not sharing any of that with her, or anyone else, for a long time did not help at all.

"When you're sober, the past starts sneaking up on you," Syd told me when we met for lunch the next weekend amid the sunshine and beauty of a January day in Phoenix. "With no warning, everything swims to the surface. Old anxieties show up."

"You're right," I admitted. "I have not managed my money or my life well or appreciated what I had when I had it. I am stressed about all of it. My old drive and relentless determination are gone. What happened to me? My killer instinct seems to have disappeared.

"God will help you to find a way to earn a living and enjoy life, keep the faith, ask around, do your research, look deep into your heart. What is important to you?" What can you live with and what can you live without?"

I feel a major event is on the horizon, titanic in nature. I suspect I am about to lose my job with yet another homebuilder, in Scottsdale this time. I've been with them less than a year. I saw it coming and didn't know how to stop it.

"You've not proven yourself the way I thought you would," Joanne, my sales manager, said as she sat in front of me. The stillness of the subdivision after closing made it the perfect time for this conversation I had been avoiding, yet I felt relieved.

"We're going to let you go. We know your heart isn't in it, and you've changed companies several times in the past few years. We will help if we can, and suggest you look at another career choice. People do burn out in this field. We wish you the best."

At first, I was stunned, but then I smiled and thanked her. I told her she had done something for me I had been trying to do for myself for months. I was considering doing something different, and now the decision was made for me. I was grateful and happy to be free. I could now walk away from a career that held so much of my drinking story.

I left within ten minutes of her saying goodbye and good luck. I locked things up quickly and never looked back. They owed me for four transactions in escrow. We agreed I would be paid eighty percent of the commission's value, since the houses were built and there was not a lot left to do to close escrow. That was just fine with me.

With no severance pay, I was on my own, unemployed, out of a career as far as I was concerned, but happy just the same.

"I was deeply troubled this year by my lack of enthusiasm for my career," I told Syd on the phone. "I don't have much money to fall back on, but I am relieved it is over."

"Congratulations. God does for you what you can't do for yourself."

CHANGE IS GOOD

NEW PLANS

"I am thinking about going to graduate school. I have always wanted to do that. I love school," I told Syd at dinner Friday night before the speaker meeting. "With five years in recovery, I feel I can handle taking on something like school."

"You have talked about it a lot. I love school, too. It is therapeutic, and a gift from God. It will enhance your chance for a permanent career change."

We headed into the meeting, greeting friends on our way to the coffee and cookie table. School was exciting to me, this would be different from school in the past. No drinking before class, or after class, or while I was trying to study. No interest in the guys in class either.

I commit today to make grad school a priority. I'm not going to let anything interfere with it. It is important to me. I pray for this to happen. I do not take this school opportunity for granted.

WHERE DO I GO?

With eight years of night school at Arizona State University under my belt, my grades reflected an average student. I had not been in the classroom for almost five years. ASU was my fifth college, having attended three schools in Michigan and one in Illinois. My transcripts transferred, and my drinking life added to a transcript that should have shown somebody else's name.

This time. school is going to be different. God help me. No going to the bars with the young guys from class. I'll work toward something I can do well and love. I'm getting my confidence back and feeling better about myself. I'll not jeopardize any of it by drinking.

The degree I wanted to pursue at ASU was Organizational Communication, and it required a graduate record exam (GRE) score. The admittance window opened only once a year.

"I picked up a copy of the GRE study guide at the ASU bookstore today, and am preparing for the test. It will take place in just a few months at the ASU campus," I told Syd quickly when we met again for lunch at Coco's. "I am getting really excited."

"Good for you. I am proud of you. Remember, God is in charge, and watching over you," she said with a hug.

That night I headed to the Scottsdale Thursday night meeting, always a busy one. I loved going to St. Barnabas Church, a beautiful setting in the desert of Paradise Valley. This meeting was sentimental for me. The Andy Capp meeting was my first, more than five years ago and, oh, how far I had come. Back then, I could not grasp anything like grad school or making independent decisions for myself. At that time, I had clung to Rusty for words of wisdom.

This time, I must be careful not to become complacent or egotistical. I had a little confidence and that's when trouble crept in for me. Humility had to be my constant companion. The drink could tap on my shoulder anytime. As a recovering alcoholic, my disease was with me always. Despite how good life looked on any given day, I knew a slip could happen. Every day, I asked God for guidance.

God help me to appreciate all that has been given to me and allow me to be open to all that is before me. Don't let me hide what is really going on with me. God help me when I get frustrated with obtaining loans. God, help me to be honest.

ARIZONA STATE UNIVERSITY

My next trip to the campus took me to the Student Services office to meet a counselor about the Organizational Communication graduate program. Although a new program at ASU in the late 1980s, it resembled the Industrial Psychology degree that had been around a long time.

Her office had nothing out of place, and her conservative, tailored look remained unruffled as she sat at attention and reviewed my paperwork.

"Since you have been a student here before, we have your records," she began in a strictly business tone. "You haven't finished a couple of courses, and will need to do that soon; and repeat a couple of others as well. After five years, Accounting and Statistics are outdated."

The revelation stunned me.

"We can process your application now for this graduate program, along with the registration for the undergrad courses. Do you have the time to do both simultaneously?"

"I work full time, but I am available most evenings. I am serious about graduate school. I will make this work," I said as I tried to comprehend how I could make it happen.

Although missing a few courses, I was not prepared to repeat anything. I tried to quickly process all these changes. With no time to call Syd or pray, I agreed to it on the spot.

"I've been ill, and that is why I dropped out of school five years ago," I said in all sincerity. "I'm ready, now, to do this."

I am sick, very sick, but no longer shamed by what has happened to me. My self-esteem has improved. My alcoholism is a disease of the mind, body, and spirit. I will figure it out. It won't be easy, but this is part of me clearing away the wreckage of my past.

"Here is the application packet. Please fill these out and return them to me as soon as possible. Your references are important. Give them some real thought," she said emphatically. "Also, your desire letter is critical to the reviewers. The department looks long and hard at your personal commitment to this program," she added as she stood up abruptly. Her wooden chair scraping across the even older wooded floor, punctuated the meeting.

I left her office a bit overwhelmed. As bright sun hit my face out on the campus's central Cady Mall, I felt invigorated. With students rushing by me to class, I was excited about school and my new life again as a student. I wanted to be like them, confident, sure and ready. I was also anxious.

Those extra classes I did not anticipate rolled over in my mind. In my other life, I would have reached for the wine bottle, walked away from the challenge, fought it, gotten angry, and blamed somebody else. Today, those were not my options. I was a sober woman with a clear mind. I put a call into Syd on her recorder and headed for the Memorial Union student community center to fill out the forms. The Union was buzzing, but an open corner table allowed me to catch my breath and enjoy a Diet Coke. The excitement of the campus was getting under my skin.

With night classes, I'm an older student. It's an escape, a release from my stress. I'll pray about my options, and plan my time, then move forward in a methodical way. The same way I'm learning to function.

Other things to consider involved financial support, and where and how to obtain it. Graduate-program student loans were going to be much more extensive than undergrad loans. My income had gone down drastically in sobriety, so I was not earning nearly as much as ten years ago. My high-powered career with high-income possibilities existed no more. I longed for a career change.

MY SPACE

On the recommendation of my first sponsor Rusty, I moved into a house with three other women in recovery. Charlotte owned the house, and was older than the rest of us by about twenty years. As a well-known artist in Scottsdale, her art had been shown for many years in the galleries on 5th Avenue in Old Town Scottsdale. She continued to sell her pieces… beautiful and colorful, like her.

She was well-liked and respected, not only for her art, but for her recovery program. She sponsored a lot of women, believed in recovery, and lived it. It seemed like a good idea to rent a room from her and, yet, a challenging concept.

There is no reason not to do this. Connie and Diana attend meetings and live happily with Charlotte. They work and go to school, too, and are serious about their recovery. It will be a very different lifestyle, but today my finances lead me here.

"Charlotte, this is Pat. Rusty told me to call you about the room for rent. Is it still available? I'm interested," I said in response to her loud, cheery hello. I could envision her mop of silver gray curly hair flying around as she spoke and balanced on her cane. A cane partially for old age, and partially from an accident she would not talk about when asked.

"Yes, it is, dear. I was expecting your call. I would love to have you," she said as her voice lowered. "If you can, come by today to see it, I am home all day. Diana and Connie live here, too. Maybe you know that, and they plan to be here all year."

Diana and Connie ran with the same crowd, a group of women I knew, too. We would all be busy and have things in common. They had been in recovery about as long as I, and did not have children either. I looked forward to getting to know them better.

The house was north of Chaparral Park, a great place to jog or bike, a good neighborhood. I moved into the house with only my clothes, books, and stereo. Everything else was sold out of the trunk of my car just months before, including the infamous china, crystal, and silver. I was "living light," which freed me in a way, but was also necessary. School was my priority, and leaving Arizona after graduate school was a possibility. This was not the place chosen by me for my career, or my life, but here I was at this time, making the best of it. My vision for myself included spending my life around water.

The noise of people coming and going in the house had to be ignored. This was Charlotte's house, and she sponsored a lot of women. I accepted there could be another woman on the couch on any given

209

morning, or the kitchen table full of laughing women enjoying themselves. That was just the way it was. A safe place for all of us, just not a great place for studying.

EXAM DAY

"I'm studying for the GRE exam this month. I take it in about six weeks," I told Connie one morning as we shared the kitchen table for breakfast. "I'm excited and scared all at the same time. It's something I've wanted to do for a long time."

"That is great. I am jealous," she said. "I have a long way to go with my community college classes to get to grad school. I wish you luck. How is it going?"

"Good, but I want a study partner. I called the campus, but they haven't found anyone yet. I studied for my real estate exam with a partner, it really helped. I'll make it work."

Exam day came quickly, with a lot of intense studying night after night. I missed a lot of my meetings to study, and made frequent trips to the library to escape the activities at the house.

I arrived at the ASU campus long before the seven o'clock start time. It was a chilly morning with frost on the grass around the old buildings, but the sun shone. A bagel and coffee at the Union and a brisk walk around campus woke me up. Things came easier to me now that I didn't suffer hangovers.

Nearing the Hayden Library, I saw the line forming outside the testing building. The security guard wasn't letting anyone into the exam room until the appropriate time. A lot of the exam takers looked younger than me. This fact did not deter me, but motivated me to change several things in my life. My career was one of them.

My age is not a factor. I am a good student, and I want this as much as they do. I have come a long way from my days of drinking before and after class, from being drunk and not making it to class. This is God's plan for me. This is my day as much as it is for them.

"You must be pre-registered and paid in full to be able to take the exam today. If you are not, please step out of the line," the security guard announced as he ushered us in the building.

"Patricia L. Brooks," I said as I waited eagerly for the packet and my turn to enter.

"Here you are. Please take a seat immediately, and check to be sure you have everything on the list placed at the front of the packet."

As I walked into the large exam room and looked for a seat toward the front, I was immediately taken back by the woman standing at the side directing people. It was Rita, the Valedictorian of my high-school class, the one who helped me through Chemistry. She now lived in the Valley, but we did not keep in touch.

I waved to her and waited for a response. It had been years since we went to lunch, but I hoped she would be friendly. She saw me with too much to drink at our tenth class reunion, and here in Arizona at a chance meeting, so I was not sure what to expect.

"This is a surprise," I said as I approached her. "Are you proctoring the exam?"

"No, I am just helping out today. I can't talk to you or anyone; please take your seat," she said and walked by me quickly, almost as if she was afraid to say hello.

Why is she here today? I've seen her twice since she moved to Arizona, and now here. What am I supposed to make of this? We were never friends really, and she certainly remembers that crazy husband of hers making a move on me, and others, at our tenth class reunion. We'd all had too much to drink. Haven't we moved on?

The exam was as difficult as I expected, but I finished it before the required time. I didn't say goodbye to Rita or anyone else, but left and went to the Union for a Diet Coke. I walked around campus again and thought about what it would be like spending four more years there in a graduate program while working full-time.

CHANGE OF PLANS

"The good news is I passed the GRE with a respectable score. The bad news is ASU has not accepted me for this fall in their Organizational Communication program. They cut off the applicants prior to my application date, and want me to redo college math again, plus accounting and statistics," I blurted out to Sydney on the phone, almost in tears.

"Slow down. There is good news here. You are getting answers and putting things in order. Now you are capable of being methodical and making decisions," she said calmly.

"You're right, I know you are, it's just hard. I don't want to wait another year, not knowing if I'll be accepted. I may seek out a for-profit accelerated university and do this in two years. A friend of mine just did that. What do you think of that idea?"

"Good luck, but don't make any hasty decisions. This is a crucial time for you, and it needs prayers and an answer from God. Give it some thought. I will see you tomorrow night at the meeting. Keep the faith, love you."

UNIVERSITY OF PHOENIX

My degree changed to a master's in organizational management in a two-year timeline, going to school evenings all year round at the University of Phoenix. Though expensive—almost twice as much—student loans were available immediately. In my typical "plow through life" fashion, forging ahead was the way, without much consultation on what I was doing. Again, no call to Syd. I was too caught up in the fast pace of meeting deadlines. Delaying gratification was not what I did, moving forward was. I would call her when I had things in place.

Was the degree as valuable? Would it be accepted as readily in the business world? Could I handle the eight-week fast-track classes with accelerated assignments? Was I able to take on such a large amount of debt? And, how long could I defer these loans to find a new career?

As a member of my recovery program, I had learned that alcohol was only a symptom of my problem, and that hasty decision-making was typical of the alcoholic personality. I was told to pray about my decisions, talk about my options, and then wait for answers. Was I willing to do that here?

I don't want to wait any longer. At almost forty years old, I'm ready to change careers, and need this for my sanity. My heart isn't in the real estate business anymore after twenty years. God, help me to remember the Serenity Prayer and to ask for help…. "God, grant me the serenity to accept the things…."

The process to enroll went quickly, and the recruiter responded to me in a few days. I had my transcripts expedited to them. The GRE exam was done, though UOPX didn't require it. All that work, and now I didn't need it. That was a bit disconcerting, but I had to let that go. I could not get angry; anger was not a productive emotion for me. Anger had been too much a part of my drinking life.

"Your classes can start in a month, but we need to decide today," the recruiter said as she ran through a list of items on the phone. I'm mailing you a packet for the student loans, most of it we have discussed, but call me with any questions. You can come in if you prefer. The sooner you get rolling, the better. We can get you in a class before loan approval, your decision."

I experienced a variety of emotions with all of this: concern about jumping ahead without the loans in place, disappointment in not going to Arizona State, and excitement about going to graduate school. Then there was the apprehension of taking on a lot of debt with student loans, coupled with the fear of what career opportunities were ahead for me. I didn't sleep well when I first embarked on this journey, and I didn't talk to Sydney. That was something I rarely did anymore, and it was not healthy.

I was pulling away from her and had no explanation for it. She was a good person and had helped me in so many ways. It was as if I was hiding in my isolation of alcohol again, not knowing if the decision I was making was the best one. I finally headed to a meeting, hoping to talk to my friend Vickie. Syd had gone on a long-overdue vacation and left me a message she was out of town. She would be happy for me in some ways, but not happy I was making these big decisions without her. That was not the sponsorship way in our program, and I knew it, but could not stop charging ahead.

THE RIGHT JOB FOR YOU

"Call me as soon as you get this. I have a work idea for you for while you go to school. This is Diane." She hung up the phone with no goodbye, in her typical fashion.

"What's going on?" I asked when I called her back.

I did not have anything lined up to coordinate with a school schedule, and I had bills to pay.

"The Russ Lyon Realty Company has a couple of high-powered agents who need a Realtor assistant. I thought of you. They are great gals. They would understand your school situation and be interested. Mention my name and call Olivia as soon as you can, at the Scottsdale office. Tell them about all your real estate experience."

I was intrigued by the idea and certainly receptive to a re-sale realty office, that was where I had started. RLR had a great reputation. I called immediately and we set-up a meeting. I had a plan to not be available on weekends or evenings, but I could work forty hours a week for them.

Their office buzzed with people when I entered the landmark adobe building at Scottsdale Road and Lincoln Drive. It felt like a gift from God that I could not have ever imagined. A place I could enjoy along with graduate school. A place for new friends.

"Hello, I'm Olivia. We want to know more about your real estate career and what your school plans are for the next few years." She gave me a warm smile and a firm handshake.

I liked her immediately as we all sat down at the large cheery wooden conference table in the back of the office. Cionne arrived just minutes later with the same warm smile. She was younger and a little more high-energy, but I knew they were both successful in their own way.

"Cionne and I have never had an assistant. We are very busy and know we need you. We are willing to split your time. Diane told us a little about you, but tell us more."

I proceeded to describe my years in the resale end of the business, and my years in new-home sales and mortgage banking for almost fifteen years. Continuing with my career change plans for after school, I told them about my college goals and the schedule I needed. They were receptive to my ideas and very supportive of my education.

I didn't tell them about my life of chaos, or about my recovery meetings at night just down the street from their office. Four women in their office of one hundred were in recovery, and attended the same meetings as I did. I wasn't ready to disclose any of that to them. As usual, my guard was up.

"We will be back to you soon... We could use you today, so we will be making a decision quickly," Olivia said as we parted ways. "Thank you for coming in, and nice to meet you."

The phone rang the next day, and the following Monday I transferred my license to RLR and became a Realtor's assistant, ready for work at eight-thirty in the morning five days a week. It was not difficult for me, I could have done more, but it was enough for the time being. I concentrated on school and left the office behind when heading to the campus. My ego didn't go to work, even though I had as much or more experience as most of the women in the office. I began to make new friends.

To mentally move on from being a full-fledged real estate agent to an assistant was easy. It felt good to let all that go because school was my game now. With no idea what I would be doing two or three years from now, I knew it wouldn't be selling houses. I could be an assistant while a student and do it well, take pride in helping these women, and be a part of this fine company. Helping these women was what I was supposed to do. It felt like life was going forward with nothing to stop me.

God was in charge. Syd was in my life more; and Charlotte, Connie, and Diana frequented the Friday night speaker meeting as I did; and Rita, once we reconnected after the test, became a friend outside of school or business.

SICK AS MY SECRETS

Within my recovery circles, I had heard ten years of sobriety can be a challenging place to be. But, I had been in graduate school for more than a year and loved my classes. Work was a comfortable place. My recovery felt good, my time with my sponsor going well. I did service work as my home-group secretary, attended conferences on recovery when I could, and spent extra time with friends.

"I live and breathe this life. It's who I am today. My self-esteem is coming back to me. Alcohol is not what I choose to feel better," I told my therapist on a day I felt really good about myself. "I have been close to death due to a lethal level of alcohol, but my battle with alcohol is now at bay."

She smiled warmly.

I'm not in the alcohol cycle anymore, and haven't been for a long time. The compulsion to drink is lifted. Who I am matters to me. Earning my annual sobriety chips is an important part of my program. Those days of losing sight of everything and focusing on alcohol no longer exist.

DENIAL

Even though anxiety and panic attacks still happened, they were fewer and farther in between. Fear was not my companion, my future looked bright. With prayer, my meetings, and my sponsor, wine no longer was my best friend, my consoler, my lover. My insecurities about myself fell away. School helped me feel more social, and my spirit healed.

"You still have a strong denial system, a lack of trust, and a feeling that you've failed in life in many ways," my therapist pointed out in my next session. "Two failed marriages, a lost career, and alcoholism can do that, I sense that about you."

"Yes, I have kept my true longing—to fill up the hole inside me— a secret. I am still waiting for someone to make me complete, to be happy."

Like the child reaching for the doll in the store window that could not be hers, I kept reaching. Emotional and psychological abandonment remained a huge issue I had not yet fully come to grips with in sobriety. I never fully understood the depth of how it impacted me daily. These abandonment issues from my childhood lingered. It stemmed from my parents' emotional unavailability, even though they did the best they could. Abandonment issues in my earlier marriages were locked in me, too. Due to my inability to truly connect with my husbands, and by feeling controlled, psychological abandonment lurked in there as well.

Sneaking around was still happening. I had lived that way almost all my adult life, desperately seeking attention at every turn, and never feeling loved enough. I often went out to clubs to dance and listen to music with my friend Sandy. I wasn't looking to drink alcohol, but to seek attention from a young man who would make me feel good. Just like the craving for a drink became too great for me, so did love addiction. I was in total denial of my unrealistic expectations; emotional demands too great for anyone to live up to anytime.

Masks

I do well in school, too. I'm always in good favor with my study group and my instructors. I love school. It's the priority in my life. I'm so happy I have made the decision to be a student again at almost forty years old.

My work as a Realtor assistant was flawless, with no complaints from anyone. Things moved along quite smoothly. I enjoyed having less responsibility than in the past, working my classes around the agents who contracted me. Still, nobody in that office really knew me.

"I don't want them to look at me. I feel ashamed by the way I think, and deny the danger of my behavior," I finally confessed to my sponsor when she least expected it.

"The Jekyll and Hyde personality of the alcoholic is rearing its ugly head," she said. "Your body chemistry is needing a fix."

My adrenaline rush came only after I found a love fantasy and lived vicariously through those thoughts. I trembled often from anxiety yet was obsessed with feeling better. I had heart palpitations, yet I told no one. I held back from my therapist and my sponsor, making things worse for my stress. This cave where alcohol lived was close by.

How did things go along so normally with my sobriety, only to now live a lie? I am falling into desperation. I feel pitiful. My love addiction has hijacked my cravings. I am humiliated.

LAUGHTER

My home group was a five o'clock on Sunday nights at the Franciscan Renewal Center in Scottsdale. We were an amazingly close-knit group of men and women of all ages and various lengths of sobriety. This group was sometimes far more hilarious than the Comedy Club on Scottsdale Road. We laughed at ourselves with self-deprecating humor. It was healing.

If we were having a tough time, we talked about it, laughed about it, forgave, and moved on. We were family. We didn't get sober to be boring. We attempted to laugh at ourselves and enjoy our new life.

God gave me what He believed I could handle. Now a strong person, I had already handled a lot. What did God have in store for me now? I missed being a so called "normal" person, but I didn't miss that drunken obnoxious person. I accepted daily that I was a recovering alcoholic.

Humor is an evolving tool healing this alcoholic from trauma, grief, and depression. I see it happening for me many times a day.

"Be direct and open," my therapist said at almost every meeting. "Give me a raw testimony of your day, how you really feel at this moment."

I took that to mean be brutally honest, but poke fun at myself, too. To not take myself too seriously, just take my recovery seriously. I did not take it far enough, though, I held on to love story secrets I was just not ready to release.

"I have many sides," I told her in response. "I'm trying to find a way to merge them into one whole person, a person I know and recognize. Someone I can love again."

"Start by looking at what has taken a toll on you with your drinking," she advised. "You say you want more humor in your life, try taking something that isn't funny and make it funny by having a new perspective. Can you try to do that?"

I laugh at myself, I have a good sense of humor. But, what is happening to me? Why this reckless behavior with men? It is dangerous the way I indulge in relationships. Does everyone relate to the opposite sex the way I do? Why now, with so many years of sobriety under my belt?

My love addiction sold me down the river just like alcohol, acting rebellious from the time I was very young. Life was supposed to be fun, but I was behaving badly. Boyfriends who should not be in my life were hurting me. I lived dangerously, finding detached sex in unintended relationships, even if I met them at a meeting.

"A lot of these guys are the same ones you met in a bar, but are now in a recovery meeting and not watching you through booze," my sponsor said when I shared tidbits of what was going on with me.

Determined to do it my way, even in sobriety, was a power position that handicapped me. Love addiction is a strong pull and an easy disguise for what it really is, a drug. I wanted to be strong and not critical of myself, asking God to help me. There was no other choice for me.

SOBER TRUTH

Life on the outside of my recovery program appeared to be wonderful at ten years of sobriety, but it was not true. I had secrets as an active member of the program. Strong recovery people filled my life. My monthly lunch date with four of those women friends always remained on my calendar. We met to keep in touch and to support one another, but I held my biggest secrets close.

My harmful secrets controlled me. I was incapable of sharing all my love addiction with my sponsor, even though she knew about some of them. My current relationship had gotten physical very quickly. Then, domestic violence became part of my secret, too.

Day-after-day, immobile with fear, nothing changed in my situation. I justified it all by taking some of the blame, and poking fun at myself for taking him back. The bruises reappeared and the calls to the police repeated after a slapping incident at home, or a shoving and pushing scene in public that lead to a fall and injury.

Many things learned in my decade in recovery circles were at odds with my life, such as taking care of myself, loving myself first, and being honest about my situation. My anger often surfaced with a vengeance. Standing with God was difficult. I was losing faith.

God chose my abuser for me, just as sure as if he introduced us. As soon as that connection was made by happenstance in a bar, my life began changing. I held on passionately. No amount of shame stood in my way for the way I was being treated, both physically and emotionally. No amount of guilt derailed me. I was not a quitter.

I'm not in love with him, I'm in love with love. I am drunk on love, obsessed with getting this right. I am blind, all over again, but in a different way. The memories of my alcohol downward spiral are diminished. What I learned about self-care is slipping away. God help me.

221

ADDICTION

We had things in common. Mr. Silk Suit was not a drinker, but came from an alcoholic home like me. He attended the Catholic Church and was divorced. Again, just like me. He had a master's degree, I was attending graduate school. We enjoyed jazz and cultural events together. We both enjoyed exercising and eating well.

He wanted to control things, when we were together, and when we weren't. We often practiced similar behavior, I had a need to control, too. That was my love addiction. I did not see my part clearly and was neither ready, nor willing, to do anything about it.

Our meeting was unexpected, but not a coincidence. After a movie, my girlfriend Sandy and I stopped at the Soho Jazz Club in Old Town Scottsdale, an upscale hotspot the beautiful people frequented. We didn't intend to stay long. I had to study the next morning. She drank very little, so I was comfortable with her. The Soho Club, a first-class place with sultry live music and a mostly friendly crowd, welcomed us.

He noticed us as soon as we sat down. I was immediately enchanted by his exotic good looks, a charming personality enhanced by his mischievous smile. He was obviously younger than me, and I could clearly tell he enjoyed attention by the way he worked the room with that smile.

He asked me to dance soon after he noticed me. With his eyes fixated on me, the games began. He wore a dark silk suit and Italian loafers. I had noticed his expensive shoes immediately, since I wore casual khaki shorts and an Oxford shirt. It wasn't what I normally wore when I went out to a club, but I had not planned to be out for the evening.

He is not really my type, too much of a pretty boy in his fancy attire, not classic enough for me. He obviously knows a lot of the women in the club by all the hellos he's getting when we dance. But, tonight, he is focusing on me.

My insecurities often soared in these situations but, with enough attention, my love addiction could jumpstart my love fantasy. I hungered for praise. Mr. Silk Suit was more than enough for me that night. I continued to dance with him in the game of lust. He persisted all night long by staying close to me and eventually pushing my friend Sandy out to another table.

"May I have your card? I'll call to take you to lunch. Is that okay?" he asked softly.

"Yes, I would like that," I chirped.

He assured me he did not have a card at the time, since he was in transition to freelance work. I did not question him. He embraced me before I headed to my car, only to have him follow me and talk for another hour standing near the vehicle. I was impressed with what he had to say. That was a dangerous place for me.

SECRETS

I attended my home-group meeting the next day as a fraud, fearing success in the relationship as much as failure. I did not love myself with this behavior, but wallowed in the excitement of it and told no one about this mysterious person.

I went to Mass with a couple friends after the Sunday-night meeting at the Franciscan Renewal Center. My secret was shared only with God. I prayed. It was hard to hide from my thoughts, and found no peace. I had learned in sobriety to allow myself the freedom to feel fully alive. Where was that now?

Graduate school was a temporary escape. With all the homework demanded of me, that responsibility was in the forefront of my mind. My drive to control worked its magic in my classes, but not always at home. Coming in the door of my condo that Sunday night I saw the phone recorder blinking fiercely. Three messages, all from him!

"I miss you, I want to hear your voice, and see you soon," he said in one breath.

He did not want to wait for the weekend to see me again. I felt wanted. That adrenalin rush came over me like a runner crossing the finish line. I was overwhelmed, but I did not call back. Not yet.

A dozen red roses awaited me at the office Monday morning. "We're meant to be together. Let's have lunch soon."

I was the center of attention, the envy of the women in the real estate office. Who was this mysterious man I had met over the weekend? What was he like? The bars of my love addiction prison began closing in on me. I made no attempt to stop it and called to leave him a message.

"Thank you for the roses, they're beautiful, and quite a surprise. Lunch is good for tomorrow, but only an hour. Can we meet close to my office in Scottsdale? That is a busy day for me."

If I had called her, my sponsor Diane would have told me, "Slow down. Ask God for guidance. If it is meant to be it will happen in God's time." She would tell me my sobriety and classes are my priorities. I work hard, don't cheat myself now.

I did not call her that night, though. Not the next day, or even the following day. To be honest with her did not even occur to me. I was losing ground, and love addiction trumped honesty. My sponsor was being replaced with a person who was not part of my sobriety journey, or was he? God was taking me face-to-face with my dirty little secret.

TEMPTATION

The new relationship began two years of disappointment, lies and deceit. He was never consistent in his plans with me or his commitment to us, often disappearing for days or weeks with no explanation. I took him back when he showed up with a new TV for me, apologizing for missing a date. Another time it was tickets for the Nutcracker Ballet at the Performing Arts I desperately wanted to attend. Those came after he cancelled with me at the last minute for a party, again with no explanation. A third time, it was a trip to San Francisco to visit my nephew Sean who was in graduate school at Berkeley. That happened after he had been out of sight for a week around the holidays. My love addiction flourished at all-time high.

We talked about working on our volatile relationship on that trip. I overlooked abusive comments and emotional abuse. His coercive control was visible every minute of the trip. I played his game when things were on the edge from the minute we boarded the train to San Francisco from San Diego for what was supposed to be a romantic adventure.

I blamed myself for most of what happened. For our not getting along, for making too many demands of him, for not giving him space. I took the victim role, the martyr, since the problems were mine. Although not terribly close to my nephew, I did share privately with him about my stressful relationship. My nephew did not comment, but wore a sad look on his face when we said goodbye that night.

I avoid the lies, the deceit, and the insanity of the abuse by pretending they do not exist. My eyes are shut and failing me. We fight constantly. I feel boxed in with no place to go, alone and very afraid. I shouldn't be with him. I don't want to drink, but I want to punch something.

"Accepting his offers and looking away from the shame of the relationship when he taunts you is becoming your norm," my therapist observed in a session after this trip. "He does not fulfill plans, but you continue to accept, then complain in our sessions. What are you going to do to change this?"

"I know it's not good. I don't know why I keep taking him back. It is sick behavior. I will do something to change things. Our trip to California was a disaster. The theatre show, the good restaurants, and seeing my nephew could not make it better."

ABUSE

Barely hiding the bruises on my arms and legs and the sadness on my face, I finally allowed the pain in my heart to be heard in my voice. I spoke briefly in a small group at a meeting the day after we returned. I desperately needed that connection, but didn't share my dirty little secret of abuse and love addiction. Those in the group were waiting for that early sobriety smile to come back to me, and to them. I tried to appear upbeat, but didn't go out for coffee for another week, pulling back further. That was dangerous.

I overreacted to questions about where I had been or what I was doing when casually asked by anyone. The self-doubt that had slipped away in my early sobriety returned with a vengeance. I was not living in the moment, I was thinking about what was going to happen that night if he came by my condo or called me. He blamed me for the trip's failure. We had taken a plane ride home after four days, almost in complete silence.

My car tires were slashed on more than one occasion, again after this trip. The police found no fingerprints, and there were no witnesses. The apartment complex where I lived had no surveillance cameras. The police did not help me because they had nothing to work with in this case. I paid twice for new tires with my high deductible. We never did prosecute anyone.

A couple months later, a toxic liquid was poured in the gas tank of my pretty yellow Chrysler New Yorker. The car was parked in the Motel 6 lot across from my apartment, adjacent to Fashion Square Mall. Hiding my car hadn't worked. The dealership said it was too toxic to work on and declared it totaled. This was a huge financial loss for me, but not a time to drink.

Accepting his invitations became more difficult. I was haunted by the car, even though he denied involvement and blamed his ex-wife. We made our relationship a priority, and I went to fewer meetings to work around his schedule. Not being prepared to buy another car, and having a hard time coming up with a larger down payment to match the funds, I received little comfort from the insurance company.

The vandalism with the toxic liquid was something only a research chemist could do, a research chemist like Mr. Silk Suit. He knew how to make a mixture that would stop a car permanently, and punish me for saying no to his lies and deceit. He denied everything to the police, continued to blame his ex-wife, and begged for me to take him back. Suddenly, he couldn't stop calling me.

With no one prosecuted for the crime, and all the expenses going to me, I festered in silence. Post-traumatic stress settled in and ached in my weary body. My alcohol recovery had worked well for a decade, but none of it seemed to work with domestic violence in my life. Many of my recovery friends left me. Or, had I left them? I did not see this coming, but it steamrolled over me just the same.

A never-ending cycle of abuse was now in place. He had no trouble breaking promises and denying me commitments. I was on a downward spiral to deep psychological wounds. The red flag of physical abuse flew high. I was on the receiving end of more hits. God revealed my reality with each blow, but I kept coming back. I lost touch with myself and became that shell of a person who protected my feelings before recovery.

UNDERSTANDING

I do not ask for his abuse or agitate to be hurt. I have unfinished business. The cycle must be broken. I do not seek to be a statistic, but silently I am one. Alcoholic thinking, that I can do this alone, hovers over me. God help me.

"How have I gone from being sober and free for more than ten years to hiding my secret of love addiction and domestic violence? How have I plunged to the depths of despair again?" I asked my sponsor, finally getting honest with her.

"The leap appears highly unlikely, but it is not. It is a natural progression for you," she said as if she had waited for our talk.

"I carried this secret long before he threw me out of a moving car after a friend's wedding, when I did not want to be left at home while he went to another party. Before he shoved me against the wall in my condo when I questioned where he had been. Before he banged my head on the trunk of my car after I didn't wait for him to enter a movie when he was half an hour late."

I survived, by the Grace of God, when he hurled me into the sharp edge of my dresser and knocked me into a white fog that sent me to the emergency room fighting for my life. Not a drink in more than a decade, but I was insane, not sober in the true sense of recovery, and living a lie. I filed a restraining order against him, but it was just a piece of paper. I was captive in my addiction, and domestic violence served as the catalyst.

My love addiction issues had never been fully addressed and yet were critical to my recovery. I had never been completely honest, even after being in harm's way and fighting with bloody hands to get free of a locked door and my abuser. The night in the emergency room, I was oblivious to how many times Death's door opened in front of me. Maybe even more times than when I drove drunk. Denial is a strange bedfellow.

I love my meetings, yet I find the most unlikely men there to bring into my inner circle. I've had several emotionally abusive relationships in sobriety, prior to this physically abusive one with a nondrinker. My sponsor advises me to say no, but that word remains unspoken by me. This assault almost took my life.

My never-ending pursuit for love cost me recovery friends, sanity, and almost my life. Thank God, my sobriety was strong in spite of me. It was a miracle I did not drink while exploiting myself. I could not quit him, and lost sight of what it was to be truly sober.

RECOVERY

It was my destiny to make a stop at a local shelter. The Sojourner Center had one last bed that night. I stayed twenty-four hours, but left out of fear while I prayed to be grateful for this relationship that tested my sobriety. I worked to forgive myself and my abuser, thanking God for the outpatient treatment program at the Chrysalis Center. I went through it with other abused women, and learned so much from them, and the women who led the group.

In many ways, it was like the out-patient treatment program I experienced with alcoholism at Desert Samaritan Hospital ten years earlier. A group of about twenty met several times a week, sharing stories and feelings. By getting to the heart of the matter, baring our souls—and eventually trusting the therapist in charge and the others in the room—we began to heal.

My individual therapy was necessary, too, to penetrate the brainwashing I had endured. I had a long way to go, but I was willing to break the cycle.

Acceptance of this trauma, forgiveness all the way around, and a reliance on God broke the cycle of domestic violence in my life. It was a lot of time and energy and work, but my abuse conversations with others like me revealed how critical it was for me to go deep into my soul. I left nothing unturned in my Twelve Step work and therapy. The other women who had walked this path, both in sobriety and in abuse circles, were there for me. I was there for them, too.

Relating to other women with this part of my love addiction recovery was paramount to my anger management, and my ability to move on to a life I could not have imagined. I did not tread carefully with my story amongst any of them. We understood one another.

Patricia L. Brooks

BREAKING OUT

BREAKING OUT

I asked a lot of questions in succession that night in the emergency room: What size is the wound? How many stitches will I need? Will I need an MRI? The temptation to blame others for how far down domestic violence had taken me had to be squashed. I dealt with my loneliness in prayers, while feeling abandoned again. This time, by my friends. Even though there were people willing to help me, I was alone in many ways.

"Our soul and spirit can be lost in trauma and abuse. We must be rekindled back to health," my therapist stated the first night we met after my assault. "It is our soul that contemplates why we are at the time of the trauma. You will see all of this to be true."

I know she is right, but this is a lot for me to handle. I'll listen. God help me to be open and hear her. I want the joy of the dew on the flowers again.

"We will start from the beginning and look at the damaged girl who became the damaged young woman." She handed me another small journal and a pen. "Take a minute to write out a couple of ways you have betrayed yourself in this relationship, and your moral code. Try not to let your pride get in the way or be too hard on yourself either. I want you ready for these trials you have ahead of you."

The room went silent as I began to write, feeling some of my stress dissipate. This exercise was not going to be easy for me. I doubted myself with him many times. Although I loved to write, this was not my normal writing. Still, I did not want to stay sick with secrets, so my writing continued. Remembering the emergency room and the ten stitches in the back of my head convinced me this was a new chapter in my life.

This was how the next eight weeks of therapy began for me. I heard what she said as if the wind was blowing through me, and I hoped for a miracle. I dug deep into my heart and prayed for answers without high expectations of myself.

I am always trying to cure my ills. I will learn how to let the angel on my shoulder into my heart. Like the wounded gull fighting to fly, I pray daily for the strength to recover.

LONELINESS

My abusive relationship was over, but the trials were pending. A criminal trial in the Scottsdale Court System, and a civil trial in Phoenix lay ahead. The city attorney in Scottsdale had not yet contacted me. I had a call in to him. He was my favorite "ambulance chaser" and had helped me before. My life appeared "normal" to others on the outside, but the dark cloud of sadness lay heavy on me. I would have to deal with Mr. Silk Suit again in another court. It would be lonely and disconnected. Who would be there for me?

Why is there this sadness I can't shake? I forgave myself, things are better. Why do I feel I have no friends? I have a new home group and have met new people. After so much isolation, can I go back to a social life?

"I'm anxious all the time. I don't feel connected," I told my therapist the next week as I tried to communicate how I felt, wanting to make the best use of my time with her.

Several people commented about my hands shaking. I was not myself at work, and had taken the day off to see her, and to rest. I was not ready to tell my story to just anyone who would listen. My insecurity about the assault, and the ten stitches in bright blue thread, concerned me.

"Do you feel this way even when you're around others?" she asked. "Your women friends at work or in your recovery group?"

"Yes, even with them. I feel out of step, as if I'm always trying to fit in. It's as if I'm looking in from the outside. Most people see me as positive and upbeat. They would be surprised to know this about me."

"Your pain and anxiety are very real," she continued. "You'll feel it emotionally and physically. Trauma is difficult to overcome, but you can do it."

This fear must be completely released from my mind, heart and soul. Especially before we go to trial. I will be ready, but I will need to work at it. God help me.

My friendships, unnurtured for many years, were missed, which was no one's fault but my own. At one time, they had my back if I needed them. I was lonely in a house with five other people, usually keeping to myself for fear of feeling like I didn't fit in, just like in high school with a lot of friends around me. I, again, became the scared rabbit in the thicket, often afraid to venture out.

"My life lacks meaning, as if nothing fulfills me. Is this depression? I withdrew socially for so long from my recovery life, I feel like I am grieving."

"You are grieving the loss of yourself in another life," she commented as the session continued.

She handed me tea, my favorite, lemon ginger. She let me take time to absorb that thought. I liked that about her. We did not rush our time together.

"I have held tears back my whole life. I'm afraid to cry for fear I'll cry myself to death. But, maybe I need a good cry before the criminal trial begins. I have been writing my witness/victim statement, crying over those words."

"You feel unstable and angry, with resentments toward him, and yourself. We'll work on all of this. Keep telling yourself you have forgiven yourself. Eventually, you will forgive him to bring you peace."

I want to give and receive love, but I can't seem to do that. I'm not really a loner, I just don't trust. My mind and spirit are shut down. I'm afraid. God help me to thwart the grief hiding in my soul.

JOURNALS

I drove over to the Coffee Plantation at the Biltmore Fashion Park in Phoenix after work on Friday night. I felt safe at the upscale shopping center, only a twenty-minute drive for me. A guitar player sat out on the patio and I found a quiet place in the corner to journal. I had met Mr. Silk Suit there many times, so I prayed he wouldn't show up. It was a public place, anyone had a right to be there. It was great to not look for him as I wanted to prove to myself I could go anywhere, anytime, and be my own person.

I started journaling by making dates with myself to go out for coffee regularly, to frequent this place and to meet new people. The smell of the new red leather cover and beauty of the cream-colored lined pages in my journal made it feel like a true gift to myself. It was all mine and would not be shared with anyone.

I wrote for an hour and enjoyed the beautiful weather, the season for being outdoors. I committed to myself to write for thirty minutes before I allowed myself to be distracted by the people milling around, or the music.

I wrote that night with fierce abandon, unaware of the tables filling up and the music flowing. Deprived of creativity and nourishment during the batterings, the writing filled me up. My soul and spirit died in that relationship, but now I was coming alive again. This writing thing was a refuge to release my creativity.

When my hand cramped, I quit and leaned back in my chair. At that point, I saw him with his new girlfriend, the other redhead. They stared at me from a table across the patio. Not smiling, but enjoying themselves, and perhaps wondering what I would do next.

I did not acknowledge them. I stood up, tossed my hair, put on my sweater, carefully packed up my things and walked to my car without so much as a second glance toward them. I knew who she was, as he had been with her many times before. It was all part of the lie, but it didn't matter anymore. God was putting his hand of grace on me to walk free. I no longer felt guilty for not loving myself, for not respecting myself. That was another time, this was now.

That night, I prayed my writing would lead me to more creative expressions and that my chronic loneliness would eventually leave me. I so desperately wanted to move toward an end where life would be easier, like the metamorphosis of the butterfly in Spring. I wanted to appreciate each day, and all the little things that came my way.

I still don't feel good about going out alone, but I need to do it, like I did last night. I survived a slight encounter with them, and I am okay today. I feel cut off from life in a lot of ways, but determined to find my way. Keep the faith and be ready to face them in court.

ILLNESS

"Please tell me this anxiety is temporary, I'll know meaning in my life soon, and that I will find it here and in my writing."

"You will dear," my therapist said as she paced a bit, then sat back slowly in one of her cranberry-colored wing-backed chairs.

I settled in, too, on the soft leather couch. Her office was cozy and welcoming, colorful but not overdone. I could camp out there for days and not feel so lonely.

"Remember, we are always alone to some degree. We come into this world alone, we go out alone, maybe this is your time to get comfortable with being alone," she added with a bit of a grin.

We talked often about my feelings of abandonment. She listened intently to my story about seeing him, but had no comment. She was ready to talk about me. I was ready to ask God for help, to give it all to God to get back to myself.

"My closest friends seemed to have moved on," I told her. "Judy is busy with her new husband Geoff, and her career. Kyle has the same type of commitments, and a young child. Diane has two boys in middle school, plus a small business. I no longer have a confidante in any of them. They don't have time for our lunches anymore."

"Write about this, and your answer will come."

God, my youngest sister is available, but she is 2,500 miles away in Michigan. Sometimes her voice at the other end of the phone is not enough. I have to be careful choosing my confidante; this illness of "loneliness" makes me vulnerable and raw. I commit here to myself to allow for God's grace and to pray for His guidance.

LADYBUGS

I started going to a new home group, Ladybugs. A group from my early sobriety and one drawing me back currently. I needed an all-women's meeting. My well-being came from my sobriety and the women in recovery. My mental state was questionable unless I asked for friendship in the meetings.

My happiness was at stake, too. Long-lasting healing was possible, one step at a time. Persistence had worked before and it could work again if I was willing. Spirituality was my life's goal, even in the dark days. Now, the dam was broken and the opportunity was before me with this special group called Ladybugs.

They met Thursdays at one in the afternoon at St. Barnabas church in Scottsdale. I had been there before, but not for a long time. The time of the meeting was now workable, my schedule being more flexible since I worked from a home office. The members represented a lot of long-term sobriety, and quite a few of the women had reached out to me early.

They were friendly and welcoming when I arrived. An older woman greeted us at the door, which was a nice touch. She was outgoing and gave me a hug. She was new to me, but we knew each other by the paths we had taken in our drinking days.

Flashbacks of talking to the police officer in the emergency room the night of the assault came back to me during the discussion part of the meeting. That was usually how it worked. I shared how important my sobriety was to me, and that no matter what happened I was not going to drink.

I was not the plaintiff. In the state of Arizona, the state is the plaintiff and the victim is the witness. Even if I did not testify, they would press charges, but it would be so much easier if I helped them. Feeling some control coming to me as the officer asked me questions that fateful day, even though I felt alone and afraid of retaliation. I could share that with these women.

After a woman spoke who talked of her experience with alcohol, we broke up into groups to share for a couple minutes, the typical meeting format. As I opened-up about my loneliness since the assault, I felt like a part of the group and, again, that connection to people who could relate to me.

There were women there who embraced me. I was home. Some of them I had met before, and some were new to me. After the sharing, we closed with Lord's Prayer. One of the women, Marcia, talked with me for a long time in the parking lot of the church. We had known each other from our early days in sobriety. She was a spiritual person, I liked her and felt safe with her. God gave Marcia back to me, to help me tell my story. We decided to meet for walks. She lived in my neighborhood.

My self-destructive nature was not judged by her or the others. I returned each week, telling my stories and sharing more. My twelve-year recovery anniversary chip came in September. Women there had walked my path with domestic violence. They knew my journey, heartache and pain, loneliness, and despair, too. The fear I had of the pending trials started waning just a bit.

I suffer some memory loss from the emotional abuse and the assault. My learning to let go and trust is going to be slow. I am making progress. I will not be hostile towards myself. I am a wounded soul. Post-traumatic stress is part of my description.

PHYSICALLY

"Your blood pressure is still high," my physician said at my annual exam. "This is not good for a woman in her late forties. I want to do an extensive exam today."

"I am trying to relieve my stress with exercise. I jog several mornings a week and play tennis, too, in a league."

When the stitches were removed, I gave my doctor the gruesome details of the assault. He was quiet at first, but began to ask me questions and showed a lot of empathy for my situation. I had been Dr. Baird's patient since he opened his practice in Old Town. He knew me well.

"High blood pressure can be life threatening," he continued as he made notes and put his stethoscope to my chest. "Your heart is a little fast, but may not be of concern."

"I do feel heart palpitations sometimes," I confessed. "Especially at night if I have had a busy day dealing with the courts, work, and the lawyers. My PTSD, I guess," I added, feeling a bit overwhelmed by this talk.

"A visit with a cardiologist could be in order, if they continue. I want to see you in three months, sooner if any of this progresses. Your cholesterol is good, but you suffer from anxiety. You need to watch this closely."

"My dad had three heart attacks before he died. My personality is a lot like his," I added. "I'm working on my anxiety with meditation, too, and journaling in the mornings."

"Keep that up and let me know if you need me. Your wound healed well. You're lucky."

The air was clear and cool as I left his office, a beautiful day for a walk and time to think. I was grateful for our talk, and that he was concerned and willing to check on me further. He knew about the head banging incident from a year ago, when my abuser attacked me in the parking garage. He also knew of the bruises from being thrown from my car that night when my abuser brought me home from a friend's wedding. I had seen my doctor with both incidents, concerned about the bumps and bruises. There was no humiliation talking to him, then or now. He was a good person and one of the few people I could trust.

Before driving home, I took a stroll up the side street by the Performing Arts Center. Exhaustion visited me that day, too, but I was determined to walk. I prayed for perseverance.

This loneliness and anxiety are my disease. I see something similar with a friend who now battles with Epstein Barr Syndrome. She acquired it from extreme stress to her body. My disease could impact my cognitive skills and physical being. Respect what my doctor says to me. Follow his instructions.

EMOTIONALLY

My therapist had me scheduled out for nine months, which would take me to the end of the year and the anniversary of the assault. The goal was to deal with my loneliness and anger, and to tie it back to the emotional abuse I endured in my first marriages. It was a lot of in-depth work, stressful and difficult, but there was no quitting now.

We addressed my current anger, and how I was going to handle it going forward. We worked at reversing my thought-patterns of blame to understanding the part I played in this unhealthy relationship.

"Write about what happened and come at it from an objective point of view."

"I will commit to changing my attitude about my part and to being open to new ideas about the situation and its impact on my life. I will keep journaling to hear and see the answers," I said willingly.

"You'll do well to participate this year in my women's group therapy. It would help you to feel connected to others who know you by your experience with both love addiction and domestic violence," my therapist suggested. "I'll make arrangements for you to join the next group with the Chrysalis Center. The sessions are held in a business building in east Phoenix. If we have to set up a carpool we will but, for sure, we will be waiting and watching for you to arrive. This is important for your anger issues."

"I don't want you to prescribe antidepressants for me. I'll try anything else first. I took them in early sobriety and they hit me hard, both physically and emotionally. I went to Dr. Goff, he was infamous for over-prescribing Arizona State athletes. I was in on his Nardil push at that time. You might remember, it was in all the newspapers."

She did not respond. She was good about not discussing the good and bad about other therapists or doctors. I respected her for that.

My diet is not good, not balanced. I need more protein. I don't cook and tend to eat vegetables and fruit. God help me to take time to eat properly and take vitamins.

To help my loneliness, I got more involved with recovery. While serving as the secretary of my new home group, I made it my goal to meet somebody new at each weekly meeting. I started chairing meetings and making it an adventure to secure speakers.

My sponsor Syd and I were moving away from each other. She was not attending the meetings I was attending, or vice versa. She was often unavailable to meet and, eventually, I stopped calling her. There was more reliance on my new home group friends and my therapist. My ego became my safeguard, for a while, until isolating showed up again. I had to connect with another woman and share my thoughts. No more hiding. I wanted to get to that deep place of honestly with myself.

"I desperately want to stop fearing my future," I told Marcia on one of our walks. "The two trials ahead are daunting, but alcohol is not even in my sight. I am more concerned with my sanity."

"Fear is powerful," she said. "It can take on a life of its own. I raged when I first came to recovery. I am so grateful I just kept talking. You have done that before, you can do that again."

"I was so fearful. Rage almost seems like a defense for me. I yell at drivers when I am in my car, I yell at the TV. I have never been someone afraid of the future."

I walked back to my condo that day and found three messages on my recorder. One from the City Attorney's Office with a time and date for the trial, even though they had never met with me. They had only read my victim's recap letter I generated and sent to them. More stress. I did not call immediately, afraid I would lose my temper.

The next message was from my civil attorney, telling me his assistant in his office would research my case. They would move forward after the criminal case, regardless of the outcome.

The third call was from the chiropractor's office in Tempe. A well-known chiropractor in town was willing to take me on for the next year, even though the trials were not settled.

This is my life: lawyers, and doctors, and courts, and stress, and questions. Please God, give me answers, and hope, and trust, and confidence I am doing the right thing.

Patricia L. Brooks

TRIALS AND TRIBULATIONS

The criminal trial did not happen as expected, and surely not on my timeline. With no call from the city attorney after the assault, I wrote a letter to him with all the memories of that night, so as not forget anything. I was not interviewed by their office and felt ashamed of myself for thinking it should be any other way.

When we were closer to the court date, the date the police had given me, I called the mayor's office. The city attorney was still not returning my calls. It was frustrating. I had to act.

The mayor agreed to talk to me and appeared appalled when I told him my story of the neglect on the part of the City Attorney's Office. I could not afford a private attorney, and did not need one in this case, being the victim not the plaintiff. I prayed my guilty feelings of regret for what had happened to me would not surface again.

The mayor agreed to approach the city attorney and tell him to call me and get the ball rolling for the trial. The same day, after meeting with the mayor, a phone call came from the city attorney. The mayor must have jumped on him the moment I left his office. They did not apologize, but that did not matter to me now. I just wanted to move forward and get on with settling things.

We talked briefly, but made no plans to meet before the trail. The city attorney told me he had sixty cases ahead of mine, and there would be no time to meet. There would be no jury, but I would be able to speak to the court with a victim's statement after the verdict was given by the judge. The defendant, my abuser, was going to represent himself.

"This 'defending himself' is typical of an abuser," the city attorney said. "I have seen it often in these types of cases. You will likely be interviewed and questioned by him."

It was unnerving, but I was happy about making my victim's statement. That night I wrote my statement to the court, and to my abuser. My defeats would not be exposed. I would not be shamed, but proud, and not sound negative, just tell my truth.

"This is going to be a strange day in court," I told my friend Kyle at lunch later in the week. "I'll be approached by him in court since he's defending himself. He'll try to humiliate me, but I won't let him."

"Are you kidding me?" she responded in a high-pitched voice. "I've heard of that happening. I'm not surprised he would do it, he's pretty arrogant."

After we finished our lunch, I stayed longer for tea and worked more on my statement.

I am not going to be intimidated by him anymore, but courageous in my words. I commit now to myself to let go of the outcome and give it to God. Please God guide my words, so I can heal from this, too. I will not be self-conscious or shamed by him again. He will not take control of my mind.

THE CRIMINAL TRIAL

My criminal trial was first on the schedule that morning for Scottsdale City Court. I was early, waiting in the lobby for the city attorney, ready to meet him for the first time. Along with the judge, he would help decide the outcome. The city attorney rushed in soon after and talked to me briefly, not really about anything new. I felt a sense of disconnection with him, everything was so matter-of-fact. My feelings of shame did not surface that day, but that was only with much prayer.

As we entered the courtroom, Mr. Silk Suit was nowhere to be found. I needed him to show up and to get this over with forever, but he was late as usual. I was scared and alone, feeling isolated. No one had come with me that day. It was a weekday, so my friends were working. I had no family nearby. I was alone in a court of law, with my legal pad filled with handwritten notes, ready to read my statement. No matter what the outcome, I hid my fear and loosened my grip on my shame.

I said a lot of affirmations in preparation for this day: "I am not a shame-based person," and "This is not my fault," and "I am not guilty of any wrongdoing." They seemed to have worked. I was feeling confident things would go my way. None of the usual "critical voices" in my head were there that day. My inner voice was not judging me.

"In cases like this, domestic violence is between those in the relationship. Without children, or cohabitation, and with this being his first offense on record, there will likely be no jail time," the city attorney explained as we sat down. "If he had met you in a bar and knocked you off a bar stool, that would be assault and battery. But, he was in your home with no sign of break-in according to the police report."

I am frustrated by the conversation. Of course, he broke into the apartment. He found my unlocked patio door, but all that didn't matter anymore. We were at the end of the line, and it will be what the judge determines after a short showdown in his courtroom. Let's rumble!

My thoughts went to my therapist visit from earlier in the week. "Stay strong," she had said. "Be authentic to who you are. You've worked hard to prepare for this day. Be gentle with yourself."

Syd helped me prepare by saying it was time to "let it go" and "move on with your life." I remembered how many times I had talked to her about wanting it to be over, but giving my power back to him. She was genuinely interested in my life and my recovery. She had empathy for my situation. I was vulnerable and shared with her what was going on with me and where I was going with my victim's statement. My life with lawyers and courtrooms was no longer going to be a negative.

I set realistic goals for myself for the trial, for the outcome, and for my life going forward. I was safe and felt adequate and full of those thoughts. Being there with my truth and my statement was not a waste of time or energy, it was my right as a victim and as a citizen.

JUST THE THREE OF US

They showed up just in the nick of time. Mr. Silk Suit came to the front of the court room and his latest girlfriend sat closer to the back. I knew her and had seen her around the clubs. In some odd way, I was not surprised to see her there that morning. She seemed to fit in. Human nature is imperfect, and it was on display there.

It was almost fitting that none of his friends were there. They all believed he never was an abuser and was falsely accused. I am sure they all thought this a joke and it would be over in twenty minutes. A new girlfriend was typical of him. She had probably been in his life for a long time. He had other women when he was with me. It was likely they were old friends.

"Shame goes together with a lack of trust," my therapist had said more than once. "He hurts and shames you with other women."

I had worked on my shame before the trial, by writing about it in my journal and sharing with my therapist and Syd. The actions prepared me for this moment. Reaching for a drink was not even a passing thought.

As expected, the judge proceeded in a matter-of-fact manner. I sat quietly with the city attorney, my abuser sat at the table to my left. The courtroom was small and basic, almost nondescript. The city attorney exchanged information with the judge in a casual and friendly manner. Then I was called to the stand and sworn in with my hand on the Bible and asked simple questions for some clarification. Questions such as where I lived, how long I had lived there, if I lived alone and what I was doing professionally.

It is Mr. Silk Suit's turn to ask me questions. He seems unprepared and nervous, and looks very foolish acting as his attorney. His questions are not relevant to the case. He is searching. Things are moving very quickly.

You could sense the frustration of the judge and the city attorney as they were forced to listen to this foolish man. Things were going my way. My abuser had dominated and controlled me for more than two years, but was now out of his element and making no headway whatsoever. I felt more alignment with my inner peace. My outside actions matched my inside feelings, my personal values. I wasn't afraid of the questions.

I did not waste the court's time and was prepared with my victim's impact statement. By testifying as a victim and witness for the plaintiff, who was the State of Arizona, I was valuable to this case. I knew what it meant to respect the court system, work with it, and accept its limitations. This was a new place in that courtroom for me with three unlikely men who would walk out of my life just minutes after the trial was over, never to be sought after by me again. I was totally in gratitude sitting there on that stand owning my fears.

Because Mr. Silk Suit was a pathological liar, he easily made mistakes with his recollections and fooled no one that day. He made it all about him, cunning but not baffling. It was obvious what he was doing. The judge let him talk himself into a hole he could not get out of no matter what he professed. It was fascinating to watch. There was no need to distance myself.

I am authentic. I know intrinsically who I am, and I show my true colors.

I left the stand feeling good about my strength, and not giving up my power. The city attorney knew it, too. He had a slight smile on his face as I passed him at the table to sit down. I did not care if there was a winner or a loser. In my heart there was no defeat.

THE VERDICT

Mr. Silk Suit did not get jail time. He received a thousand hours of community service, and a fine that was not disclosed nor paid to me. It went to the court.

"There is no restitution to you because you are the victim, not the plaintiff. The monies go to the Scottsdale City Court. He's convicted of a misdemeanor and not a felony, due to this being his first conviction of this type," the city attorney explained.

Apparently, the other times we had run-ins with the law, no record had been made, or the charges were dropped. He was also ordered to attend eight four-hour anger management classes through the City of Scottsdale, and to complete them within a thirty-day period.

"It is now time for you to read your victim's statement to the court, Miss Brooks," the judge said in an inviting voice. "Please, there will be no interruptions."

I thanked him and moved to the front of the courtroom, turning to face everyone with my back partially to the judge. With twelve pages of legal pad in front of me, I changed the narrative I had carried inside for a long time and rewrote my life story. No longer a victim, but a survivor with a victory in the judicial system, my statement resonated for me.

I read loudly and clearly and did not hesitate, talking about my missed career opportunities and the many times I was coerced into believing he cared for me, and took him back against my better judgement. I talked about how he abused my friendship, and the friendship of my friends.

I had rhetorical questions with no answers regarding the relationship, how men should treat women, and how a relationship should be. It was therapeutic and cathartic to read each line and not be interrupted by Mr. Silk Suit or anyone else. It was my time to seize the opportunity to make a fresh start in my life with my new voice. I read each word with purpose and passion for where life was taking me from there.

I could see her, the other woman, head bowed but looking at me with one eye… almost wondering if she could be me someday, or even today. What was she reflecting on as I read on about incidents that were so cruel and unfair? My inner voice encouraged me. I did not need an answer to every question I posed. I just needed to say what I had to say at that time.

I talked about my post-traumatic stress and all the complications from it, and how it was not going to control me like he had for so long. I was stronger now, he would never hurt me again.

THANK YOU

Mr. Silk Suit asked the judge if he could rebut my statement and, of course, he was told no. The judge declared the case closed and told him to remain for sentencing details. I was asked to leave and thanked for being a witness for the State.

I felt liberated, and thanked the judge before I left the courtroom, as well as the city attorney. I left the courtroom with my attorney for a small conversation in the lobby. My sobriety allowed me more clarity than my DUI courtroom days. It was a good day. Although not completely happy, I was happy enough, and not going to go back to court on any of it. It was all good.

"You might want to get a civil attorney and go after him where it really hurts, in his wallet," the city attorney advised as we left the building. "I have seen this happen on many occasions. That court will be in Phoenix."

"Thank you. I am pursuing the idea and have somebody to help me. He represented me twice in car accident cases and has a partner who works with these kinds of cases." I spoke proudly, feeling like a grown-up.

Just as I turned to walk away, Mr. Silk Suit and his girlfriend walked by us, hurrying to two cars. It was a surreal moment, but with no pangs of jealousy or anger toward either of them. I felt sorry for him, and even sorrier for her. My connection to God gave me a new freedom. This time I was on the winning side. He had the conviction, even if it was only a misdemeanor. It validated the verdict just the same.

I went home to write in my journal, with no criticism, to validate my feelings and acknowledge my anger. My sanity depended on it. It was my truth and it needed to be recorded. My voice needed to be transferred to paper. Someday it would be vocalized as the healing progressed.

In my darkest hours of isolation and loneliness, I had a plan to survive and found the words and thoughts, hopes and dreams to put on paper. I would no longer be silenced, but make a difference soon for other women on my journey. The new me would take long, slow, deep breaths and learn to relax and expel negative energies. I would go back to yoga with enthusiasm, exercise, stay slim, and maintain a structured life.

These ideas were exciting to me, some were already a part of my anti-stress regimen. Slowly, I was allowing time for myself and improving my life, one day at a time. I was living that tried-and-true recovery mantra, and counting my blessings, with a holistic view of sobriety. Pray, write, and meditate.

My therapist watched for my old coping patterns to return, but they were dissipating. That shutting-down mode, the blank stare and the going numb, were not me anymore. I was feeling emotions. The desire to drink never surfaced, and my anger rose to the top less and less. I followed my intuition and listened to my inner voice. My spirit came back to God with the faith that the civil trial would go well, too.

PHOENIX SUPERIOR COURT

"Are you sure you want to pursue another trial? This could prolong the agony of the past two years, especially since he's egotistical enough to represent himself," my therapist reminded me as we settled down for our first session since the criminal trial.

"Yes, I do. I've had several months to think about it. I can handle it. It will be closure for me, since he has not done any jail time. He might 'pay' this time. It is for the other women victims, too, not just me."

We talked at length about the criminal trial, about the weeks ahead adjusting to closing out that chapter of my life. We analyzed letting go of the shame of being addicted to him just like the chaos with alcoholism. I gave my burden of being needy to God.

"You'll never have to go through any of this again once it is all over," she said in closing. "We'll put the focus of your life where it belongs, on you and your successes."

It would take many months for me to accept my new life, for now the project at hand was the civil trial. Feeling hopeful, I called my attorney.

"Dean, I am ready to pursue the civil trial, what do we do next?" I asked as soon as he answered the phone.

"I am happy to hear that. I want to learn all the details of the criminal trial and what led up to it. When can you come in?"

I was in his office within twenty-four hours, telling him everything I could remember. We made plans to meet again the next week after he did research. I soul searched to make sure my subconscious remembered it all. We set a trial date for two months out. We were not going into this with unrealistic expectations, but with faith.

As a recovering alcoholic, unrealistic expectations are dangerous, and lead me down a path I can't afford to go, a path of anxiety and stress. I take each day as it comes, do what Dean suggests and pray about the rest. He tells me there is no precedent for a domestic violence case without children involved winning restitution in Superior Court. I will change that fact.

I did not discuss this plan with Syd. She was of the opinion, like my therapist, that we were taking control of a futile situation that should be left to God. It was out of the realm of "recovery talk," so I kept it quiet and began feeling alone as we moved forward.

The idea of drinking did not cross my mind. God was taking care of me. The tools of prayer and faith with more than ten years in recovery helped me maintain a relationship with Him. I had other options such as meditation, journal writing, yoga class, daily exercise, and a sponsor if I chose to use her.

THE COURT ROOM

The Phoenix Superior Court building was historic, the security a bit more elaborate. My lawyer was of my own choosing. Someone eager to help. He had not been a part of the criminal trial as that was not his area. I felt better represented than in Scottsdale Court. My abuser was ready to pounce on me—again, representing himself. We were in a larger court room with a judge and no jury. It was de ja vu, though different.

I was not offered a victim's statement by the judge, only asked questions on the stand. My abuser did not ask me questions, nor did my

251

attorney. The judge asked my abuser questions. It was informal and quick, an amazing process. Then, it was over. There would be no negotiations.

"The court awards the plaintiff, Ms. Brooks, the amount of twelve thousand dollars. The defendant, Mr. Collins, please approach the bench."

It was over in a heartbeat, a jaw-dropping moment in which I experienced heart palpitations, but I had nothing to be concerned about then. I was happy and wanted to show it, but that would come later. My lawyer wore a small smile on his face. It went better than we could have imagined. With no idea what else was said to my abuser by the judge, Dean and I headed out the door to talk privately. I felt light on my feet, almost in a daze, as I grasped what just happened.

"We did it. You won. This is unusual. You have set a precedent with the amount of money you will receive. Congratulations!"

He vigorously shook my hand. I responded with a good handshake and a smile. It took me a minute to say anything and compose myself. My mind was rushing through all that had just occurred.

"What happens now?" I asked anxiously.

"The judge is assigning him a timeline to pay. It will funnel through my office. We will pay your chiropractor, the private investigator, and our office first. The rest will go to you. You should end up with more than fifty percent. The court costs will be paid by the defendant."

We walked to my car, discussing a few more minor details, then we parted. It was a beautiful Friday afternoon with the sun shining and a slight breeze. I mustered up some humor and left my friend Marcia a message from a nearby phone to meet me at the Friday night speakers meeting. No self-loathing today. "I hit the jackpot. Help me celebrate," were my words.

I stayed on task driving in Friday traffic downtown Phoenix, not letting my mind wander back to the courtroom and what just happened. This win was an unexpected victory in Superior Court for domestic violence, for recovery, and for me. My feelings of guilt and shame for being a recovering alcoholic, a victim of domestic violence, and a twice-divorced woman did not exist. I had put myself out there, and it worked.

RECOVERING RESTITUTION

"It has been six months since the trial and we don't know where he works or lives. He has not paid a dime of the twelve thousand dollars I was awarded in court," I told my friend Judy at lunch on a Friday. "I get so angry, I am sometimes afraid of my feelings. Not that I will drink, but that I will do something stupid. He is still controlling me."

"I thought you had a private investigator?"

We turned to our lunch at Tokyo Express on 7th Street and began to eat. "I do, and he's not doing anything. I'm ready to take it on myself. I've a plan."

I proceeded to tell her my idea about going to the car dealership where he took his BMW, to see if they had a new address for him. Since he had changed companies after the civil trial, it might be a challenge to get someone to help me, but why not try?

"That sounds illegal, do you really think somebody will do that for you?" she asked. "I would be careful, don't get yourself in trouble or in danger."

"I'm not afraid anymore. My PTSD is still there, but I have techniques to help my anxiety. Taking control is one of them. There's a BMW dealership just down the street from here. I'm going to go there after we finish lunch and play my own investigator."

We talked about it a little more, finished lunch, and hugged goodbye. I was feeling confident with God's power behind me. I had to do this. If not, the restitution would never be mine. It would never end with him if my role was not played out here.

CAMELBACK BMW

"I need your help, I hope you will help me," I announced to the young woman at the reception desk at the dealership. "Please tell me if this person brings his car in here, and if you deliver it to his workplace." I handed her a small note. "I am a domestic violence survivor. He owes me money from an assault case. I need to find him."

There it was. *Boom!* I put it out there on her desk with nothing held back.

She stared at me, swallowed, and said "just a moment." She turned toward her computer and, in a couple of minutes, handed me back my note with a phone number and address on it.

"He was just here a couple weeks ago. I remember him. We delivered his red sedan to this company, ON Semiconductor," she said in a soft voice, pointing to the note. "Please, take this and go, and tell no one you were here or talked to me. I should not be being doing this. Good luck to you."

"Thank you and God bless, you have done a good thing," I said hurrying out of the showroom before anyone realized we had a conversation.

I was stunned and, for a fleeting moment, felt like celebrating and calling somebody to hoist a glass. I realized quickly those days were not my days anymore, not for more than ten years.

There was no time for celebration. This was only the beginning, I had a lot of work to do. The next step was to go to ON. I would pretend to be somebody else, get a confirmation that he worked there. Then I would call my attorney and pray to God my idea of garnishing my abuser's wages could happen with a contract employee.

"Hello, I am calling to confirm one of your employees," I said from their lobby phone. My heart was pounding, praying Mr. Silk Suit did not walk through the lobby and blow my cover.

"Yes, Mr. Collins is here on contract for the next six months, until December fifteenth," she said casually.

I was almost dumbfounded. She did not ask my name, or why I was inquiring about him.

It was done. I left there, drove to the Circle K across the street, and called my attorney. My sleuthing got his attention. He listened and responded only after I slowed down.

"Good work," he said with a bit of a chuckle in his voice. "We can use this. I will get on it right away with a garnishment. You had a good idea, took a risk I would not have recommended for you, but it worked. Congratulations. Call me back tomorrow."

It did work, and within three days three thousand dollars was delivered to my attorney by messenger. Mr. Silk Suit was looking to negotiate a pay schedule for the rest. The answer was no. By the end of the week, all the money was delivered, and it was over. I ended up with about seven thousand dollars after the others were paid, including the private investigator who did very little for me.

THE LETDOWN

There is a letdown when the chaos stops. I had it with alcohol, the DUIs, the jail time, the newness of recovery, and with the domestic violence ending. Now, I have it with the trials ending, the restitution paid, and the lawyers leaving my life after several years. It is a relief and a withdrawal from the chaos. Chaos I've been addicted to for a long time.

I embarked on a new life, one of peace and hope, and meditation and recovery, in a new way. A quiet life. What would that be like, and who would be on that journey with me? Only God had that answer. It was not for me to ask for a special request. The attitude of "let go and let God" was necessary here.

Patricia L. Brooks

FORGIVENESS

" **F** orgiveness is the action of forgiving. Sounds simple, but it's not," my therapist Ann commented as we settled in for our hour session. We had been together for more than three years, but met now only twice a month. "To stop feeling angry toward those who have done something wrong toward you, has been our goal, and you have made progress."

I nodded my head in agreement. It was partly a conscious decision after ending up in the emergency room the day I was assaulted. It was a culmination of many incidents of violence with my abuser.

"To stop blaming others, like your parents, ex-husbands, and former boyfriends, was a priority for a long time. Congratulations! We are getting to the end of the list," she said with a big smile.

That made me feel I had done the work needed. I played a part and was owning up to staying with him too long. To stop feeling anger toward my alcoholism had taken time, but I was closer to that goal, too. It was a disease, but I could change my behavior, and I had. There was so much shame about that part of my life; I had to let that one go—the shame put on me by others who did not understand I was sick. Only with the release of that anger could I fully enjoy sobriety the way it was meant to be enjoyed. I deserved forgiveness.

I made a conscious and deliberate decision to release my anger toward those who had not been there for me, or who had abused me in some way. That is one of the steps of a recovery program. I wrote diligently for hours and hours to see clearly where I had been wrong, too. The vengeance I carried after the assault, or after a divorce, or after a break-up with one of my many boyfriends, was eventually squelched in my writings, but not without a fight. Many men had harmed me deeply. I had a hard time releasing those feelings.

"Forgiveness is not glossing over what happened to you," Ann assured me on many occasions when I struggled to forgive. "Forgiveness is not denying the seriousness of the offense either," she added emphatically. "You don't have to forget anything that happened to you. It will make you stronger. It has already."

"I do feel a bit stronger, and I want to forgive, especially my abuser, but that is going to take time. It's been so painful to conceive it."

"You don't have to condone anything that happened to you, either harmful or abusive. There are no excuses for these offenses."

I will hear those words in my head for the rest of my life. I trust her. With the love addiction, I yearn for someone to fill the hole inside of me. I learned so much the hard way through my experiences. The lessons are already helping me to see how I hurt myself. There are many learning relationships in my story, some chosen for me by God.

These are the good and the bad, the successes and the failures. Yet, I was under no obligation to reconcile with any of these men, or release them from legal accountability. My quest to forgive was for my peace and healing. I made sure of that with the criminal and civil trials, pursuing my abuser with a clear mind, knowing it was the right thing to do. I was now able to forgive him for his shortcomings, his mistakes that harmed me, and his ego. His evilness and deceit were left to God.

THE PLUSES

"Forgiveness will bring you peace of mind," my sponsor said the next week as we talked further about this new approach to my life. "It frees you from anger and lets you go deeper into releasing negative feelings. It is part of your recovery journey; it is God's way."

"I feel good about working on forgiveness. It's important to me to clean my side of the street. The hard part will be to work more on forgiving myself. I still have a hard time doing that, even at this stage and I have fifteen years of sobriety this year."

"You don't have to have positive feelings toward your abuser, or anyone else who has harmed you, for that matter. Remember, forgiving him is for your peace of mind, not his," she added with a smile. "It will empower you to recognize the pain you have endured and own."

"I don't want to let the pain define me anymore, or to call myself a victim again. I want to heal and move on. It's possible. I have come so far and have seen it in others in recovery."

The best way for me to practice forgiveness was to do kind acts, acts of mercy. To do work in the jail where I had been incarcerated was a first step. To forgive them for any wrongdoings I may have experienced or perceived, such as food deprivation, was the next step. It had been fifteen years, and I was ready to go back and speak to the women. I wanted to extend compassion to them, show them what long-term sobriety looked like, even after a detour with domestic violence. My story needed to be told, and I wanted to tell it to them and help them. This was now my life's purpose.

ESTRELLA JAIL

Within six months of that decision, I met Sandra, a poet and a creative type, at a writing workshop I attended through Scottsdale Community College. She was about my age and we hit it off at the break. She shared one of her poems with me. Many of them, she said, were about women she had met while working in the jail system. I shared an excerpt from the memoir I had written about my sister, and my plans to write more. We decided to meet for lunch the next week at the Arcadia Farms restaurant in Scottsdale to talk further about our writing and why we chose our topics. I was also ready to share my jail story with her.

At lunch, one thing led to another and I found out quickly she had recently retired from the Sheriff's Office. She had been instrumental in setting up several programs for the jailed women to learn life skills and communication before their release. After listening to her, I asked if she could help me get into the jail as an educator, an inspirational speaker for the women.

"My writings are memoir. I have a story to tell that might surprise you. I spent time in the Estrella Jail fifteen years ago, for a second DUI. I want to go in again to give back to the women," I said as if that was everyday talk." I have an inspiring story, I know I can help them."

"That is terrific. I can do that easily, after they do a background check, fingerprints, and search for warrants on you. Have you been behaving yourself?" she asked with a bit of a twinkle in her eye.

After filling her in on the details of that part of my life, I explained my mission of forgiveness. To go back to be of service to the women was part of my indirect plan to seek forgiveness, for both my anger against the guards and the police, and against the jail system.

Within a month, she had me set-up to spend eight hours at the Estrella Jail at 35th Avenue and Durango, teaching a life-skills workshop over a four-week period to twenty-five women nearing the end of their sentences. I entered the jail that day with confidence, ready with a new attitude to be supportive of the women. Only for an instant did I experience a twinge of PTSD when the bang of that heavy metal door closed with a clanging sound behind me. The flashback of days gone by, when I was locked inside, came rushing back to me. I held my breath and moved forward with the woman guard who greeted me and ushered me inside.

The place was sterile and plain, with gray and white paint and a lot of chrome. Not quite the way I had remembered it but, then again, this was the training area now and not the detention area where I was held. Nothing like this positive training program existed when I was in there. They offered a whole new program of rehabilitation. I was proud to be a part of it, proud to be delivering information and inspiration within these walls.

The three guards in the training room greeted me with a handshake and asked a few simple questions, reminding me of the format and what to expect. They told me not to approach the women or to touch them in any way. While they spoke, I heard a familiar shuffling in the hallway just outside the training room door, the sound of shackles being unlocked in the hallway. A few minutes later, the women entered all in a row, heading directly to their seats.

They wore their blue pajamas and worn-out flip flops. Most of them looked disheveled, but clean, yet not too concerned about their looks. They did not seem like a group of women ready to graduate from anything. Some slouched in their chairs as they looked me up and down, but did look curious and a bit eager. That was a good sign. Quite a few were younger than me, and one of them was pregnant. This cross-section of Arizona represented at least four races of the general population: Black, White, Native American and Hispanic.

Pauline, a strong and positive woman and the main guard in charge, introduced me briefly. She was prepared and had an agenda. For the first ten minutes, I told my recovery story without hesitation.

"I was here for DUI just like many of you, and I did not want to be here either. But, I had to pay for what I did," I said in my introduction. "I am a recovering jailbird and a recovering alcoholic. I am grateful today I did not kill myself, or anyone else, or I would have gone on from here to Perryville prison."

We talked about goals, being positive, honoring what we can do when we put our minds to it. I stayed on the task of educating them about time management and goal setting, about further educating themselves on the outside in any way they could: earning a GED, a community college degree, or technical school certification. They wrote affirmations about believing this jail time was a stepping stone to a good life, and did not define them.

"This is not the end, it is the beginning. My life has changed in so many ways I could not have imagined. I had to pay for what I did with fines, time, loss of my license, and amends to a lot of people, but today I am a proud woman. You will be, too, if you believe you can be, and listen to those who want to help you."

The guards assisted me in planned activities such as writing a short goal, discussing it, and visualizing their lives in five years. Several participated verbally and were quite articulate, others were nonverbal, but listened. We clearly shared a productive afternoon, because none of them asked to leave, many thanked me personally, and asked to comment on what they learned. They had all been chosen for this program.

"My story is like your story," I told them. "I hurt a lot of people, but I hurt myself more."

It is a scary and exciting time for me. It is also good for me. I feel happier than I have in months. My health is improved by the endorphins gleaned when giving back as a volunteer at the jail. I am a successful woman in recovery and a domestic violence survivor. I am proud. The stress is there, but a good stress with the excitement of it all.

I went back the next week, the week after, and the last week, which included their simple graduation with cookies, punch, and a few family members. A celebration experience I am glad I did not miss. Mary, the pregnant one, went into labor at the end of the program and delivered her baby later at the County Hospital.

I sustained a relationship with the program director for the rest of the year, since we now shared a feeling of trust.

I forgave myself during that time for getting to jail in the first place, and for driving a wedge into so many relationships due to drinking. Graduation day—with no caps or gowns, but colored ribbons and their smiles—revealed a small difference I had made in their lives. With this experience, I was less vindictive about jail, more willing to resolve conflicts with friends, and found myself so much more grateful for my life.

I was given a much shorter sentence than most of these women had for DUI. I had a job and a pretty condo and close friends waiting for me. Though the experience happened almost twenty years before, I still remembered it vividly. I prayed for each of the women in this special program.

During those four weeks of training time with this group wanting to improve their lives, I came and went very comfortably. I was not depressed at all by going back to the scene so devastating to me earlier. My gratitude made me feel more satisfied with my life just the way it was every day.

CULTIVATE FORGIVENESS

In the weeks following the training for the jail, I found my capacity for forgiveness growing. It became a choice, not something my therapist suggested, or my sponsor said was part of the recovery way and I had to do it to stay sober.

It was now second nature for me to forgive. I not only began to forgive myself for my transgressions, such as getting angry when having too much to drink, but I started to forgive others for how they had harmed me. My plan was to seek out opportunities to forgive. I felt good about the idea. It represented growth.

To me, forgiveness was a gift from God, something of an honor that made me a better person. I journaled about forgiveness, its health benefits of lower blood pressure, its psychological benefits of less anger, and the changes happening in my life as positive events.

Forgiveness thoughts brought me peace and closure. Not only with the men in my past life who had harmed me directly, both physically and emotionally, but also with many others who had harmed me indirectly. I found closure and reduced my suffering by cultivating forgiveness. It would now be my life's work.

I articulate my emotions more and am willing to express them. This is where I will make a path for myself to true happiness. The challenge now is to make a list of people I will forgive but, more importantly, to make a list of the ones I will ask to forgive me. My sisters and my parents, my husbands, and my friends.

THE SILVER LINING

If I learned anything about forgiveness… it had to come from the heart and be authentic to earn personal benefits. In seeking these opportunities for forgiveness, I had to journal about them first, and pray about them, to make an effective and sincere apology. I prepared and wrote out everything I meant to say. I had to be sure to not leave anything out.

"Please forgive me for the times I hurt you and was unkind to you. I am in recovery for alcoholism and working to be the person I can be. I do not blame my drinking, I mention it only as a point of reference. I take responsibility for my actions. Please forgive me when you can, so we can start again."

The only way to ask for forgiveness was to acknowledge the offense. Like when I had borrowed money and took months or even years to repay it, even when I had the money. To own up to what I had done, big or small, and say it out loud, was critical.

The person to start with was my longtime friend Ellen, my former roommate and co-worker. Many times, during my drinking days, I had borrowed money from her, and used her, often when it was not convenient for her. Ellen cared for my condo and my dog during my stint in jail. She visited me there and helped pick me up when I was released. At the time, it was a lot to ask of her. She had been quite ill, but I asked anyway. She never complained. It was time to do the right thing and seek her out. I made the call.

"Ellen, do you have time for lunch?" I asked. "My treat. What's your flying schedule?"

Ellen was a flight attendant for America West, something she chose as a third career. I admired her for that choice, doing what she wanted to do. "We're overdue to get together."

"I have personal leave this week. How about Friday?" she asked with enthusiasm.

We had been new-home salespeople together. She often covered for me with my hangovers, but I never appreciated it. Being selfish in the middle of my addiction, it was all about me. I took advantage of her.

"Great, let's meet in Tempe at Trick's, by the campus. I know you know the place, it is a good one for lunch. I will see you there early, say eleven thirty? I will make a reservation, they are always busy."

I was prepared to not only acknowledge my offenses with not paying back money I owed her due to car troubles, but for also having borrowed money from her, one too many times, to take a trip. This day, I carried a cashier's check for her.

I will explain to her why I was not reliable at that time. That my alcoholism controlled me. My goal is to show genuine concern for our friendship, and not feel shame or guilt. To own up to what I did and ask for forgiveness. To be sure I will pay her back all the money I've borrowed. I am willing to take care of any past debts.

She probably never expected me to ask for forgiveness, and as a Christian church-going woman, she may have long forgiven me for taking advantage of our friendship. She told me on the phone she had forgiven herself, too, for allowing me to do what I did. She was a long-time member of Al-Anon, and still attended periodically.

We greeted each other with a hug. As usual, the food at Tricks was delightful. We sat outside under the large trees in their courtyard in front of the old historic house, just off the campus of Arizona State University on a beautiful spring day. A perfect setting for forgiveness.

In this win-win situation, I cultivated empathy for admitting what I did, and I truly showed my remorse when I said to her, "Please forgive me for taking advantage of our friendship?" I became a new person.

We were friends for many years. She lived with me once for six months in my early sobriety, when she was making a personal transition. It worked well for us financially, although strained at times. We were two very different people, and still are.

Our longevity showed in our conversation, we saw each other's humanity in our stories as we caught up on our lives. My time with my abuser had isolated me from so many people, especially someone like Ellen who was an honest and good person who could see through me.

She had tried to talk me out of going to San Francisco with him one Christmas, afraid of me being alone with him on an out-of-state trip and away from friends. I insisted on going and minimized what he would do, but she was spot-on. He was abusive, hurting me both emotionally and physically on that trip, even causing a scene on the airplane. I never told her the whole story until this lunch date.

265

"I feared he would leave me in California and not give me my return plane ticket. In the end, though, that did not happen," I began. "I never told you the truth about that trip, thanks for caring and being concerned. It is time to do that now, and to forgive myself in the process."

While asking for her forgiveness for using her repeatedly, I could not let myself off the hook too easily. Sick and in the throes of my abusive relationship, I described how I had to reflect honestly on how I ignored her friendship and concern, and followed my addiction to him one more time. Together there, twenty years later, I saw forgiveness as even more necessary to strengthen our relationship.

This lunch was to seek a lasting peace between us, not justification for anything I had done. My alcoholism was no excuse. I could have helped myself, but I was just not ready. We had both moved on with our lives, yet remained eager to share what was new and different and exciting for us.

"I love flying for the airlines. I always wanted to fly. The money I inherited from my mother made it possible. I love the travel and the new friends I have made."

"That is wonderful, I envy you with the travel and no more time in an office," I said as we finished our lunch. "I am ready to start writing and pursuing my creative side. I love teaching at the college level. No more direct sales for me either."

This was a process. It would take time to heal our friendship, but it would be worth it.

"Thanks for being honest," she said, wiping her lips with the cloth napkin. "You had to go through what you needed to go through, and I couldn't help you. I had to practice my Al-Anon teachings of letting go one more time with you," she said smiling.

"I had to do what I did and get to the ER to realize it was enough, and to let go of trying to control my life. Please forgive me for all the times I took advantage of you. I appreciate you seeing me today. It means a lot."

"Of course, I forgive you, I did a long time ago. That is the way I live my life."

MEDITATION

Meditation came into my life about that same time. I prayed it was part of my connection to God and my recovery, but meditation was different. For me it was going deeper into my soul.

I also started reading about Mindfulness, staying in the moment. This was another new concept for me, but one I related to as a part of recovery. Then, at the point in my sobriety where I enjoyed more peace, my recovery program was solid, close to God. To feel a spiritual level, a deeper sense of being, opened my mind to new ideas with forgiveness in focus. I made a connection to myself and felt contentment with these tools.

Mindfulness, for me, was about learning to be more compassionate, forgiving, and generous, and to be of service to others. I felt at home with all of that and grabbed onto forgiveness. Still healing from my secrets and my suffering caused by the alcohol and the abuse, my suffering lessened. My spiritual program began to blossom.

The next step was to concentrate on making wise decisions, not fly-by-night decisions like I had made in the past. I meditated daily, and grew mindful of the consequences and benefits of my decisions. I continued my path of seeking out opportunities to ask for forgiveness.

"I want to have more compassion for others, to be available to give back and sponsor other women, not only in recovery, but also in domestic violence. The idea of being there for somebody else God puts in my life is energizing to me," I told my friend Marcia in a grand announcement.

Instead of saying "slow down," as she often did, she agreed.

"You want a life of well-being. I can hear it in your voice. You have seen it in others, so you can see it for yourself. It will give you a freedom you have never known before. Start a practice of healthy behaviors of service to others and be mindful of where you can be generous."

"I want to accept whatever comes my way and move forward. To be aware of what a difference my last abusive relationship has made on me, and how sharing my secrets in my recovery has freed me. Ending up in the emergency room got my attention. To learn more coping skills, like

I learned in the classes I took after the assault, is even more critical to my success in helping other women."

As time went on that year, I realized I had developed an innate ability to grow, transform, and heal with the tools I found in my meetings, and from others who shared with me on my journey. Because of those things, I went further with my plans to forgive and to never live with harboring resentments again. Safe to explore the deepest parts of myself and learn who I needed to forgive to be free, I forgave myself first to be able to be valuable to others.

GRATITUDE

A gratitude journal in early sobriety taught me the healing potential of writing. The opportunity to write for five minutes every day improved my health and wellness, not just my emotions. I found deeper relationships with these writings and grew happier.

"It's being thankful, being ready to show appreciation, and kindness," my therapist clarified. "Do you feel more optimistic when you journal gratefully? Does your spiritual side emerge?"

"Yes, I'm feeling spiritual today. I like it."

I am grateful to be alive, and feeling less materialistic, sleeping better, and see success in my relationships in recovery. But, am I deeply grateful?

"We practice gratitude for psychological and physical wellbeing," she continued as the session progressed. "You will have increased energy and visit the doctor less as you continue with your regimen. You will want to exercise more and bounce back more quickly from injury."

I immediately professed my gratitude for my sobriety, reminding myself of those who don't make it. The ones who go back out there and often take their lives, or die early, because of the disease of alcoholism. Grateful for my health, both physically and mentally, and satisfied with my life, I felt good most of the time. This attitude boosted my optimism about future joy. I was not envious of others, but I felt pleasure in the little things and relaxed with myself. I was more enthusiastic and friendlier, and I looked better.

I reflected on Chuck and his kindness, driving home from my session. He was the man who brought me to my first meeting quite a few years earlier. I was truly grateful for him, he could have saved my life. Although I could not understand why, after he was many years sober, he walked away from sobriety. Even so, Chuck remained important to me.

MEETING CHUCK

I was referred to Chuck by my sales manager Denny as part of a deal to not fire me for my drinking and unprofessional behavior. He was with the ad agency that represented Wood Brothers Homes, the home builder I worked for at the time. He was ten years sober, and ten years older than me when I picked up my second DUI. Denny arranged my outpatient treatment at Desert Samaritan Hospital in Mesa, and a chance to keep my job if I quit drinking and connected with Chuck about recovery.

An outgoing charismatic guy, he presented ad campaigns to our sales meetings on Monday mornings. I didn't know his story until he drove me to the meeting that night at St. Barnabas Church in Scottsdale.

That was the first time I said, "I am Pat and I am an alcoholic."

He immediately introduced me to Rusty and invited her to become my first sponsor. She was a friend of his and I liked her immediately. According to Chuck, she was going to be tough with me, but not to worry. I needed somebody else watching out for me besides him. A woman in recovery was a good idea as she would understand me at a deeper level. Once we talked awhile, I needed her. She was straightforward and committed to recovery.

Chuck, like Rusty, included me in recovery groups who went out after the meetings for coffee at Coco's, or for ice cream at Spencer's Ice Cream Parlor. He was witty and kept the conversation upbeat. He talked incessantly, but we learned a lot about the recovery program from him, and we laughed a lot.

Soon after those first few years, he was around less and less. He left his wife unexpectedly and filed for divorce, now with a woman he met through golf. She was not in recovery, and surrounded herself with quite an active social circle that included him.

Since I spent much of my adult life trying to fit in, I appreciated his nonjudgmental friendship. If he chose to drink again, God was his judge, surely not me. It was hard for me to imagine going back to the drink after all those years.

Being in gratitude helps reduce my anxiety. I am thankful to be alive and feeling healthier, busy with graduate school and working full-time. A place of thankfulness is very good for me. These benefits help me to heal and stay sober, and to pray for Chuck.

I sensed he was in trouble the night he called me out of the blue to say hello. He had that sound of hopelessness in his voice, that longing that comes when the right words are hard to find. Ice cubes clinked in his glass. They played an old familiar sad song. I loved him, he was my friend.

I was thankful it wasn't me all alone with a drink late at night calling friends from days gone by. Many positives filled my life, one being my sobriety. Chuck wanted me to talk about my classes in Organizational Management, and my goals to teach college students. No tales of my dysfunction here, that was the past.

"I had it all, and I let a night of fun at the golf course take me back to the old days. I forgot all the bad times in a minute when I was offered a drink. It was that easy. I had no resistance," he finally said after a long pause. "It's not at all the place where I should be at this stage of life, right back where I was many years ago struggling with the drink."

"Come back to the meetings, we all miss you. You know you will find answers there, you know you're welcome."

THE LETTER

Chuck's misery saddened me. Maybe he regretted his second marriage and leaving his recovery friends behind, but he never really said. I didn't prod, but waited for more information from him that did not come. It was unpleasant for both of us to have our conversation end in silence. I truly felt sadness for him, he was in a bad place. I feel his call opens an opportunity for me to write a letter to him to express my thanks for his

271

help, even though he is fighting for his sobriety. She also wants me to deliver it to him in person.

"It will have a real impact on him and on you. It might move him to reach out to his recovery friends again. Imagine him not here anymore," Marcia said as we talked briefly the next day. "Write in your journal first about what might have happened to you had you never met him and gone to that first meeting. You'll be much more in gratitude when you see him."

"That's a great idea, I will."

Three days before calling Chuck to make our date to meet, I wrote in my gratitude journal, "It's not what you are given, it's how you take it.' I had read that somewhere and couldn't get it out of my mind. Writing fiercely at first and discovering my gratitude while developing the letter, I remembered how his friendship and kindness helped me at a desperate time in my life.

Marcia suggested a simple one-page letter, so I revised it many times to meet that goal. I took my time, reading it aloud to myself to prepare to read it to him. Not to fix him, but to further grow on my journey with him and in service to God. I anticipated his reaction while writing, and imagined the time to meet when I called Marcia to say the letter was ready.

"I don't want it to look like a plea for attention, I want to be genuine. He's a strong life force, a little eccentric, like me. He's changed, I have, too, and I need to be me," I told her.

My sober experiences were gradually accumulating. I was a survivor. What had happened to Chuck? What problems had derailed his life? I took one more look at the handwritten letter and put it in an envelope.

He was skeptical about my call, but accepted my invitation. We met at the Coco's restaurant near Fashion Square Mall in Old Town Scottsdale. A safe place we both knew and had been to many times with each other, and with friends after meetings.

"Good to see you," he said warmly with a hug.

"Same here, it's been too long."

He immediately admitted to having a problem with sobriety. "It's not the alcohol really. I've failed to work a good program and follow the steps that make a difference for me. I'm a phony. I don't practice what I preach."

I am amazed how easily he is saying these things. It takes a conscious effort to listen and let him talk. Our meeting is awkward.

"I'm here to say thank you, to tell you I'm grateful for our friendship. I've something to read to you," I began in a serious tone.

I took the letter gingerly from my purse. It was personal and focused on him rather than on things he had done. He was watching my every move, curious but not fearful.

I heard Marcia's words in my head. "This will be an unexpected event that will add depth to your life, even if he has been drinking."

"Dear Chuck,

You came into my life for a reason, and that was to introduce me to recovery, and to be my friend. For that, I am forever grateful. You were also meant to share time with me and others in our early sobriety. You have done that many times. For that, I am grateful.

Your friendship over the past five years has meant a lot to me. It is one I could never have anticipated. I am humbled by and grateful for it. Thank you."

"Thank you," he said. "This is really beautiful."

Tears began to well up in his eyes. I continued, reading the last three paragraphs without stopping. Although sure he had been drinking that day, I was undeterred. No one is good or bad, but a mix of both. Chuck showed himself to me that day and yet chose to deny his drinking. He never admitted it.

No motive is pure, I saw that in myself while selfishly reading the entire letter before we spoke to each other. I was gaining so much at that moment, hoping he was, too. My grandmother used to say, 'Life gives to you by taking away' and this time proved her right. We shared a simple hug goodbye and, as I pulled away, saw Chuck reading the letter again in his car, slumped over in emotional overwhelm.

GRIEF

After going through a lot of those first five years of recovery, the hardest part of recovery became dealing with grief. I lost several people. Chuck was the first one. A year after I read him my letter, he was gone. His death certificate said acute alcoholism. I learned quickly not to complain about my life. That would be selfish and ungrateful. I began to live to the fullest, thankful for all who had crossed my path and helped me in their own way.

"Chuck is gone, did you know?" I asked Diane in a phone call as soon as I heard.

"Yes, I just heard this morning." Longing tinged her voice, as if she could have said or done one more thing.

"There's a lid for every pot," she once said, quoting somebody she enjoyed, but thinking more about Chuck. She was rarely willing to examine this part of her life.

My gratitude for Chuck's impact on my recovery goes deep. My level of appreciation for him is strong. I want to keep that a priority in his memory, but choose not to go to his memorial. His death is sad for me on so many levels, and unnecessary in so many ways.

"I am disappointed in him and do not want to admit that to anyone else, at least not yet. I am still angry with him for not putting his sobriety first, and expecting that from all of us," I told Diane on the phone when she called to offer to go with me to the memorial.

"I understand, I am angry, too, but I need to go. This will be some closure for me."

It all happened too quickly for me to grasp. Chuck knew I cared before he left this Earth. That was enough for me that day, and hopefully enough for him, too.

MEMORIALS

On the day of his memorial, Chuck's words came to mind: "You don't have to like the meetings, you just have to go." Had that been a clue to his unhappiness in sobriety? Was it harder for him than it appeared? Or, were they words for me to live by?

He had also said to a group of us one night, "Resentments lead to drinking our poison and, if we drink, we die." Those words now sang to me.

Later, gratitude filled me for his words, all of them. This was not useless information. He had challenged me, and others. He did not die in vain.

I remember him every September 23, since 1983, along with my recovery program anniversary. I'm appreciative to him for the courage it takes to face the challenges of sobriety alone when you know there are solutions and people to help. It takes a lot of stamina to be so proud, but more to not be ashamed and admit you need help. I ask God to bless his soul each time my name is called to share my story. Sometimes around the time of this reflection, I write in my journal about the stigma of being an alcoholic and how it might have been too great for him. He went out with a social circle of people who drank.

Chuck faded some from the conversation as the years went on but, on occasion, his name would come up in my meetings. A feeling of sadness would permeate the air. We all knew it could have easily been us, but for the grace of God and one day at a time.

We chose being upbeat in sobriety and accepted that everybody doesn't make it. The estimated statistics say about thirty-five percent of the people who come to treatment and recovery make it. The figure is estimated because no real records are kept, due to anonymity. That's not because it's built for failure. It's because it's a humble program, a willingness program, needing a complete life change for the one seeking sobriety. This is often too much for people, yet the same promises and opportunities are offered to everyone.

I read once, *"We seem to find heaven by backing away from hell."* There is humor in that statement. That is alcoholic behavior, coming at life from the back door. That attitude has saved my life, and for that I'm grateful. Chuck didn't intend to risk his life by leaving his wife and marrying someone else he may not have truly loved or even known. He just wanted to change the sound volume on his life and looked in the wrong direction. He wanted to smooth out the rough edges and, unfortunately, the drink seemed like his only option.

I had no intention of risking my life by moving away socially from my recovery friends. I just wanted to tone down my life, spend more time in prayer, and write in my journal. I longed to smooth out my anger. Low self-esteem had crept back in, and I was isolating. I prayed to learn from others' poor decisions.

"With much gratitude, I thank him in my prayers for his part in helping me to stay sober. Today I can hardly remember his face, or the sound of his voice, but I feel the impact on my life almost daily." I shared this comment with Diane a year after his memorial when she mentioned the anniversary at a meeting. Almost as a tribute. "I am grateful for the way it all turned out, and that Chuck was in our lives early on in sobriety," I added.

"This outcome was inevitable for him," Diane said. "If we hadn't had our time with him, we would have been cheated out of a good friend. He had a lot of friends."

'Thank you. I just couldn't go to his memorial service, but was there in spirit. I'll remember the joys and benefits of knowing him," I added. "How would I feel if I denied them?"

I think about all the laughter, the jokes, the get togethers. They keep me from feeling lonely. If I had not met him, I might never have crossed paths with the many people he introduced me to who are here for my benefit.

My therapist continued this gratitude conversation with me to help me grieve, and to prepare me for the loss of others to come.

"Notice the positives, the sights and the sounds that surround your memories, and acknowledge them," she suggested. "Ask yourself why they're pleasurable to you. Write about them in your journal."

"I like to run and hike and be with nature. I am on my bike a couple times a week and hike Camelback Mountain on the weekend. I enjoy trying new places when I hike, to keep it interesting. Physically, I felt better. Chuck often asked me about the hikes, as he never attempted the mountain, he was afraid of heights."

My blood pressure lowered, and writing in a gratitude journal helped me immensely. My aches and pains from exercise seemed to be less and less when gratitude for the little things was present. It was all beginning to work for me.

Patricia L. Brooks

ACCEPTANCE

GRIEF

"**T**ry to embrace your grief without agreeing to it," my therapist Ann said as we discussed my sister's passing. "Accepting is consenting and, with her lung cancer, that is all you can do."

I finally accepted my sister passing away. I could not help her, sometimes even comfort her. At fifteen years sober, she was ten years away from a drink, yet terminally ill. She was forty-two years old, married, and the mother of two teenage boys.

I surrender to God after initially fighting. Acceptance is the only answer. This situation is unchangeable. She is not going to beat stage-four lung cancer with its ten percent survival rate for women over forty, even if they take her lung out, which she has agreed to do. That move gives her two or three years. God help her.

"There is power in accepting. It means we stop resisting and find the lesson," my therapist continued.

"What possible lesson could there be? She quit smoking for twelve years before they discovered she had

279

lung cancer and was terminal," I quipped. "I'm not concerned about drinking. That it is not the answer, but it is so hard to process why her and not me. Why her, after she turned her life around?"

Ann went on to talk to me about how things happen that transform us, and once the lesson appeared, my transformation could begin. Was the lesson to live each day to the fullest? To appreciate my life just as it was? To be more grateful for all I had?

My sister's life hadn't always been easy. She often said she wanted to pinch herself because it had become so good. I had more to do with my life, to live for both of us, and be transformed by that responsibility.

"Look at what happened to her in a positive light," Ann said on another occasion. "You have a chance to do great things with another chance at life. The chance she didn't get, do well with it."

I opened my arms to accept grief. It was not easy. When I lost my friend Charm in a dreadful car accident at a young age, I began to understand grief. Now, it was my sister, to lung cancer. Grief was hard to do, painful. My parents passed away in my early sobriety, I never fully grieved my unfinished business with them. I didn't want to fight and resist the loss of my sister, but the heartache was unbearable. More than my two divorces in my twenties, or the acceptance of my alcoholism.

"Acceptance is a choice, difficult, but a choice," Ann said to finish our session.

I commit to myself this day that I am not going to ask why. God has called my sister home. I am not going to complain about my life. She lived a happy life in her later years and accepted her fate.

ABUSE

Being ten years sober in an abusive relationship was complicated, hard to understand, and hard to explain. I had kept it a secret from almost everyone.

"Find the lesson or God's purpose behind every challenge," Ann suggested to me when we met soon after the assault. "It'll help you embrace your vulnerability, not fight it."

I had been angry and frustrated in that relationship for two years, trying to fix an unfixable situation. By ignoring all the red flags of lies and deceit only to my detriment, I kept my secret safe, hid my bruises, and lived in fear. The sober way of peace, love, and openness was not my life.

After a lot of meetings and talks with my sponsor, I accept God's plan and don't judge myself. My acceptance is not a weakness. It allows me to believe better things will happen to me. I am safely away from him and the chaos, and accept my mistakes.

"Unless you accept life on life's terms, you'll never be happy," Diane, my sponsor, said after my physical healing began and the stiches were removed. Ending up in the emergency room and calling my sponsor was humbling. A had a lot to accept. I said many times, in my denial, it will never get so bad that he'd try to kill me. I was wrong.

Removing the stigma of abuse changed my attitude. I journaled each day with the question 'What needs to be changed with me?' While focusing on what was right with the world, and how I had been treated as a victim, I accepted my status as a domestic violence survivor. My empathy grew toward the other survivor women, too.

"Find a greater contact with God, your higher power, than you've had in the past," Diane, suggested on the phone, as we discussed where I was one night. "I'm meditating a lot these days, I suggest you make meditation important to you, too."

"It's been hard for me to concentrate, but I will."

"Acceptance is the ability to effectively deal with things beyond our control," Diane said as a definition for me to contemplate. "Your attitude is in your control."

"I'm focusing on acceptance in my gratitude journal. I am determined to move beyond the old victim status and to understand why love addiction is a part of my persona, part of my addiction to alcohol," I offered. "Somedays my progress in sobriety is slow, but it was steady."

"Be the best person you can be in any situation," she continued. "That's all you can do."

"I'm trying to be more cognizant of my thoughts. I want to morph into what I want to be and not what somebody else wants me to be. I have done that all my life."

The post-traumatic stress disorder that accompanied the abuse was beyond my control, but I accepted it was there, and dealt with it head-on. Determined to heal and be useful to others, I recognized my limitations and worked at being positive through prayer and meditation, searching for information to understand trauma.

"Accepting your PTSD is not resigning yourself to anything. You have this disorder. He didn't win," my therapist presented at our next session. "You've won."

"I'm not running from the struggle. I'll do whatever you suggest I do to break through this cycle to feel safe."

"Acceptance is not a part of helplessness, you're not helpless," she continued. "Feel your feelings. You'll gain much emotionally and learn to cope, no matter what happens next."

I pray to get a handle on my strong emotions, especially my anger. I'll live in the moment and not worry about my future any longer. And, to deal easily with those mood swings I know so well, even if the strong stressors come along again. They always do. That is life.

My day started by praying for a deeper relationship with the women I saw regularly at my home group: Marcia, Vickie, and Lizz. I prayed, too, for God's will, a large part of acceptance of the way life is destined. I didn't want to be reduced to one with depression, as before. It would be so easy to slip into despair, now that my sister was gone. I often felt very alone, knew PTSD, and had memories of my domestic violence relationship. This was my grief.

VICKIE

On the recommendation of my therapist Ann, I nurtured a mindset of acceptance and agreed to sponsor someone who was terminally ill. My friend Marcia asked me to drive Vickie home from our Thursday meeting, since she was busy. I gladly accepted. Vickie had a pleasant personality, and with about as many years of sobriety as Marcia and I.

"I'll be happy to drive you home after the meeting, but I'll need to pick up my husband Earl at Papago Park Golf Course first. Is that okay with you?"

"Sure, I'm in no hurry, just grateful to be here, or anywhere, actually," she said with a quick grin. "I'd like to meet your husband."

"Earl is very supportive of all I do with recovery. He has been to many open meetings with me and understands what recovery is all about. We've been together for ten years now in a sober relationship, and were married six years ago. He is a gift from God. He will want to meet you and get to know you. He loves to meet my sober women friends."

Vickie smiled at the idea.

She was a petite Italian woman, a few years older than me with gray hair and a gaunt look due to her lymphoma. Her dark eyes seemed darker today. She was terminally ill as far as Marcia knew, but I wasn't going there with today's conversation. She had a brace on her leg and walked with a cane or a walker. She had a story to tell.

Vickie appeared older than she was, but her delicate hands were quite feminine, possibly lovely at one time. The ravages of chemotherapy and radiation took their toll on her, just as they had on my sister. I prayed for her.

"I like this women's meeting and hope to come more often now that I'm feeling a little better. My treatments just ended," she said with a heaving chest. It was not easy for her to breathe.

I liked her spirit.

"If Marcia, or someone else, drives you to the meeting, I will drive you home. We all live pretty close to each other," I said while carefully adjusting her seatbelt, hoping not to be too helpful.

Mindfulness meditation class taught me to accept what is there in the present moment. This was quite a moment. I was ready to be there for her, reflecting deeply on my experiences with my sister and praying quietly about my time with Vickie.

"Do you mind if I put the top down on the car?" I asked. "It's a beautiful day, is it okay with you, or too much for you?"

"I'd love it! I have so little hair now, why not!" She laughed.

The sun shone down on us at eighty degrees to make it an almost perfect day. We had a twenty-minute drive. For a fleeting moment, I sensed she had hope. Her slight smile and relaxed manner said she had finally settled down for the ride in my red Mustang. Her troubles were far away.

My meditation thoughts remind me to work around obstacles, and Vickie's disability and ill health is an obstacle to a normal relationship, but one I can handle. This is a chance to do for her what I couldn't do for my sister who was too far away during her illness. I accept the challenge of my new friend, and this gift from God.

"Will you sponsor me?" she asked at our next meeting.

I took a beginner's attitude and committed to care for her. Distance had forbidden me from caring for my sister or her boys after her death, this was an opportunity for me.

"We can face the world together and sponsor each other."

She fills a void for me and a chance to be of service to her and to God with this friendship. I accept her failing health. It is just the way her life is, but it in no way changes the beautiful person she is inside.

Our relationship humbled me quickly. Vickie soon became too tired to attend meetings and the need to visit her at home was the next phase. It was a blessing in disguise, a chance to get close to her.

"Come back in an hour," I told my husband as he dropped me off at her house. "She'll be tired by then; an hour will work for us."

I recognized the limitations of our meetings, her mother was always nearby, often listening to us. But, I vowed to make the best of these times, greeting her with a big smile as she lay on the couch in pain. She smiled when I arrived and, on occasion, had special European chocolates for me sent from the old country. We talked about a lot of things, from recovery to marriage—my three and hers unrealized—and a little bit about her years in a cult before being rescued by her sister.

She entered the cult as an adult through a friend at the airlines where she worked, and was controlled almost immediately—mentally, emotionally and physically—by the woman who led it all. Vickie was searching for community and spirituality not found in a recovery program.

Vickie was lost to the cult until her sister spent a lot of money, time, and energy to get her out. Obtaining her release was not easy. Both the leaders fought her release, and so did Vickie. Her sister was strong.

She never told me all the details. Mindfulness helped me accept I needn't voice my thoughts about the cult. Vickie held supportive views of the people, the place, and their philosophy long after her "lost years" ended. Maybe out of brainwashing, maybe out of pride.

"I've long given up the delusion I know everything," I told her. "I am not here to judge. I just want to do the right thing. Spending time with you is the right thing."

"Right things happen," she said. "My sister rescuing me when I became ill in the cult, and you being willing to spend time with me now, are right things."

I didn't reject anything I was asked to do for her, by her or her mother. Sometimes, my husband and I took her to the hospital for her drugs or a doctor's appointment. When we met, we talked about whatever she wanted to discuss, sometimes just observing her pain and the realization of how she had lived her life. God had put her in my life to accept and support, not to judge. And, to learn patience.

Vicki died a year after we began our relationship. She was at a Hospice facility in Scottsdale when she drew her last breath. Her mother called me to come to say goodbye to her. What an incredible twelve months it had been for both of us, and it had flown by quickly.

As one who practices meditation, I had a sense of well-being as I whispered "goodbye" in her ear. Leaning down close to her still body lying in that dimly lit room, I was grateful for our sober friendship. Tears welled up in my eyes. It was a sad day, even though it had been coming.

Her eyes fluttered, and she twitched, but she heard me. Her mother also wanted me to tell her it was okay to go, and I did. Feeling freer myself, I squeezed her hand and then let go. A heavy feeling of weight in the room lifted.

I don't fear my emotions today. This is her time and not mine. Her mother sits quietly with me next to her bed, accepting this is God's plan. With a few short wheezes, as if she is seeing her life passing before her and going to the light, Vickie slowly leaves us.

Her funeral, with a traditional Mass, was at a Catholic Church in Scottsdale, St. Maria Goretti. The priest spoke, and a church member read scriptures. It was a very impersonal ceremony. No one sang "Amazing Grace," or anything else. I was saddened and disappointed.

To accept this, I acknowledged her family's wishes. Her burial was in a nearby cemetery in South Scottsdale. Again, only the priest spoke. Dinner at the Olive Garden franchise did not allow for a lot of socializing, no podium, no agenda and no plans to allow for any of us to really say goodbye to our friend, the petite woman who had made a difference in our lives.

PURPOSE

THE ALCATHON

"There comes a time in recovery when we look at how we will be responsible for not only ourselves, but others, too. It is what we call service work, giving back to others in some small way," said the main speaker. "Having integrity and character is the cornerstone of a good and solid recovery, and serving others is a good way to start."

Several years before meeting Earl, back in 1999, I had attended the Alcathon on Christmas Eve, and the hotel ballroom was filled for the eight o'clock speaker. Carol S. from Los Angeles, a longtime sober woman, was carrying a strong message of hope. Not only was she a captivating speaker, but also employed a sense of humor. I loved to laugh at the meetings, and especially at myself, as I related to the speaker's stories.

The Alcathon runs twenty-four hours from noon on Christmas Eve to noon on Christmas Day, with meetings going on continuously. It's a time for fellowship, sharing pot-luck style food and a lot of good support for those who have nowhere to go over the holidays. It's also for people like me who seek to be with recovering friends at Christmas rather than anyone else. I usually spend three to four hours there on Christmas Eve, after early outdoor Mass at the Casa. The two seem to go together.

Having attended the Alcathon for most of my sobriety, I looked forward to it with the holidays. This night, remembering the first time I went, I had looked in amazement at all the people choosing to attend on Christmas Eve. My sponsor Rusty had driven me and her son Andy into downtown Phoenix to the Hyatt Regency. That was a special night, just like tonight, with a sense of community in the air. I remember being inspired by the speaker and gaining so much from small conversations with people we met, people from all walks of life we might have never met anywhere else.

"Service work can be going to meetings, making coffee, bringing cookies, or cleaning up the room. It can be sponsorship, serving on a committee for a big meeting like this one, or it can be taking calls on a late-night shift at Central Office," she said easily since she had done so much of this work.

I listened carefully and nodded. I enjoyed service work, and had done quite a bit, especially with chairing meetings, speaking, or getting the speakers lined up. I felt satisfied with my service work, but I could do more, and had a game plan to grow in my recovery.

One of my positive traits was not judging others, or myself. We were taught in meetings to do our service work when we were ready and able. My purpose in the program was to always be passionate about recovery, to serve as a walking example of what happens if you stop drinking and work to turn your life around. Like so many times in my life, I played to win and, with recovery, it was that way, too.

"Alcohol is your opponent in the game of life," she said as she wound down her talk. "It ravages society. We need to be vigilant and on the attack with alcohol. It can easily take over."

My main goal for the New Year was to maintain my sobriety. To never be humiliated with a DUI again, to never go to jail again, and to never feel "less than" others in society because I had broken the law.

My intention for the New Year is to make a commitment to more service and to achieve another year of sobriety by giving back. My expectations are realistic. I have a sponsor and a homegroup and go to meetings regularly. I speak at meetings a few times a year, and serve the homeless through my church, The Franciscan Renewal Center, with others in recovery at the Andre House.

ANDRE HOUSE

We went to the Andre House once a month, a small home in downtown Phoenix run by priests sent from Notre Dame to serve God. We fixed the meals in the basement of St. Mary's Church—daunting to say the least, with a full flight of steep concrete stairs as the only way out, but we did it.

Usually, we numbered 800 to 1,000 paper plates with black felt marker to keep a count, and often used all of them. We prayed for gratitude, to serve God, and grow as a person. I chose to be humble before God and do whatever it took to make this a happy experience. For me, my passion to help others was enhanced by this experience. It made me grateful to be a part of life, no longer on the outside looking in on where life was really happening. Service work gave me hope.

We transported the meals in large aluminum pans up the basement stairs to waiting vans. The food was taken down to the corner of 11th Avenue and Jackson where the homeless community of South Phoenix anticipated a hot meal on Sunday night.

My new-found passion for helping the less fortunate was easily satisfied as the homeless population seemed to need so much. I appreciated them as "but for the Grace of God go I." I had met many women and men in recovery who had lost everything before they ever got to a meeting room. It was only by God's Grace I didn't drink myself out into the street.

The women serving the homeless were asked to not wear flashy or expensive clothes and to not wear their hair down or accessible to the people coming through the food line. I tied my long hair back each night while serving food. We had heard some of the men would reach over and touch long hair.

I also left my black-leather bomber jacket at home on cold nights, even though it would have been my first choice for warmth. My brown wool coat worked out just fine. I was on a mission on those nights and it wasn't to get attention. They owed me nothing. There in the presence of

God to be of service for them, I committed to my own character development through this work.

"Accept his challenge whole heartedly, it is an opportunity," Father Alejandro, the priest on duty at St. Mary's, said to us that Thanksgiving night.

He blessed the meal before we took it out to the vans. It was not our regular night, we were the Sunday night group from the Franciscan Renewal Center. But, they were shorthanded on holidays as many people had places to go. Not me, I was destined to be at the corner of 11th Avenue and Jackson serving pumpkin pie to eager hands. Having not attended a Christmas or Thanksgiving with my family in Michigan for about a decade, this was where I was supposed to be.

My recovery friend Ellen was with me, as she usually was for the Andre House meetings or St. Mary's work duty. We kept each other excited about the night as we cut piles of vegetables.

"Each Thanksgiving, I come away satisfied, even though exhausted. I can't remember feeling happier for being a part of serving a thousand Thanksgiving dinners here in the street," I told her when we had a little time to chat.

"Me, too," she said. "I am getting to know a few of them, and like the smiles on their faces when I give them a little extra potato or a larger piece of pie."

We both agreed we fall asleep after these evenings with big smiles on our own faces. The conversation changes to recovery talk to keep us going as we organize seemingly endless piles of bread rolls for the dinner.

"When are you going Christmas shopping for yourself?" she asked with a laugh.

"Maybe this weekend, but not for much more than one thing, maybe a new purse. Not much money to spend these days, but I want one Christmas gift. How about you?"

"Me, too. My kids do give me a few things, but it is about buying for them. I am just so grateful to be sober with them in my life."

Sobriety is one-day-at a time. What we do here for the homeless is important. We can have no misunderstandings about the value of this time together. We are here for each other and for our service commitment.

Sad men in dark and dirty attire began to appear. The women came unkept and timid, helping the fearful children. People, from all walks of life, moved slowly through the food line, often with their heads down. Even a little girl carrying her worn-out doll entered slowly. I felt gratitude and sadness at the same time, remembering I still had all my childhood dolls.

My passion was to help others. That night would be joyful, I would keep smiling, no matter what sadness showed up. It was our job to be a positive light for these people. This night made me feel grateful for my life. I greeted each one equally with a warm hello. There was no need to ask how they were. That was obvious, and disconcerting.

"Find encouragement and demonstrate it in a small way," Father Alejandro said to us after the prayer. "They may not respond, but they are listening."

That is not a radical approach for me but, with a group of homeless women, it is a challenge. I am close to their situation in so many ways. I am only beginning to have my confidence back. I believe alcohol is but a symptom of my problems, and there's a lot of work to be done now that I've put down the drink.

SERVICE

"We've moved beyond even thinking about having a drink," Ellen said with a smile as we drove home that night, cold but content. "Going to meetings is almost second nature. We call each other."

"Yes, I avoid my triggers, but I don't want to get complacent. I'm not better than any of those women we saw tonight. That is why I want to be of service to them. To never forget how close I came to being on the other side of that table."

"We showed up tonight on a very chilly Thanksgiving evening when we could have been someplace else like having a nice dinner ourselves at Tomaso's. That is pretty good service in my book," she said as she snuggled into the seat. "We get up and get going. We don't feel sorry for ourselves."

We both laughed. We knew each other's thoughts about years past... Drinking too much brandy on Thanksgiving and Christmas. Or, saying something we regretted, like telling off friends over politics or religion, topics best kept to ourselves.

"Thanks, talking about all of this keeps me joyful and grateful without alcohol. Your enthusiasm is good for me. I'm glad we share our stories about past mistakes, that we confide in each other about our imperfections. We're good for each other. This homeless work allows me to be unselfish."

I looked out over the city of Phoenix, at all the beautiful Christmas lights on the buildings around Central Avenue, especially the tree on top of the Hyatt Regency Hotel that could be seen for miles. I was truly humbled.

By surrounding myself with those I trusted, like Ellen, staying sober was easier now than other times, and it was fun. We were heading home to our warm beds and not back to that cold park across from the Andre House like the homeless women. We were miracles.

I go to at least three meetings a week, turn things over to God and don't react quickly. Life is working. When needed, I rework the steps with my sponsor. I oversee my own thoughts through prayer and meditation. I am happy this holiday season and feel blessed.

AUTHOR'S NOTE

In my thirty-fifth year of sobriety, I honor the women in recovery I have written about in this memoir, and those who are in my life now. They are family and women I consider some of my dearest friends.

Marcia is still in my life as a confidante. We take time to talk privately at our home group meetings. Ellen is someone I see on occasion, but when I do our friendship is as it has always been, a strong bond in recovery. Vickie is not as available as the others, but I do see her. Sometimes we connect at a holiday party given by a mutual friend. We cherish a closeness that has endured decades.

Lizz came into my life later in recovery, but at just the right time. We met in a situation that was business related, but soon learned how much more we had in common. Today, we meet regularly on Thursday for tea before our home group meeting. This time spent is important to me and has been critical to my sense of where I am at this juncture in my sobriety.

Molly is a gift from God, entering my life just over three years ago. She offers me a chance to walk my years of sobriety again through her story. I will always be grateful for her trust in me and the opportunity to share her life and her early sobriety as we trudge the road of happy destiny.

There are many other women who have come and gone in my recovery—such is life. Rusty, Diane, and Syd were there for me on my journey at the time they needed to be. One thing is for sure, many of these relationships are enduring friendships... a sisterhood that cannot be broken. Rusty and I still see each other at recovery functions and it is a special reunion. For her and all the others, I am truly grateful in this anniversary year of recovery.

DEDICATION STORY

CHARMING

C harm's name you could not forget: Charmeon. Named after a French protagonist from a novel her mother loved, she came from a creative family. Charm sang like no one else I knew, and loved to write. We enjoyed talking about the creative things we wanted to do in our lifetimes. She wrote personal essays. Her enthusiasm was infectious as she talked about them, along with her singing and her faith.

My first husband Alan and I met Charm and her husband Murray at the University of Dubuque in Iowa at their Presbyterian Seminary. They had come from Oklahoma, we had come from Michigan. Our husbands became ordained ministers.

Charm had competed in the Miss Tulsa pageant a few years earlier. With a full head of long blonde hair, a luscious complexion, and a lot of energy about her, she put life in any room. Charm was curvy and pretty, in an all-American girl sort of way. She had hoped to compete for the Miss Oklahoma title, but when Murray asked her to marry him she said yes. So instead of another pageant, they made plans for Iowa.

She is my dearest friend, a confidante. I tell her how I feel about this place, about a lot of things. She is a big factor in my confidence. She encourages me to follow my dreams, even though she knows they are far from here. She confessed to me she left some of her dreams in Oklahoma.

THE MEETING

We met early in seminary life. The Murray's lived in the married housing unit next to ours, and since the insulation was almost nonexistent, we quickly got to know each other. The units were old WWII barracks once used for military married couples, and later moved to the campus. Although more than forty years since the war ended, they were still used.

These one-room bungalows had a small stoop, but no porch or patio. The parking lot lay nearby. I spotted Charm going to her car the day we moved in to our unit. She quickly came over to say hello, flashing her beautiful smile and offering her help. I liked her immediately.

Maybe it was her infectious smile, or the pretty blonde hair and blue eyes, or that deep voice I did not expect, but she intrigued me. I commented to my husband how beautiful she was as soon as she hurried off.

"She seems pretty on the inside, too. Beauty is only skin deep, you know," he commented in his usual "I know best" demeanor.

"She seems genuine to me, I hope we become good friends," I said immediately, thinking about when I could make a conversation happen with her.

I was already feeling lonely and not a part of seminary life. It was very different from what I had anticipated. The feel and look of Iowa provided a stark contrast to Michigan, and this campus was not at all like the campus where we met near Lake Superior. Everyone seemed so serious, so cautious about their every move.

THE VOICE

I woke up thinking it was the radio playing. The sound of the Fifth Dimensions' *Wedding Bell Blues,* from The Age of Aquarius album, but it came from next door. One of my favorite songs was being sung as beautifully as if Marilyn McCoo was in the next building.

Moving closer to the small kitchen window, I realized only then it was live. My new neighbor Charm was singing at the top of her lungs, in perfect pitch and with the sheer joy of a stage performer. She was uninhibited, belting it out as if it was the most important performance of her life.

What is she doing this for anyway? Does she sing all the time? Does she sing in a choir? I've so many questions, I must talk to her. This is my chance to ask her about this song. Why this song? I love this song.

I threw on a dress and went outside my door, dragging a chair from our small chrome kitchen table with me so I could sit on the stoop and listen more easily. When she stopped, I waited, pretending to enjoy the

II

warm fall air. I didn't wait long. She saw me through the window and came out the door humming.

"May I join you?" She brought a blanket and plopped herself down on the nearby grass.

"I love that song. You are very good," I blurted out. "I love their music. Do you sing in public?"

"Yes, I am in the Dubuque Talent Fair at The Grand Opera House in a few weeks, in downtown Dubuque. I saw it announced in Sunday's paper and I immediately applied to compete."

"That is wonderful!"

"I have sung in other competitions in Oklahoma. I would love to have you and your husband come that night."

That was the beginning of a close friendship I never could have anticipated blossoming in the Bible Belt of Iowa. Charm was delightful and fun, talented and ambitious. All those qualities made me want to be around her. I also admired her desire to be a professional singer and asked her a lot of questions about her creative life. I wanted that, too, a professional career in the arts with writing. She was motivating.

We spent time together chatting when we could, and took turns sharing dinners with our husbands in their place or ours. Even if the menu was as basic as spaghetti and marinara sauce with cheap red wine, we had a good time and made the best of the night. Each couple had a lot to talk about from religion to politics, as it was 1969. We wondered what our futures were going to look like. It seemed our present situation was a stepping stone. Charm and I had big ideas, even though our husbands merely raised their eyebrows when we talked about fame.

We didn't drink a lot of wine around them because they only drank a little. The State Liquor Store laws controlled us. She had grown up in a strict religious upbringing. Her dad was a minister and, at home, she abided by all his demands. My upbringing included alcohol at all family gatherings. Wanting to impress my new friend, I followed her lead with a single glass of wine at dinner. My second glass came after they left, to help me sleep.

III

THE BIG NIGHT

Alan went with me to the talent show at The Grand Opera House. I was excited, and dressed in my best dress, a cream-colored crepe shirt-waisted dress with a large ruffle in front. The outfit included matching shoes and purse in ostrich. The whole outfit was a gift from my mother-in-law. I added a light green shawl since the air held a bit of chill now that it was fall. I looked good in this ensemble, worn for only the best of occasions. Alan liked me to dress smart, as he was one to dress well. That night he wore a brown Nehru jacket with matching pants. Quite a sophisticated man, he often appeared aloof to others.

Our seats were in the balcony, comfortable at front-row center. We had a great view in the old quaint intimate theatre. I loved waiting for the curtain to go up. Charm was the third act to come on stage. She rushed at us with her big smile and blonde hair streaming behind her like a palomino on the run. She, too, had on a cream-colored dress, but it was more flowing, and fit her entrance perfectly.

As that familiar music began, her commanding voice took over the stage. I welled up with pride watching the audience respond lovingly to my friend. Charm nailed it with every note and sent chills down my spine. Alan was impressed, even though he didn't say much. He just smiled. Murray sat up-front beaming. She made *Wedding Bell Blues* her song. The crowd loved it and rose to their feet as she took a sweeping bow and floated off the stage.

"The winner of tonight's performance is Charmeon Richie," the announcer said with confidence. We knew who had won even before the other acts finished. He proudly handed the glass trophy to Charm as she smiled and waved to the crowd, back on its feet and cheering.

By now I was crying. We had just seen an incredible performance, a Miss Tulsa talent-award winner, and a success story happening before our eyes. I was proud to call her my friend and anxious to get backstage to congratulate her.

"You were terrific!" I said reaching in to give her a hug. "I loved the song even more tonight. It was perfect."

IV

"Thank you so much for being here, it means a lot to me," she said. In the next instant, the local *Telegraph Herald* reporter pulled her away, wanting a story. This was where she belonged, in the spotlight.

Our husbands chatted in the corner. Murray looked proud but, in another way, almost insecure. He married a diamond in the rough—a tiger that, if let loose, would certainly roar. He watched her from afar, as we all did, talking with the newspaper reporter and others from the audience. She was going to be a star, going to be somebody.

FT. LAUDERDALE

"I entered a writing contest and won, and I want you to be there when I accept my award," Charm said excitedly as we met up in the front yard, heading to our cars.

It was a snowy December day in Iowa.

"The thing is, it's at a conference in Ft Lauderdale where I will receive the award."

"Ft. Lauderdale, Florida?" In dismay, I scraped the thick snow off the windshield of my little blue Ford Maverick. Florida sounded good to me. "Are you serious? Do you mean drive all that way?"

"Yes, but I thought if three of us drove around the clock, we could do it in three days with good weather. My Volkswagen gets good mileage. What do you say?" she asked in her usual cheery voice.

The cold snap on my face helped me consider a yes to this stunning question. I had never been to Florida and wanted to go. I immediately saw the two of us doing this.

"Who is the third person?" I asked with a bit of trepidation. "I can't imagine any of the other gals here doing this, just me and you."

"No, it would be Darlene, from the Osco Drug Cosmetics Department. You met her when you came in the store to meet me for lunch," she said confidently. "The three of us can do this, get along and have fun, if our husbands agree," she added.

It took a lot of sweet talk to convince our husbands we should take this trip, and that the three of us could drive down and back in her red VW bug.

V

Also, it took a lot of conversations between the three of us girls to decide what to pack since space was so limited. Swimsuits, hats, towels and sunglasses were a must, two pretty dresses each and of course shorts. In the car, jeans. We would sleep four hours, drive four, and ride shot-gun for four. It was going to be an adventure.

We left in the snow of January with the sun shining. We made good time, getting into our groove more the second day than the first. We hit more snow in Atlanta, its first snow in sixteen years. We sailed past a lot of cars off to the side of the road. It was a light powder, not anything to us, we were from Iowa. We just kept going.

We promised each other when we saw our first orange trees, we would be sure to wake the sleeper. We shared our first glass of fresh orange juice together and toasted the Florida state line. *"Welcome to Broward County"* read the sign along the Sunshine State Parkway. It was three in the morning and the air smelled of citrus at the truck stop off the first exit. We were exited.

THE AWARD

Charm was awarded the highest contest honor at the Dr. Charles W. Shedd Conference for Writing Excellence. She had previously met Shedd in Oklahoma. He was a Presbyterian minister for both country churches and big city cathedrals around the country. He was a prolific book writer and wrote a syndicated column. I knew him by his most famous book, *Letters to Karen*. He wrote in the religious/spirituality genres, so he was a perfect match for Charm.

Darlene and I cheered her on at the dinner. We were honored to be there, and to meet this famous man. We enjoyed the other winners and hearing about their writing, too. More importantly, we saw Charm win. She had written about her faith and her life in the church, and what God meant to her now as she embarked on the life of a seminary student's wife. She was always the humble servant.

Before returning to Iowa, we spent a morning at Ft. Lauderdale Beach Park. It was a day of salty warm breezes and cool ocean temperatures, but we wandered into the ocean anyway. It was not anything like unsalted Lake Michigan, even the sand felt different to me. For a few hours, we relaxed and enjoyed the sun. It was cooler than expected and not a lot of people were at the beach, which was just fine with us. We took in the beauty of the Atlantic and enjoyed our first trip to the east coast. It was also a time for me to reflect on my unhappy marriage, my secret affair, and my journals that held those secrets.

Darlene and Charm took the afternoon off from the beach that last day to visit a relative of Charm's family living in a retirement area. I spent it window shopping near where we were staying—the Aqua Hotel, North Beach Village—and went out to lunch. It was unusual for me to have my space, peace and quiet, and to do what I wanted to do.

"I really don't want to go back," I told Charm when it was just the two of us awake in the night heading back up I-75 the next day. Darlene was fast asleep, and I needed to talk.

"I guess you can tell, Alan and I do not have a great marriage and we don't spend a lot of time together."

"I know things are tense between the two of you. It's not easy being in the situation we are in with seminary. Maybe you need to get some counseling before it goes too far," she suggested. "I will pray for you that things get better. Seminary is demanding."

Charm is committed to seminary life while I am already planning how I am going to get out. It has hardly been two years, but I am ready to go. My affair with Jack is ending; I can feel it. It is not going to end well. My secret drinking here or there is now moving toward a need to drink. I feel it pulling on me. Does she want to hear this?

"I am thinking of leaving and going back to Michigan this summer, after the school year is over. I don't fit here. I know I don't." I said it as if I was making an announcement to an employer to resign, and not to my best friend about my marriage. "Alan can see it, we do not have a marriage of anything but convenience. It has always been that way."

Charm was saddened. Her pretty smile disappeared, she started to speak but stopped. She saw Darlene sit up in the back of the VW. I did not want to share my angst with anyone but Charm. She respected me for that, squeezed my hand, and kept driving.

We arrived home safely and told a few tales of the beach, the awards dinner, and the drive, but most of the trip was kept between the

VII

three of us. It was our "girls go to Florida" trip. We cherished whatever it was we had, even if it wasn't with boys and drinking, or beach parties, like it could have been in college when we were single. This trip was ours, and ours alone.

SUMMERTIME

"We are going to Branson, Missouri, for the summer to counsel at a Christian camp. We will spend a couple months there before school starts in the fall. We leave in a week," Charm revealed as she peeked into our kitchen window with that beautiful smile. "We heard about the place from friends back home. We can be of service, and Murray needs a break from his classes."

"I will miss you. Be safe out there," I said and went outside to hug her goodbye. "Alan is registered for summer school, and I will be working. We have no plans to go back to Michigan on vacation."

Sadness came over me as I watched her pack their car over the next few days, knowing they would be gone until September. Would I still be in Iowa when she returned? How much was going to change over the summer months? We had not discussed my leaving since Florida.

LEAVING HOME

Iowa was never home to me. Being married to Alan was never a marriage, and the affair with Jack ended after a threat to Jack for the job he could not afford to lose. I was told to leave Apple River Chemical Company and given no choices.

I do not love my husband, I do not believe I love Jack. I'm not even sure how much I love myself.

Where would I work? Where would I go? I wanted to make a good decision, but there was nobody to help me. Charm called after leaving for camp, but I did not bother her with all of this. She sounded so happy with their life there. So much of it was already done, there was no reason to bother her.

VIII

I did not call my parents. They would be very upset, since they had taken out a loan to pay for my wedding and had only started to pay for it. This would be too much for them to hear over the phone. I was alone.

My husband was humiliated and hurt. He agreed seminary life was not for me, and our problems were not going to be resolved. Marriage counseling was futile. This was the wrong place and he was the wrong person for me.

A friend from work helped me move to an apartment in downtown Dubuque.

The summer did not go along as well as hoped. I had a different job at the same company and was told not to communicate with Jack, though he would not take no for an answer. He found out where I lived through the employee records at the office and stalked me. He called me and came to see me. I felt sorry for him and tried to deal with it on my own. It was embarrassing, downright tiring at times to keep avoiding him and telling lies, but it was for the best.

THE CALL

"She's gone, Pat," Alan's solemn voice said as soon as I answered. "It was a horrendous car accident. Charm and Murray were hit head-on by two drunk kids in a stolen truck."

The words stung so hard I could hardly breathe. I sat down to try to speak. My legs grew numb and I feared I might fall down. My voice was not functional for questions, and my heart pounded.

Please God don't make it true. Tell me it's a dream, wake me up from this nightmare.

"Murray is in the hospital in pretty bad shape, his legs are crushed, he was thrown from the car about thirty-five feet, but they say he is going to live. It is too soon to tell," Alan continued.

I can't breathe. I can't stand. I can't sit. I need to lay down to take what's coming next. This is a nightmare.

"Charm was killed on impact," he continued as if reading a report from the newspaper. "She was decapitated and never knew what hit her. The truck came up over a hill and crossed the line. With that little VW, they did not have a chance. You know the engine is in the back on those things, there was nothing to protect them."

I could not bear to hear another word, but I could not stop listening, while trying to grasp the fact that my friend died on a highway, killed by drunk drivers. How horrific a crime this was… how would Murray survive without her?

"Murray is in a coma, he doesn't know she's gone. It's God's will Murray is alive."

"This can't be true. Dear God, how can this be true?" I kept saying as I started to cry, sobbing so hard I started choking. "I have to see her again."

"I can come over tonight if you don't want to be alone," he offered. "You should be with somebody tonight, stay with somebody."

"I don't know, I don't know. I can't think."

"I will have more information tomorrow. I do know it happened at dusk. They were heading back to the camp where they were counseling. They had gone out to dinner."

I feel guilty. Did I show her how much she meant to me? Was I truly the friend I wanted to be for her? God help me.

Some things change our lives like none other. This was one of those times. A life full of energy and love was taken too soon. A life of creativity and beauty snuffed out in a flash in the night by a stupid act of teenage drunkenness and speed behind the wheel. I was angry at God, and angry at myself for not calling her more that summer. Sobbing uncontrollably, I spent the night alone in my little apartment, too distraught to call anyone and drinking a lot of wine.

I made no plans to go to Oklahoma to the funeral. My husband went. He asked me to go, but I said no. I was too upset, or was it too selfish? I did not contact her family, send flowers, nor write a letter. Why did I not do anything? I wallowed in my own grief instead of looking for a way to console her family, or her husband who was my friend, too. I could not explain my behavior and talked to no one about any of it. There were no words when I tried to digest any part of this painful and senseless story. Even writing about it didn't help me.

X

GRIEF

About six months later, when I went back to Iowa to finalize our divorce, Alan told me that a Stop Drunk Driving Campaign had been developed with her picture at the center. He said billboards with her beautiful smiling face lined the highways in Missouri.

I wept when thinking of all the talent and creativity lost that summer night in July, the Fourth of July weekend, no less. Our beautiful blossoming friendship had died, too.

Would this be her legacy? Stopping drunk drivers with her smile?

I will take my grief inside and bury it, move back to Michigan to go to school, start fresh and pick up the pieces. Someday I will do something worthwhile in her memory, to honor her life, but starting today I will value her friendship all my life.

XII

ABOUT THE AUTHOR

Patricia L. Brooks, MAOM
Award-winning Author, Speaker, Advocate, and Survivor

In her latest memoir *Sick as My Secrets,* Patricia L. Brooks candidly looks at her life, that swirled around alcohol consumption, and offers solutions to a huge problem that grips many females. She is passionate about storytelling and her third foray into memoir writing as she lovingly supports other women in recovery by openly telling her story.

In her second memoir, *Three Husbands and a Thousand Boyfriends*, she shares her story of love addiction, domestic violence, and post-traumatic stress. Patricia advocates for progress in domestic violence and recovery awareness.

Her first memoir, *Gifts of Sisterhood – journey from grief to gratitude* is her tribute to her sister who passed away from lung cancer. Patricia earned a prestigious Arizona Authors Association Literary Contest Nonfiction award for this work.

With a master's degree in organizational management (MAOM), Patricia facilitates workshops on writing memoir, and marketing and publishing books. She's also available to speak on grief, recovery, and domestic violence survival. Her goal is always to communicate wellness through writing and speaking.

Patricia is the president of Brooks Goldmann Publishing Company, LLC, serving as a publishing consultant for nonfiction and memoir books. More than a dozen years ago, Patricia created the highly successful Scottsdale Society of Women Writers, and continues to serve as its president.

An Arizona resident for more than forty years, Patricia is originally from the Upper Peninsula of Michigan at the Straits of Mackinac. She resides in Old Town Scottsdale with her author husband, Earl L. Goldmann, where they enjoy the arts and cultural vibe of their community.

Contact Patricia at:
480-250-5556, patricia@plbrooks.com
www.brooksgoldmannpublishing.com

AUTHOR'S REQUEST

Photo: Cassandra Tomei, TomeiStudios.com

PATRICIA L. BROOKS

It is my hope you will give me feedback now that you have read my story and taken this arduous journey with me. Please send comments not only on the book itself, but also on your reaction as a witness to my breaking free from the prison of alcoholism.

I do want to hear from you, either in a review on www.Amazon.com or in a personal email.

Thank you and God bless.

Patricia L. Brooks
www.brooksgoldmannpublishing.com
www.Amazon.com

Sick as My Secrets
www.sickasmysecrets.com

ISBN 13 0-978-09817881-6-6
ISBN 10 0-9817881-6-5

Acknowledgements

When I see a new book being launched by one of my writer friends or by strangers I know it's taken an army of proofreaders, editors, designers, and friends to critique it and mold it to the book we want to read. My gratitude for my supportive team goes in this order.

To my husband Earl L. Goldmann who is always optimistic about what I am writing. He has been my rock and my soulmate on this journey to carry the message of recovery through my speaking and my writing. Earl is brave and never judges me. He allows me to be myself. He supports me and my sobriety wholeheartedly.

Secondly, thank you to my friend and colleague Ann Videan who has painstakingly edited my manuscript with much care and attention to detail. Her keen eye has kept this memoir focused. She also added her expertise in book layout and cover design to finish out the project. Her shared creativity makes this memoir a thing of beauty and a book I'm most proud to share.

Many thanks go to my critique group women who spent countless hours over the past several years giving me feedback on these pages: Sherry Kesling, Kitty Kessler, Shannon Tyree, and Suzanne Diamond. I am truly grateful for their friendship and encouragement. They helped me polish the manuscript and define my purpose for the book. These women were always patient while challenging me to be more concise with my words.

Thank you as well to my dear friends in sobriety who help keep me sane and sober each day as we trudge the road of happy destiny. I appreciate all their spiritual wisdom and faith in me. They have been mentors to me when they did not realize it and have made my life a joy.

A special thank you to all of you reading my book. Your support of what I do and what I represent is incredibly important to my mission in life, and that is to help others. I thank God for his presence in my life each day and the opportunity I have to spread my story of hope. I look forward to all the blessings this book will bring to me and my husband, to you, and to the alcoholic who finds answers here in these pages.

Recovery Resources

- **NCADD: National Council on Alcohol and Drug Dependence**
  800-622-2255, 24-hour hotline
  www.ncadd.org

- **AA: Alcoholics Anonymous**
  www.aa.org

- **Drug Alcohol Hotline**
  855-435-5596
  www.drugalcoholhotline.com

- **Al-anon Family Groups**
  757-563-1600
  888-425-2666, toll free
  www.alanon.org

- **SLAA: Sex and Love Addiction Anonymous (Arizona)**
  602-337-7117
  www.slaa-arizona.org

- **SLAA: Sex and Love Addiction Anonymous (National)**
  Fellowship-wide Services
  www.slaafws.org

- **CODA: Co-dependents Anonymous**
  602-277-7991, Arizona
  888-444-2359, national
  888-444-2379, Spanish
  info@coda.org
  www.CODA.org